THE HISTORY OF FREEMASONRY

ITS LEGENDS AND TRADITIONS

ITS CHRONOLOGICAL HISTORY

BY ALBERT GALLATIN MACKEY, M.D., 33°

VOLUME FIVE

PART 2. - HISTORY OF FREEMASONRY

CHAPTER XLIII

THE UNION OF THE TWO GRAND LODGES OF ENGLAND

THE fusion of the two rival Grand Lodges - the "Ancients" and the "Moderns" - was the most important event that has occurred in the history of Speculative Freemasonry since the organization of 1717.

The mutual denunciations of two bodies, each practicing almost the same rites and ceremonies, each professing to be actuated by the same principles, and each tending to the accomplishment of the same objects, and each claiming to be the supreme Head of the Masonic Institution while it accused its antagonist of being irregular in its organization and a usurper of authority, could not have failed eventually to impair the purity and detract from the usefulness of the Institution.

The sentiment of active opposition on the part of the "Moderns" had grown with the increasing success of their rivals. In 1777 the constitutional Grand Lodge had declared "that the persons who assemble in London and elsewhere in the character of Masons, calling themselves Ancient Masons, and at present said to be under the patronage of the Duke of Atholl, are not to be countenanced or acknowledged by any regular lodge or Mason under the constitution of England; nor shall any regular Mason be present at any of their conventions to give a sanction to their proceedings, under the penalty of forfeiting the privileges of the Society, nor shall any person initiated at any of their irregular meetings be admitted into any lodge without being re-made."[1]

This anathema was followed at different periods during the rest of the century by others of equal severity. The " Modern Masons," knowing the legality of their own organization and the false pretensions of the " Ancients," are to be excused and even justified for the intensity of their opposition and even for the harshness of their language. Feeling assured, from all the historical documents with which they were familiar, that the Grand Lodge organized in 1717 was the only legitimate authority in English Masonry, it was natural that they should denounce any pretension to the possession of that authority by others as an imposture.

The "Ancients," who, notwithstanding the positiveness with which they asserted their claim to a superior antiquity, must, unconsciously at times, have felt their weakness, never displayed so acrimonious a spirit. On the contrary, they were unwilling to enter into discussions which might elicit facts detrimental to the solidity of their pretensions.

Hence, we find Dermott saying: " I have not the least antipathy against the gentlemen of the modern society; but, on the contrary, love and respect them; "[2] and though in a subsequent edition he complains that this amicable sentiment was not reciprocated, he admits the equal right of each society to choose a Grand Master, and expresses the hope to see in his life-time a unity between the two.[3]

In 1801 the Grand Lodge of "Ancients," in a circular addressed to the Craft, made the following declaration:

"We have too much respect for every Society that acts under the Masonic name, however imperfect the imitation, to enter into a war of reproaches; and, therefore, we will not retort on an Institution, established in London, for some years, under high auspices, the unfounded aspersions into which a part of their body have suffered themselves to be surprised."[4]

About the beginning of the 19th century many leading Masons among the '*Moderns" began to recognize the necessity of a union of the two Societies. I am compelled to believe, or at least to suspect, that at

---

[1] Preston gives this degree in full; Northouck only summarizes it. see Preston, " Illustrations," Oliver's edition, p. 242, and Northouck, " Constitutions," p. 323.
[2] "Ahiman Rezon," edition of 1764, p. 24.
[3] Ibid., edition of 1778, pp. 43-44
[4] Ibid., edition of 1807, p. 124.

first the success of the "Ancients" was a controlling motive in this desire for a fusion of the two Grand Lodges.

At this time there were Grand Lodges of "Ancients," or as they styled themselves, "Grand Lodges of Ancient York Masons," which had emanated from the London body, in Canada, Pennsylvania, Maryland, South Carolina, New York, Massachusetts, Nova Scotia, Gibraltars and most of the provinces and islands of the East and West Indies, and a recognition by the Grand Lodges of Ireland and Scotland.[5]

Elated with this success and with the diffusion of their authority, the "Ancients" did not at first incline favorably to the idea of a union of the Craft. They were willing to accept such a union, but it must be without the slightest compromise or concession on their part.

Long before the close of the 18th century the "Ancients" had made an important change in the character of the claim for regularity which they had advanced in the beginning of the contest.

Some time after the Grand Lodge of England, according to the "Old Institutions," was organized by a secession of several lodges from the Constitutional Grand Lodge, Lawrence Dermott, writing in its defense, sought to attribute to it an origin older than that claimed by the Grand Lodge which had been instituted in 1717, and asserted that that organization " was defective in number and consequently defective in form and capacity."[6]

Again he declares that when this Grand Lodge was about to be established, "some joyous companions," who were only Fellow-Crafts, met together, and being entirely ignorant of the "Master's part" had invented a "new composition" which they called the third degree.[7]

At a later period the "Ancients" appear to have abandoned, or at least to have ceased to have pressed this claim to a priority of existence and to a greater regularity of organization. More mature reflection and the force of historical evidence led their leaders to the conviction that both of these claims were wholly untenable.

After the death of Laurence Dermott they began to confine their claim to legality, and their defense of the secession from the Constitutional Grand Lodge upon the single ground that the latter had made innovations upon the ancient landmarks, and by their change of

---

[5] Ahiman Rezon," edition of 1807, p. 117.

[6] Ibid., edition of 1778, p. 14.

[7] Ibid., p. 35. It will be noted that Dermott did not make these grave accusations in his previous editions of the "Ahiman Rezon." They are first advanced in the edition published in 1778.

words and ceremonies had ceased any longer to maintain the pure system of Speculative Freemasonry.

While these "variations in the established forms" were maintained by the Grand Lodge of "Moderns," the Grand Lodge of "Ancients" declared it to be impossible to hold Masonic intercourse with those who thus deviated from the legitimate work of tithe Order.

Hence, though, as has been seen, the Ancients were less agressive in their language toward their rivals and did not indulge in the harsh censures which characterized the Constitutional Grand Lodge, they were, until after the commencement of the 19th century, more averse than that body to a union of the two divisions of the Fraternity, and met all advances toward that object with something more than indifference.

The evidence of this fact is abundantly shown in the transactions of both bodies.

We learn, on the authority of Preston, that in November, 1801, a charge was presented to the Constitutional Grand Lodge against some of its members for patronizing and officially acting as principal officers in a lodge of "Ancients." The charge being proved, it was determined that the laws should be enforced against them unless they immediately seceded from such irregular meetings. They solicited the indulgence of the Grand Lodge for three months, hoping that they might be enabled in that time to effect a union between the two societies. This indulgence was granted, and that no impediment might prevent the accomplishment of so desirable an object, the charges against the offending brethren were for the time with. drawn. A committee of distinguished Masons, among whom was the Earl of Moira, who was very popular with the Craft of " Moderns," was appointed to pave the way for the intended union, and every means were ordered to be used to effect that object.

Lord Moira declared, on accepting the appointment as a member of the Committee, that he should consider the day on which such a coalition should be formed as one of the happiest days of his life, and that he was empowered by the Prince of Wales, then Grand Master of the " Moderns," to say that his arms would be ever open to all the Masons in the kingdom, indiscriminately.[8]

This was the first open and avowed proposition for a union of the two Grand Lodges. It emanated from the " Moderns," and up to that date none had ever been offered by the 'Ancients," who were silently and

---

[8] Preston, "Illustrations," old edition, p. 329.

successfully pursuing their career - in extending tending their influence, making lodges at home and abroad, and securing the popular favor of the Craft. [9]

The effort, however, was not successful. After suspending all active opposition, the Constitutional Grand Lodge learned in February, 1803, that no measures had been taken to effect a union; it resumed its antagonistic position, punished the brethren who had been charged with holding a connection with the " Ancients," and unanimously resolved that "whenever it shall appear that any Masons under the English Constitution shall in future attend or countenance any lodge or meeting of persons calling themselves Ancient Masons under the sanction of any person claiming the title of Grand Master of England, who shall not have been duly elected in the Grand Lodge, the laws of the Society shall not only be strictly enforced against them, but their names shall be erased from the list and transmitted to all the regular Lodges under the Constitution of England."[10]

What were the means adopted by the Constitutional Grand Lodge to accomplish the much-desired object are not now exactly known. But that they were highly distasteful to the "Ancients" is very clear from the action of their Grand Lodge adopted on March 2, 1802.

This action was evidently intended as a reply to the proposition of the rival body of "Moderns," tendered in the preceding November.

The declaration of the Grand Lodge of "Ancients" is printed in Harper's edition of the Ahiman Rezon, published in 1807.[11] As this work is not generally accessible to the Fraternity, and as the document presents a very full and fair expression of the position assumed by the "Ancients" at that advanced period in the history of their career, I shall copy it without abbreviation.

"It was represented to this Grand Lodge, that notwithstanding the very temperate notice which was taken in the last Quarterly Communication, of certain unprovoked expressions used toward the Fraternity of Ancient Masons, by a Society generally known by the appellation of the Modern Masons of England, that body has been further prevailed on to make declarations and to proceed to acts at once illiberal and unfounded with respect to the character, pretensions, and antiquity of this institution. It was not a matter of surprise that from the

---

[9] There is no doubt that at that day, in America certainly, the "Ancients" were more popular than the "Moderns." Hence there appears to have been a settlement of expedience exhibited in the desire of the latter to effect a coalition.
[10] Preston, "Illustrations," old edition, p. 330.
[11] Pages 125-131.

transcendent influence of the pure and unchanged system of Ancient Masonry, practiced in our regular lodges, the solidity of our establishment, the progressive increase of our funded capital, the frequency and extent of our benevolence, and, above all, from the avowed and unalterable bond of union, which has so long and so happily subsisted between us and the Ancient Grand Lodges of Scotland, Ireland, America, and the East and West Indies, it should be a most desirable object to the body of Modern Masons to enroll the two societies under one banner by an act of incorporation; but we did not expect that they would have made use of the means which have been attempted to gain the end.

Bearing, as they do, the Masonic name, and patronized by many most illustrious persons, we have ever shown a disposition to treat them with respect, and we cannot suppress our feelings of regret, that unmindful of the high auspices by which they are, for the time, distinguished, they should here condescend to the use or language which reflects discredit on their cause. Truth requires no acrimony, and brotherhood disclaims it. It is a species of warfare so inconsistent with the genuine principles of Masonry, that they may wage it without the fear of a retort. Actuated by the benignity which these principles inspire, we shall content ourselves with a tranquil appeal to written record. It is not for two equal, independent and contending institutions to expect that the world will acquiesce in the apse digit of either party. We shall not rest our pretensions, therefore, on extracts from our own books, or on documents in our own possession - but out of their own mouths shall we judge them."

In their Book of Constitutions, quarto edition, anno 1784, p. 240, they make this frank confession: "Some variations were made in the established forms." This is their own declaration, and they say that these were made "more effectually to debar them and their abettors (that is, us, the ancient masons) from their lodges." Now what was the nature of these changes? Fortunately, the dispute did not rest between the two rival bodies; it was not for either to decide which had the claim of regular descent from the ancient stock of the "York Masons." There was a competent tribunal. The Masonic world alone could exercise the jurisdiction and pronounce a verdict on the case. Accordingly, after frequent visitations made to our lodges by the brethren from Scotland and Ireland, who repaired to England, the two Grand Lodges of these parts of the united empire pronounced in our favor and declared that in the Ancient Grand Lodge of England the pure, unmixed principles of Masonry -the original and holy obligations - the discipline and the pure science, were preserved. It was not in the forms alone that variations had been made by the modern order. They had innovated on the essential principles, and consequently the Masonic world could not recognize them as brothers.

"In the strict and rigorous, but beautiful, scheme of Ancient Masonry, every part of which was founded on the immutable laws of truth, nothing was left for future ages to correct. There can be no reforms in the cardinal virtues; that which was pure, just, and true as received from the eternal ordinance of the divine Author of all good, must continue the same to all eternity. In this grand mystery, every part of which contributes to a sacred end, even the exteriors of the science were wisely contrived as the fit emblems of the white and spotless lamb, which is the type of Masonic benignity.

"The Grand Lodge can not be more explicit. They will not follow the blameable practice of entering into a public discussion of what ought to be confined to the sanctuary of a regular lodge. Suffice it to say, that after mature investigation by the only persons who were authorized to pronounce a judgment on the subject, resolutions of correspondence were passed by the Ancient Grand Lodges of England, Ireland, and Scotland, which were entered in their respective archives, and which the Fraternity will find in our Book of Constitutions.

"These resolutions have been constantly acted upon from that time to the present day. We have since been further strengthened by the formal accession of the Grand Lodges of America and of the East and West Indies to the Union. And it may now be said, without any impeachment of the modernized order, that the phalanx of Ancient Masonry is now established to an extent of communication that bids defiance to all malice, however keen, and to all misrepresentation, however specious, to break asunder. May the Eternal Architect of the World preserve the Edifice entire to the latest posterity; for it is the asylum of feeble man against the shafts of adversity, against the perils of strife, and what is his own enemy against the conflict of his own passions. It draws more close the ties of consanguinity where they are, and creates them where they are not; it inculcates this great maxim as the means of social happiness, that, however separated by seas and distances, distinguished by national character or divided into sects, the whole community of man ought to act toward one another, in all the relations of life, like brothers of the same family, for they are children of the same Eternal Father, and Masonry teaches them to seek, by amendment of their lives, the same place of rest.

"The Ancient Grand Lodge of England has thought it due to its character to make this short and decisive declaration, on the unauthorized attempts that have recently been made to bring about a union with a body of persons who have not entered into the obligations by which we are bound, and who have descended to calumnies and acts of the most unjustifiable kind.

"They desire it therefore to be known to the Masonic world and they call upon their regular lodges, their Past and Present Grand Officers, and their Royal Arches and Masters, their Wardens and Brethren throughout the whole extent of the Masonic communion, to take notice, that they can not and must not receive into the body of a just and perfect lodge, nor treat as a Brother, any person who has not received the obligations of Masonry according to the Ancient Constitutions, as practiced by the United Grand Lodges of England, Scotland, and Ireland, and the regular branches that have sprung from their sanction. And this our unalterable decree, 'By Order of the Grand Lodge."

A careful perusal of this document will show that the position which had been assumed by the "Ancients" at the middle of the 18th century, when they organized their Grand Lodge, was abandoned by them at its close. Dermott maintained that his Grand Lodge was regular in its organization on the ground that the organization of the other body was irregular and illegal, and illegitimate. One of the reasons he assigned for this illegality was that it had been formed by a less than lawful number of lodges. There were but four lodges engaged in the organization of the Grand Lodge at London in the year 1717. But, says Dermott, with the utmost effrontery, knowing, as he must have known, that there was no such law or usage in existence nor ever had been, "to form a Grand Lodge there must have been the Masters and Wardens of five regular lodges;" and he adds that "this is so well known to every man conversant with the ancient laws, usages, customs, and ceremonies of Master Masons, that it is needless to say more."[12] Hence the Grand Lodge of 1717 "was defective in number and consequently defective in form and capacity."

Another charge made by Dermott against the "Moderns" was that they were ignorant of the true Third degree and had fabricated a mere imitation of it, a "new composition" as he contemptuously calls it.

But at the close of the century both these charges were abandoned and a new issue was joined. The ground on which the

---

[12] "Ahiman Rezon," edition of 1778, p. 13.

"Ancients" rested the defense of their secession in 1738 from the Constitutional Grand Lodge was that that body had made "variations in the established forms;" in other words, that it had introduced innovations into the ritual.

Now this would seem to be a singularly surprising instance of mental aberration, if we did not know the perversity of human nature. When charging the "Moderns" with the introduction of innovations, the "Ancients" appear to have completely forgotten that far more serious innovations had been previously introduced by themselves.

The "Moderns" had only made a transposition of a couple of words of recognition; the "Ancients" had mutilated the Third degree and fabricated out of it a Fourth, hitherto unknown to the Craft. It ill became these bold innovators to condemn others for the very fault they themselves had committed to a far greater extent.

We are ready to exclaim with the Roman satirist: "Quis tulerit Gracchos de seditione querenges.?"[13] "Who could endure the Gracchi when they complained of sedition ?"

Having thus, by implication, at least, admitted the legality of the original organization of the Constitutional Grand Lodge and the correctness of its primitive work, and restricting their charge of irregularity to the single fact of the existence of innovations, the "Ancients," notwithstanding the emphatic language in their address of 1802, in which they had declared the impossibility of recognizing their rivals, had certainly made the way more easy for future reconciliation and union.

Had they continued to maintain the theory of Dermott that the Grand Lodge of 'Moderns" was an illegal and un-Masonic body, which had never known or had the Master's part, I do not see how the "Moderns" could, with consistency and self-respect, have tendered, or the "Ancients" listened to, any offer of union and a consolidation.

But about the beginning of the 19th century there were many Masons, especially among the "Moderns," who felt the necessity of a reconciliation, since the protracted dissension was destructive of that harmony and fellowship which should properly characterize the institution. We have seen that the Prince of Wales had in 1801, when he was Grand Master of the "Moderns," expressed his willingness for a union of all English Masons. This sentiment was shared at a later period by his brothers, the Dukes of Kent and Sussex.

---

[13] Juvenal, Satire II., 24

But of all the distinguished members of the Constitutional Grand Lodge, none was so zealous and indefatigable in the effort to accomplish a reconciliation as the Earl of Moira, who in 1795 had been Acting Grand Master under the Grand Mastership of the Prince of Wales.[14]

In 1801 he had been appointed one of a committee to attempt to effect a union of the two Grand Lodges - a mission which was unsuccessful in its results. But he was more felicitous two years afterward in his efforts to induce a good understanding between the Grand Lodge of Scotland and the Constitutional Grand Lodge of England.

It has been heretofore seen that at an early period in the career of the Atholl Grand Lodge, the Grand Lodges of Ireland and Scotland had been induced, through the influence and misrepresentations of Dermott, to take the part of the "Ancients" and to recognize them as the only legal Masonic authority in England.

In 1782 the Constitutional Grand Lodge, supposing, it seems fallaciously, that there was some prospect of establishing a friendly correspondence with the sister kingdoms, concurred in a resolution recommending the Grand Master to use every means which in his wisdom he might think proper, for promoting a correspondence with the Grand Lodges of Scotland and Ireland, so far as should be consistent with the laws of the Society.[15]

As this last provision necessarily required, on the part of the Irish and Scottish brethren, a denunciation of their friends the ancient Masons," we may infer this to have been the cause of the unsuccessful result of the negotiation. Notwithstanding this resolution, says Preston, the wished-for union was not then fully accomplished.[16]

But twenty years had to elapse before a spirit of conciliation was shown by the Grand Lodge of Scotland, and eight more before the Grand Lodge of Ireland exhibited a similar spirit.

At the annual session of the Grand Lodge of Scotland in November, 1803, the Earl of Moira being present, addressed the Grand

---

[14] To no person, says Preston, had Masonry for many years been more indebted than to the Earl of Moira (now Marquis of Hastings). Toward the end of the year 1812 his Lordship was appointed Governor-General of India; and it was considered by the Fraternity as only a just mark of respect to invite his Lordship to a farewell banquet previous to his departure from England, and to present him with a valuable Masonic Jewel, as a memorial of their gratitude for his eminent services. Preston, "Illustrations of Masonry," old edition, p. 346.

[15] Northouck, "Constitutions," p. 340.

[16] "Illustrations," old edition, p. 257.

Lodge in what Laurie calls an impressive speech, equally remarkable for the eloquence of its sentiments and the energy of its enunciation.

As the account contained in Laurie's History is a contemporary one, it may be considered as reliable and is worth giving in the very words of the author of his work.[17]

"The Earl of Moira stated that the hearts and arms of the Grand Lodge of England had ever been open for the reception of their seceding brethren, who had obstinately refused to acknowledge their faults and return to the bosom of their Lodge; and that though the Grand Lodge of England differed in a few trifling observances from that of Scotland they had ever entertained for Scottish Masons that affection and regard which it is the object of Freemasonry to cherish and the duty of Freemasons to feel. His Lordship's speech was received by the brethren with loud and reiterated applause the most unequivocal mark of their approbation of its sentiments.[18]

It was afterward stated by the Earl of Moira, that at that communication the Grand Lodge of Scotland had expressed its concern that any difference should subsist among the Masons of England and that the lodges meeting under the sanction of the Duke of Atholl should have withdrawn themselves from the protection of the Grand Lodge of England, but hoped that measures might be adopted to produce a reconciliation, and that the lodges now holding irregular meetings would return to their duty and again be received into the bosom of the Fraternity.[19]

This was certainly an unqualified admission by the Grand Lodge of Scotland that in its previous action in respect to the contending bodies in England it had been in error. It did not now hesitate to style the "Ancients" whom it had formerly recognized irregular Masons, and to acknowledge that their organization was illegal.

The inevitable result was soon apparent. The Grand Lodge of Scotland entered into fraternal correspondence with the Constitutional Grand Lodge of England and recognized it as the Supreme Authority of English Masonry. This good feeling was still further augmented by the election in 1805 of the Prince of Wales as Patron and Grand Master of the Grand Lodge of Scotland and the appointment of the Earl of Moira as Acting Grand Master, both of which high offices were respectively

---

[17] Laurie's "History of Freemasonry" was published at Edinburgh in 1804 - the last entry in the book is the account of this speech.
[18] Laurie's "History," p. 295.
[19] Preston, "Illustrations," old edition, P. 338.

held at the same time by the same persons in the Constitutional Grand Lodge of England.

Here then was a thorough reversal of the conditions which had previously existed. In the year 1772 the office of Grand Master, both in England and in Scotland, had been filled by the same per son, the Duke of Atholl. But it was over the irregular and illegal English body that he presided. The result was a close and friendly alliance between the Grand Lodge of Scotland and the schismatic Grand Lodge in England.

Again in the year 1805 we see the Grand Lodge of England and the Grand Lodge of Scotland united under one and the same Grand Master, the Prince of Wales. But now it was the regular Grand Lodge of England that shared the honor of this royal headship with the Scottish Grand Lodge. The result in this latter case was of course exactly contrary to that which had ensued in the former.

From this time there was no question as to the relations existing between the two Grand Lodges.

Still further to strengthen the cement of this union, if such strengthening were necessary, was the occurrence soon after of an event in Scottish Masonry.

Schism, which had wrought so much evil in English Masonry, at length made its appearance among the Scottish lodges.

In the year 1808 several lodges had seceded, from political motives, it is believed, from the Grand Lodge of Scotland. They had organized an independent body with the title of "The Associated lodges seceding from the present Grand Lodge of Scotland " and on July 4th had met in the Cannongate Kilwinning Lodge room, and elected a Grand Master.[20]

The Grand Lodge of Scotland announced this rebellious action to the Grand Lodge of England, which expressed its fullest sympathy with the Grand Lodge, approved of the methods it pursued to punish the seceders and to check the secession, and proclaimed the doctrine now universally accepted in Masonic law, that a Grand Lodge, as the representative of the whole Craft, is the sole depository of supreme power.

---

[20] It is unnecessary and irrelevant to enter here into the history of this secession. The details will be found at full length in Bro. Lyon's "History of the Lodge of Edinburgh," pp. 264-281. We are here interested only in its supposed influence upon the relations of the Grand Lodges of Scotland and England.

Thus was the union of the two Grand Lodges still more closely cemented, and the Grand Lodge of Scotland became an earnest advocate and collaborator in the effort to extinguish the English schism.

In the same year the Grand Lodge of Ireland addressed a communication to the Grand Lodge of England, in which it took occasion to applaud the principles of Masonic law enunciated by that Grand Lodge in its reply to its Scottish sister. The Grand Lodge of Ireland also expressed its desire to co-operate with that of England in maintaining the supremacy of Grand Lodges over individual lodges It also pledged itself not to countenance or receive as a Brother any person standing under the interdict of the Grand Lodge of England for Masonic transgression. It thus cut itself aloof from its former recognition of the Atholl Grand Lodge.[21]

It is scarcely necessary to say that this act was received by the Constitutional Grand Lodge with a reciprocal feeling of fraternity.

Thus from the year 1808 the three regular and legitimate Grand Lodges of Great Britain were united in an alliance, the prominent object of which was the extinction of the schism which had prevailed in England for three-quarters of a century and the consolidation of all the jarring elements of English Freemasonry under one head.

With such powerful influences at work, it is not surprising that the happy and "devoutly wished-for consummation" was soon effected.

The leading Freemasons of England, on both sides of the contest, readily lent their aid to the accomplishment of this result.

The Prince of Wales having been called, in consequence of the King's mental infirmity, to the Regency, the established etiquette required that he should resign the Grand Mastership, a position which he had occupied for twenty-one years.

On his retirement the Duke of Sussex was elected Grand Master of the Constitutional Grand Lodge. He was recognized as an ardent friend of the proposed union. Through his influence, as Preston supposes,[22] the Duke of Atholl, who was Grand Master of the "Ancients," had been led to see the desirableness of a union of the two societies under one head.

A similar desire for union began now to prevail among the Freemasons of both sides, especially among the "Ancients," who had

---

[21] Preston, "Illustrations," old edition, p. 340.

[22] Ibid, p. 358.

hitherto rejected all proposals for a compromise of any kind that did not include the concession of everything on the part of the "Moderns."

In 1809 a motion looking to a union was submitted to the Grand Lodge of "Ancients," but ruled out by the presiding officer, who refused to put the question.[23]

Nevertheless, the right spirit prevailed, and in 1810 a " Union Committee " was appointed by the Grand Lodge of "Ancients," which held a joint meeting with a similar committee of the Grand Lodge of "Moderns," on July 21, 1810, on which occasion the Earl of Moira, Acting Grand Master of the Constitutional Grand Lodge, presided.

At a meeting of the Grand Lodge of "Moderns" on April 12, 1809, that body rescinded all its former resolutions which forbade the admission of the "Ancients" into their regular lodges,[24] and thus really took the first step toward a formal recognition of the seceders.

In 1810 the "Ancients" began to make concessions. They directed all resolutions relating to the union to be published and submitted to the Craft for their consideration. They also made alterations in their regulations to conform to those of the "Modern."[25]

But the time had now arrived when the necessities of concord and harmony imperatively demanded a cessation of the antagonism which had so long existed between the two rival Grand Lodges and their consolidation under a common head, so that Speculative Freemasonry in England should thereafter remain "one and indivisible."

The "Moderns" had long been desirous of a union, which, on the other hand, the Ancients" had always strenuously opposed. "It is," says Bro. Hughan, "to the credit of the 'Moderns' that they were the firm supporters of the Union, even when the 'Ancients' refused the right hand of fellowship." [26]

It is not to be denied that the success of the "Ancients" in winning popularity among the Craft, especially in America, where they had largely extended they influence, was a principal reason for their rooted aversion to any sort of compromise, which would necessarily result in the extinction of their power and their independent position.

---

[23] Haghan's " Memorials," p. 14.
[24] Hughan's "Memorials," p. 15.
[25] Their regulations, says Hughan, were also altered so as to conform as much as possible to those of the regular Grand Lodge."Memorials of the Masonic Union," p. 15.
[26] Ibid.

But many events had recently begun to create a change in their views and greatly to weaken their opposition to a union of the two Grand Lodges.

In the first place, the charge that the "Moderns" had made innovations on the landmarks was losing the importance which had been given to it in the days of Laurence Dermott. It was still maintained. but no longer urged with pertinacious vigor. History was beginning to vindicate truth, and those "Ancients" who thought at all upon the subject, must have seen that their secession from the regular Grand Lodge had preceded the innovations of that body, and that they themselves had been guilty of far greater innovations by the disruption of the Third degree and the fabrication of a Fourth one.

In the second place, the theory maintained by Dermott and accepted by his followers, that the regular Grand Lodge of England, instituted at London in the year 1717, was an illegal body, defective in numbers at its organization and without the true degrees, had long been abandoned as wholly untenable. History was again exercising its functions of vindicating truth. It is very evident, and the "Ancients" knew it, that if the Grand Lodge organization of 1717 was illegal, their own of 1753 must have been equally so, for the latter had sprung out of the former. It was felt to be dangerous, when men began to investigate the records, to advance a doctrine which logically led to such a conclusion.

A third reason, and a very strong one, which must have controlled the "Ancients" in arriving at a change of views, must have been the defection of the Grand Lodges of Scotland and Ireland. These two bodies which had at first entered into an alliance with the Atholl Grand Lodge at the expense of the Constitutional Grand Lodge, had changed sides, and had now recognized the latter body as the only legal head of Freemasonry in England, had admitted that the "Ancients" were irregular, and had refused to give them recognition as Masons.

A fourth reason was that the Duke of Atholl, who had long been at the head of the Grand Lodge which bore his name and that of his father, and who for two generations had been identified with its existence, had been won by the arguments or influenced by the friendship of the Duke of Sussex, the Grand Master of the Constitutional Grand Lodge, and had resolved to resign his Grand Mastership in favor of the Duke of Kent, for the avowed purpose of preparing for a union of the Craft.

Yielding to these various influences and perhaps to some others of less note, the Grand Lodge of "Ancients " in the year 1813 abandoned its opposition to a union, and accepted the preliminary measures which had been adopted by the friends of that union.

At a special meeting of the "Grand Lodge of Free and Accepted Masons of England, according to the Old Institutions" held on November 8, 1813, at the "Crown and Anchor Tavern," in the Strand, a letter was read from the Duke of Atholl intimating his desire of resigning the office of Grand Master in favor of his Royal Highness, the Duke of Kent.[27]

At the same meeting the resignation of the Duke of Atholl was accepted and the Duke of Kent was unanimously elected to succeed him as Grand Master of the Grand Lodge of "Ancients."

Edward, Duke of Kent and Strathcarne, the fourth son of George the Third, was then forty-six years of age. He was initiated into Freemasonry in a lodge at Geneva, in Switzerland. At the time of this election he was and had long been the Grand Master of the "Ancient Masons" of Canada. He was, therefore, identified with the cause of the "Ancients," but like his brothers, the Prince of Wales and the Duke of Sussex, he was greatly desirous of a consolidation of the two Grand Lodges. At as early a period as January, 1794, he had expressed this sentiment in his reply to an address from the Masons of Canada, when he said: "You may trust that my utmost efforts shall be exerted, that the much-wished for union of the whole Fraternity of Masons may be effected."[28]

On December 1, 1813, the Duke of Kent was installed as Grand Master of the "Ancients." On this occasion the Duke of Sussex, as Grand Master of the Constitutional Grand Lodge, was present with several of his Grand Officers. To qualify them for visitation they were previously "made Ancient Masons in the Grand Master's Lodge No. 1, in a room adjoining."

The transactions on that day must be considered as a conclusive settlement of the vexed question of legality. The fact that the Grand Master of the Grand Lodge of "Moderns" was present, and by his presence sanctioned the installation of the Grand Master of the Grand Lodge of "Ancients," and that to qualify himself to do so had submitted to an initiation in the system of the "Ancients," forever precluded the "Moderns" from making a charge of irregularity against their rivals; these in turn were equally precluded from denying the Masonic legality of a body whose Grand Master had been made participant in their mysteries.

---

[27] The minutes of this meeting will be found in Hughan's "Memorials of the Union," p. 16.
[28] Freemasons' Magazine, vol. iii., July, 1794, p. 14

and had taken a part in the solemn ceremonies of installation of their presiding officer.

Indeed, the union had already been virtually accomplished, and all that was now needed was its formal ratification by the two Grand Lodges.

On September fist the Duke of Kent, not then Grand Master, had been associated by the Grand Lodge of Ancients" with Deputy Grand Master Harper and Past Deputy Grand Masters Perry and Agar as a Committee to take the preliminary steps for effecting a union of the two fraternities.

This Committee had held several conferences with the Duke of Sussex, who was assisted by three of his Grand Officers, Bro. Wright, Provincial Grand Master of the Ionian Isles, and Past Grand Wardens Tegart and Deans.

The joint committee had drawn up articles of union between the two Grand Lodges which had been signed and sealed in duplicate at Kensington Palace, the residence of the Duke of Sussex.

Early in December, at the Quarterly Communications, these Articles had been submitted to both Grand Lodges and solemnly ratified, and the following Festival of St. John the Evangelist had been appointed for the Assembly of the Grand Lodges in joint communication to carry out the provisions which had been agreed upon.

Each Grand Master had appointed "nine worthy and expert Master Masons or Past Masters," to whom were assigned by the Articles of Union the following important duties.

Under the Warrant of their respective Grand Lodges they were to meet together in some convenient central place in London, when each party having opened a lodge according to the peculiar forms and regulations of each, they were reciprocally and mutually to give and receive the obligations of both Fraternities, deciding by lot which should take priority in the giving and receiving. They were then to hold a lodge under dispensation, to be styled the "Lodge of Reconciliation," or they were then to visit the different lodges and having obligated their officers and members to instruct them in the forms of both the systems.[29]

These and other preliminary arrangements having been complied with, the two Fraternities, with their Grand Lodges, met on December 27, 1813, at Freemasons' Hall, which had been fitted up

---

[29] See "Articles of Union," Article V.

agreeably to a previously devised plan, and the whole house tiled from the outer porch.[30]

On each side of the room the Masters, Wardens, and Past Masters of the several lodges were arranged on benches, and so disposed that the two Fraternities were completely intermixed.

The two Grand Lodges were opened in two adjoining rooms, each according to its peculiar ceremonies, and a Grand Procession being formed, the two bodies entered side by side the Hall of Assembly, the Duke of Sussex closing one procession and the Duke of Kent the other.

On entering the Hall the procession advanced to the Throne, and opening inward the two Grand Masters proceeded up the center and took seats on each side of the Throne.

The Past Grand officers and illustrious visitors occupied the platform, and the two Senior Grand Wardens, the two Junior Grand Wardens, and the two Grand Secretaries and Grand Treasurers occupied the usual stations in the West, South, and North.

Silence having been proclaimed, the services began with prayer, offered up by Rev. Dr. Barry, the Grand Chaplain of the "Ancients."

After the act of union had been read by Sir George Naylor, Grand Director of Ceremonies, the following proclamation was made by the Rev. Dr. Coghlan, Grand Chaplain of the Grand Lodge of "Moderns."

"Hear ye: This is the Act of Union engrossed in confirmation of Articles solemnly concluded between the two Grand Lodges of Free and Accepted Masons of England, signed, sealed, and ratified by the two Grand Lodges respectively: by which they are hereafter and forever to be known and acknowledged by the style and title of THE UNITED GRAND LODGE OF ANCIENT FREEMASONS OF ENGLAND. How say you, Brothers, Representatives of the two Fraternities? Do you accept of, ratify and confirm the same ?" To which the whole Assembly answered: "We do accept, ratify any confirm the same."

The Grand Chaplain then said: "And may the Great Architect of the Universe make the Union perpetual." To which all the Brethren replied: "so mote it be."

The Articles of Union were then signed by the two Grand Masters and six Commissioners, and the seals of both Grand Lodges were affixed to the same.

---

[30] This account is condensed from Oliver's edition of Preston, pp. 368-373. The "Order of Proceedings" to be observed on the occasion are given by Bro. Hughan in his Memorials. They do not essentially differ from the details by Preston, and the latter has the advantage of being in the past tense.

Proclamation was then made by Rev. Dr. Barry in the following words:

"Be it known to all men that the Act of Union between the two Grand Lodges of Free and Accepted Masons of England is solemnly signed, sealed, ratified and confirmed, and the two Fraternities are one, to be henceforth known and acknowledged by the style and title of "The United Grand Lodge of Ancient Freemasons of England: and may the Great Architect of the Universe make their Union perpetual."

The Brethren all responded "Amen," and a symphony was played by the Grand Organist, Bro. Samuel Wesley.

The Ark of the Masonic Covenant, which had been placed in front of the Throne, was then approached by the two Grand Masters, their Deputies and Wardens.

The Grand Masters standing in the East, the Deputies on their right and left, and the Grand Wardens in the West and South, the square, level, plumb, and mallet were successively delivered to the Deputy Grand Masters and by them presented to the two Grand Masters, who having applied the square, level, and plumb to the Ark and struck it thrice with the mallet, they made the following invocation:

"May the Great Architect of the Universe enable us to uphold the grand edifice of union, of which this Ark of the Covenant is the symbol, which shall contain within it the instruments of our brotherly love and bear upon it the Holy Bible, Square, and Compasses, as the light of our faith and the rule of our works. May He dispose our hearts to make it perpetual."

And the Brethren all responded, "so mote it be."

The Masonic elements of consecration, corn, wine, and oil, were then poured upon the Ark, according to the ancient Rite, by the two Grand Masters, accompanying the act with the usual invocation.

This constituted the impressive ceremony by which the union of the hitherto rival Fraternities was consecrated.

The Grand Lodges of Scotland and Ireland were not represented, in consequence of the shortness of the notice, but letters of congratulation were received from each, with copies of resolutions which had been passed by both.

As the two Fraternities differed in their forms and ceremonies, it was necessary that some compromise should be effected so that a universal system might be adopted by the united Grand Lodge. The determination of what that system of forms should be, had been entrusted to the "Lodge of Reconciliation " as its most important, and doubtless its most difficult duty.

This duty was accomplished in the following manner: After the ceremonies of ratification had been performed, the "Lodge of Reconciliation" retired to another apartment, accompanied by the Count Lagardje, Past Grand Master of the Grand Lodge of Sweden, Dr. Van Hess of the Grand Lodge of Hamburgh, and other distinguished Masons, when the forms and ceremonies which had been previously determined upon by the "Lodge of Reconciliation" were made known.

On their return to the Assembly-room, Grand Master the Count Lagardje announced that the forms which had been settled and agreed on by the "Lodge of Reconciliation" were "pure and correct."

They were then recognized as the only forms to be thereafter observed and practiced in the United Grand Lodge and by the lodges under its obedience.

The recognized obligation was then administered by the Rev. Dr. Hemming, standing before the Bible, Square and Compasses lying on the Ark, and repeated by all the Brethren, who solemnly vowed, with joined hands, to abide by the same.

The next step was the organization of the new Grand Lodge by the election of its officers.

For this purpose the Officers of the two Grand Lodges divested themselves of their insignia, and the chairs were taken by Past Grand Officers of the two Fraternities.

The Duke of Kent addressed the assembly. He stated that the great object for which he had taken upon himself the office of Grand Master of the Ancient Fraternity, as declared at the time, was to facilitate the accomplishment of the union. He then nominated the Duke of Sussex as Grand Master of the united Grand Lodge.

The Duke of Sussex was unanimously elected and placed upon the throne by the Duke of Kent and Count Lagardje.

The Grand Master nominated the Grand officers for the year ensuing.

The Grand Lodge was then called to refreshment, and on returning, some necessary business having been transacted, the Grand lodge was closed in ample form.

It is impossible to arrive at any absolutely accurate knowledge of the numerical strength of the two Fraternities at the time of the union. This arises from the fact that the lists made by both Grand Lodges at that date contained the names of many lodges which were either extinct or had passed over to other jurisdiction.

Thus in the list of the "Moderns" ending in 1812, as given by Bro. Gould in his Four Old Lodges, the number of lodges runs up to

640; but of these many, as the list commences with the year 1721, must have long ceased to exist, and several are recorded as being in Germany and France, where the English Grand Lodge had no longer any jurisdiction, and nineteen are credited to the United States of America, where independent Grand Lodges had long been established.

In the same inaccurate way we find that the list of the "Ancients," published in 1813 in their Ahiman Rezon, records 354 lodges as being under its jurisdiction.

Many of these, however, had passed from its jurisdiction or must have ceased to exist. Ten lodges, for instance, are credited to the United States, and some to other foreign countries where the Grand Lodge no longer possessed any authority.

We may, however, estimate the comparative strength of the two Fraternities at the union by the registry of lodges made at that time, when the members were assigned by lot.

In that list, which is given by Bro. Hughan in his Memorials of the Union, 636 lodges are enrolled. Of these, 385 were "Moderns," and 251 "Ancients." If, however, it be considered that the former had been in existence for ninety-six years and the latter only sixty,[31] it will be seen that the relative proportion of successful growth was greatly in favor of the "Ancients."

Notwithstanding that the Constitutional Grand Lodge had secured the adhesion of a much higher class in the social element, that from the fifth year of its existence it had been presided over by an uninterrupted succession of Peers of the realm, and that at the very period of the Union its Grand Master was a son of the reigning monarch, and that its acknowledged Patron was the heir apparent of the Crown,[32] the Atholl Grand Lodge without these advantages enjoyed a much greater share of popularity among the masses of the Craft.

This popularity can properly be attributed only to that innovation on the accepted ritual of the Constitutional Grand Lodge which produced the secession. The dismemberment of the Master's degree and the fabrication of a Fourth degree called the Royal Arch, gave to the seceders a prestige not-enjoyed by their rivals. Candidates eagerly

---

[31] The Grand Lodge of "Moderns" was instituted in 1717, that of the "Ancients" its 1753. The former commenced with four Lodges, the latter with seven.

[32] Whatever influence these circumstances must have naturally exerted in a monarchy, its importance will hardly be appreciated at its full value by the citizens of a republic. Anderson says that at first the Freemasons were content "to choose a Grand Master from among themselves, till they should have the honor of a Noble Brother at their head."

repaired for initiation to the body, which promised them a participation in a larger amount of mystical knowledge.

The "Moderns" soon became aware of this fact, and it was not very long before, notwithstanding their outcry against innovation, they adopted the same degree or at least quietly suffered its intrusion into their own system. A Royal Arch Chapter and then a Grand Chapter was established by some "Moderns" about the year 1766, and though it was not actually countenanced, it was not denounced by the Constitutional Grand Lodge.

It has been supposed by some writers that the "Ancients" were sustained by and indeed represented the Operative element of the Craft in opposition to the purely Speculative, which was represented by the "Moderns."

But of this there is no satisfactory historical evidence. In 1723 the Operative Freemasons who, in 1717, had taken a part in the organization of the Grand Lodge, had been laid upon the shelf by that body, nor is it likely that at a long interval they would renew the contest in which they had been so signally defeated.

The excellent results which followed from the union of the two Fraternities, in the restoration of peace and concord, and the consequent strengthening of the Institution, have preserved the method in which this union was effected from adverse criticism.

The union was a compromise, and in all compromises there are necessarily mutual concessions. But it is a question whether these concessions by both parties did not involve the sacrifice of certain principles which both had hitherto deemed important.

The "Articles of Union" which constituted the groundwork on which the consolidation of the two Grand Lodges was framed, are twenty- one in number. Most of these relate to local regulations made necessary by the circumstances. Only three - the second, third, and fourth - have reference to the concessions made in the ritual and in the system of Speculative Freemasonry. These articles are in the following words:

"II. It is declared and pronounced that pure Ancient Masonry consists of three degrees, and no more, viz.: those of the Entered Apprentice, the Fellow-Craft, and the Master Mason, including the Supreme Order of the Holy Royal Arch. But this article is not intended to prevent any lodge or Chapter from holding a meeting in any of the degrees of the Orders of Chivalry, according to the Constitutions of the said Orders.

"III. There shall be the most perfect unity of obligation, of discipline, of working the lodges, of making, passing and raising, instructing and clothing the Brothers; so that one pure, unsullied system, according to the genuine landmarks, laws and traditions of the Craft shall be maintained, upheld and practiced, throughout the Masonic World, from the day and date of the said union until time shall be no more.

"IV. To prevent all controversy or dispute as to the genuine and pure obligations, forms, rules and ancient traditions of Masonry and further to unite and bind the whole Fraternity of Masons in one indissoluble bond, it is agreed that the obligations and forms that have, from time immemorial, been established, used and practiced in the Craft, shall be recognized, accepted and taken, by the members of both Fraternities, as the pure and genuine obligations and forms by which the incorporated Grand Lodge of England, and its dependent lodges in every part of the World shall be bound: and for the purpose of receiving and communicating due light and settling this uniformity of regulation and instruction (and particularly in matters which can neither be expressed nor described in writing), it is further agreed that brotherly application be made to the Grand Lodges of Scotland and Ireland, to authorize, delegate and appoint, any two or more of their enlightened members, to be present at the Grand Assembly on the solemn occasion of uniting the said Fraternities; and that the respective Grand Masters, Grand Officers, Masters, Past Masters, Wardens and Brothers, then and there present, shall solemnly engage to abide by the true forms and obligations (particularly in matters which can neither be described nor written), in the presence of the said Members of the Grand Lodges of Scotland and Ireland, that it may be declared, recognized and known, that they are all bound by the same solemn pledge, and work under the same law."

An examination of these three articles will clearly demonstrate that both Grand Lodges made concessions to each other, which involved the sacrifice in turn of the very points of ritualism on which each had, for nearly three-fourths of a century, maintained its right to supremacy.

In Article II. the Royal Arch is recognized as an inherent portion of "Ancient Craft Masonry." Yet when about 1738 the Freemasons began soon after to call themselves "Ancient Masons," their lodges were erased from the roll and their members expelled because they had practiced this same degree. Nothing then and long after so much incensed the "Moderns" as this innovation, as they called it, of a new degree. "Our society," said their Grand Secretary, Spencer, "is neither Arch, Royal Arch, nor Ancient."

On this point the "Ancients" certainly achieved a victory. The attempted qualification in the declaration that Ancient Craft Masonry consisted of only three degrees, which was a concession to preserve the consistency of the "Moderns," was without meaning, since it was immediately followed by the admission that there was a Fourth degree.

In Article III. it is declared that the methods of initiation and instruction should be according to the genuine landmarks, laws, and traditions of the Craft. But the United Grand Lodge adopted the changes in the words of the degrees, which had been introduced by the Constitutional Grand Lodge, to prevent the intrusion of the seceders into the regular lodges. The preservation of these words and certain other changes was certainly not in accordance with the "landmarks," supposing these landmarks to be the usages of the Craft, adopted at or soon after the organization in the year 1717.

The result has been to create in these respects a difference between the Continental and the English-speaking Masons, the former adhering to the original forms.[33]

This would be a victory for the "Moderns," but not one of so much importance as that achieved by the "Ancients" in the recognition of the Royal Arch degree.

The assertion in Article IV. that the obligations and forms which were agreed upon at the Union were those which " from time immemorial have been established, used and practiced by the Craft," is thus found to be merely a "façon de parler" too much in vogue even at the present day, when referring to the antiquity of usages.

The "time immemorial" thus vaunted, dwindles down, in fact, to the date of the organization of the "Lodge of Reconciliation," to which the regulation of these "obligations and forms" had been entrusted.

The confirmation of this new system by the Grand Lodges of Scotland and Ireland, which was provided for in the same article, was not carried into effect, for no representatives of these bodies were present.

The Grand Lodge of Ireland, it may be presumed, as the Irish Masons had long favored the high degrees, would give its implicit assent

---

[33] The Gordian knot presented by the change in the Master's Word made by the "Moderns" was cut, by the adoption or sanction of both words, and they are still so used in English lodges. In the United States of America the word of the "Moderns" has long since passed out of the memory and the knowledge of the Craft, and the original word of Desaguliers and his collaborators alone is used.

to the First Article in which even the degrees of Chivalry were recognized by sufferance.

But the Grand Lodge of Scotland had always contended that Ancient Craft Masonry, or as it was styled, "St. John's Masonry," consisted of only three degrees.[34] In 1800 it had prohibited its lodges from holding any meetings above the degree of Master Mason under penalty of the forfeiture of their charter.[35] And only four years after the United Grand Lodge of England had recognized the Royal Arch as a part of Ancient Craft Masonry, the Grand Lodge of Scotland resolved that no person holding official position in a Royal Arch Chapter should be admitted to membership in the Grand Lodge.[36]

But in fact we must look for a defense of these compromises by the two Grand Lodges of England to the peculiar and threatening condition in which they were placed. Without compromise and mutual concession of many things the maintenance of which both had once deemed essential, no union could have been effected, and without a Union the success and permanency of one, if not of both bodies, would be seriously endangered.

It must therefore be acknowledged, notwithstanding any criticism on the methods pursued, which were demanded by the claims of historic truth that, here at least, the generally to be condemned maxim of the Jesuits, which justifies the means by the end accomplished, may find some excuse.

Looking back, at this distant period, upon the history of the Craft from the middle of the 18th to the beginning of the 19th century, when the passions and prejudices which distracted the Fraternity have ceased to exist, we recognize the fact that the rivalry of the two factions was destined to be ultimately of advantage to the institution.

Oliver, speaking of this and other secessions which occurred in the 18th century, says: " I am persuaded that these schisms, by their general operation, rather accelerated than retarded the outward progress of Masonry; for at the precise time when they were most active, we find the science spreading over all the European nations and exciting the attention of all ranks and classes of mankind."[37]

Antagonism, in the long run, leads to development. The protracted struggle which finally terminated in the recognition of the Royal Arch, not only gave to the Master's degree a completeness which it

---

[34] "The Constitution of the Grand Lodge of Scotland."
[35] Lyon "History of the Lodge of Edinburgh," p. 293.
[36] Ibid., p. 295.
[37] "Historical Landmarks," ii., p. 313

had before wanted, but by the establishment of a new ritual, which more nearly approached perfection than the old one, tended to develop a more philosophic spirit in the system of Speculative Freemasonry. Of this fact ample evidence is given in the lectures of Dr. Hemming which were adopted by the United Grand Lodge, and which are much more intellectual than any that preceded them.[38]

The old and comparatively meager ritual of Desaguliers, and Anderson, with the slight additions of Martin Clare, of Dunckerley and Preston, presenting only an imperfect system, would, but for the Union, have been continued to the present day, if Speculative Freemasonry had not long before died of inanition.

The rivalry of the two bodies gave an active expansion of that spirit of charity which is incidental to every Brotherhood. Neither could afford to be less kindly disposed to the distressed of their fold than the other. And this spirit of charity, thus developed during the struggle, was vastly strengthened and made of more practical utility by the consolidation of the Fraternity.

But the most important advantage derived from the long antagonism was the development of the science of symbolism, which has given to the Institution a just claim to the title of Speculative Masonry, which it had long before assumed, and elevated it to the rank of a system of moral philosophy.

Now, for the first time since the disseverance, in the beginning of the 18th century, of the Speculative from the Operative element was it announced as the accepted definition of Freemasonry that it was "a system of morality, veiled in allegory and illustrated by symbols."

It was Hemming who proclaimed this sublime definition in the Union lectures which he framed and which has awakened the thoughts and directed the Speculations of all Masonic scholars who have written since his day.

There are, it is true, some few defects in the lectures of Dr.Hemming, but they are on the whole superior to those of Preston - superior because more philosophic and more symbolical. Preston's system was the germ, Hemming's the fruit, and the fruit always is better than the germ.

---

[38] It is to Hemming that we are indebted for that sentence which defines Freemasonry as "a system of morality, veiled in allegory and illustrated by symbols." It must be confessed, however, that he made some omissions and alterations in the old lectures, which had better been spared. But "nihil est ab omni parte beatum."

In conclusion it may be said that the rivalry of the two factions was productive of this good, that it stimulated each to seek for a higher plane of action and of character; and the union which finally took place, no matter what was the actuating motive, was the most fortunate event that had ever occurred in the Masonic Society, since it developed a higher plane for its action, and secured it a long and prosperous continuance of life which one or both of the antagonizing parties must have long since forfeited had there been no Union effected.

Peace, harmony, and concord firmly established, a consolidation of interests - a more enlarged practice of charity and brotherly relief, and a more elevated character of Speculative Freemasonry - these were the results of the Union in 1813 in England, which was speedily imitated in all other countries where the rivalry had previously existed.

CHAPTER XLIV

THE GRAND LODGE OF FRANCE

It has, I think, been conclusively shown in a preceding chapter that in the year 1732 there were but two lodges in the city of Paris, one of which had received a Warrant from the Grand Master of the Grand Lodge of England and the other had been formed, we may suppose, by a secession or, as we should now say, a demission of a portion of the members of the first lodge, grown, numerically, too large.

There is no authentic record that the Grand Master or the Grand Lodge of England ever granted a Deputation for the establishment of a Provincial Grand Master or a Provincial Grand Lodge in France.

Indeed, it has been very plausibly urged that the granting of such a Deputation to the titular Earl of Derwentwater, a convicted traitor to the English Government, whose execution had only been averted in 1715 by his escape from prison, would have been a political impossibility.

Kloss, in his History of Freemasonry in France, says that " the unfortunate international political relations which existed between England, the mother-country, and France, the daughter, prevented that free intercourse and development which might have been looked for."[39]

And yet the French authorities claim that to him such a Deputation had been granted.

Thus, we are met, on the very incipience of our investigation of the history of the institution of a Grand Lodge in France, by contradictory statements from the English and French authorities.

---

[39] "Geschichte der Freimaurerei in Frankreich aus achten urkenden dargestellt," von Georg Kloss, I., 336.

There is no way of reconciling these contradictory statements. We must utterly reject the impossible or the improbable, and accept only that which has the support of reliable authority and as to which there is no conflict between the writers on both sides of the channel.

But the adoption of this rule will not always save us from the pressure of critical difficulties. The authority of the English writers is generally of a merely negative character. With the exception of the statement of Anderson, that Viscount Montagu granted two Warrants for lodges - one at Paris and one at Valenciennes, in the year 1732 - there is, in the contemporary English records, an absolute silence in reference to all Masonic affairs in France.

The French writers are more communicative, but they have so often mistaken fable for fact, and tradition for history, that we seldom find satisfaction in receiving their statements. One of them admits that the absence of any historical monuments of the first lodge has cast some obscurity over the early operations of Freemasonry in Paris.[40]

In fact, the history of Speculative Freemasonry in France, until the year 1736, may be considered as almost hypothetical and traditionally. It is said that there was a Provincial Grand Lodge and a Provincial Grand Master, but the evidence on this subject is altogether wanting - at least such evidence as a faithful historian would require.

In the "Historical Instruction" sent in 1783 by the Grand Lodge of France to its constituent lodges, it is said that Lord Derwentwater was considered as the first Grand Master of the Order in France.[41]

Rebold is more circumstantial in his details than any other Frenchwriter. He says that "Lord Derwentwater, who in 1725 received from the Grand Lodge at London plenary powers to constitute lodges in France, was, in 1735, invested by the same Grand Lodge with the functions of Provincial Grand Master, and when he quitted France to return to England, where soon after he perished on the scaffold, a victim to his attachment to the Stuarts, he transferred the plenary powers which he possessed to his friend Lord Harnouester, whom he appointed as the representative, during his absence, of his office of Provincial Grand Master."[42]

---

[40] Ragon, " Acta Latomorum," 1., p. 22.
[41] Thory, " Histoire de la Fondation du Grand Orient," p. 12. Findel.
[42] "Histoire des Trois Grandes Loges," p. 44. Ragon, who is less imaginative or inventive than Rebold, though he, also, too often omits or is unable to give his authorities merely says that Derwentwater was chosen as their Grand Master by the brethren at the time of the introduction of Freemasonry into Paris. " Acta Latomorum," p. 52.

Lalande, in his article on Freemasonry in the "Encyclopedie," places the affair of Derwentwater's Grand Mastership in the true light, when he says that as the first Paris lodge had been opened by Lord Derwentwater, he was regarded as the Grand Master of the French Masons, and so continued until his return to England, without any formal recognition on the part of the brethren.

Considering the political condition of England, which had only a few years before been the scene of a rebellion in which the family of Charles Radcliffe, the titular Earl of Derwentwater, played an important part - considering that he himself was nothing more nor less than an escaped convict, liable at any moment when apprehended to undergo the sentence of death which had been adjudged against him by the law, and considering the existence of a party of Jacobites who still secretly wished for the downfall of the House of Hanover, and the restoration of the family of Stuart to the throne, it is really absurd to suppose that the Grand Lodge of England, which claimed at least to be loyal, could have selected such a person as its representative among the Freemasons of France.

We may, therefore, I think, unhesitatingly look upon this story of the premier Grand Mastership of the titular Earl of Derwentwater as a myth, with no other foundation than the mere fact, which will be admitted, that he was a chief instrument in establishing, without Warrant, the first lodge in Paris, and that by his family relations he possessed much influence among the English Freemasons in Paris, who were for the most part Jacobites or adherents of the House of Stuart.

Rebold, who has accepted every tradition of those days of myths as an historical fact, proceeds to tell us that the four lodges which were then in Paris determined to establish a Provincial Grand Lodge of England, to which, as the representative of the Grand Lodge at London, the lodges which might in future be constituted should directly address themselves. This resolution, he says, was put into execution after the departure of Lord Derwentwater, and this Grand Lodge was regularly and legally constituted in 1736 under the presidency of Lord Harnouester.[43]

The hypothesis, universally advanced by the French writers, that Charles Radcliffe, commonly called Lord Derwentwater, was Grand Master from 1725 to 1736, therefore is not tenable. There is no testimony, such as is worth accepting in an historical inquiry, to support it. That he was not so appointed by the Grand Lodge of England can not

---

[43] Ibid.

be denied. The existing political condition of the country would make such an appointment most improbable if not impossible, and, besides, there is no reference in the records of the Grand Lodge to an act, which would have been too important to have been passed over in silence.

The condition of French Freemasonry was such as to render it extremely difficult, indeed almost impossible, to attain any accurate or reliable account of its history.

French historians do not deny this. Thory, who had the best opportunities as an historical investigator, and who was more familiar than any of his contemporaries with Masonic documents, does not hesitate, when referring to a period even a little later, to give this opinion of the chaotic condition of French Masonry in the earlier part of the 18th century.

"Masonry was then in such a disordered condition that we have no register or official report of its assemblies. There did not exist any bodies organized in the nature of Grand Lodges, such as were known in England and Scotland. Each lodge in Paris or in the kingdom was the property of an individual who was called the Master of the lodge. He governed the body over which he presided according to his own will and pleasure. These Masters of lodges were independent of each other, and recognized no other authority than their owner. They granted to all who applied the power to hold lodges, and thus added new Masters to the old ones. In fact, it may be said that up to 1743 Masonry presented in France under the Grand Masterships of Derwentwater, Lord Harnouester, and the Duke d'Antin the spectacle of the most revolting anarchy."[44]

Such a description, whose accuracy, considering the impartial authority whence it is derived, can not be doubted, must render it utterly useless to look for anything like a constitutional or legal authority, in the English meaning of the term, for the administration of the Masonic government during the time in which Derwentwater played an important part in its affairs.

Until 1732 there was no lodge in France which derived its authority to act from the warrant of a Grand Lodge. The one formed in 1725, by Derwentwater, Harnouester, Maskelyne, and Heguetty, and

---

[44] "Histoire de la Fondation du Grand Orient," p. 13. Clavel confirms this testimony He says that "all the lodges which were afterwards established in Paris and the rest of France owed their constitution to the societies (the primitive lodges) of which we have just spoken. Most of them assumed the powers of Grand Lodges and granted Letters of Constitution to new lodges." - "Histoire Pittoresque de la Franc-Maconnerie," p. 108.

those which had been previously founded in other parts of France - at Dunkirk and at Mons - must have been instituted under the old principle of the Operative Freemasons, which ceased to be recognized in England, in the year 1717, that a sufficient number of brethren might assemble for Masonic work, without the authority of any superintending power. Warrants were not known or recognized in England until that year. They had not yet been extended into France. The first Warrant known in France was that which was granted by the Grand Lodge at London to the lodge in the Rue de Bussy at Paris, and numbered in the English list as No. 90.

But for years afterward lodges continued to be organized, as we have just seen, in France under the old Operative system of lodge independence.

During all this period there was no Grand or Provincial Grand Master in France. But Charles Radcliffe, who had, it seems, been the introducer of Speculative Freemasonry into Paris, must have been very popular with his English companions, who, like himself, were adherents of the exiled House of Stuart. After the death of his nephew he assumed the title of Earl of Derwentwater, and as such was recognized by the French king and the Pretender. He was a leader of the Jacobite party, and it is very generally supposed that it was in the interests of that party that he organized his lodge at Paris, the first prominent members of which belonged to the same political party.

It is not, therefore, astonishing that his connection with Freemasonry, as the founder of the first Parisian lodge, has led to the traditional error of supposing him to have been the first Grand Master of the French Freemasons. In his day there was no Grand Lodge nor Grand Master in that kingdom.

The astronomer Lalande, who wrote a very sensible history of Freemasonry for the French Encyclopedia, recognizes this fact, when he says that Lord Harnouester was the first regularly chosen Grand Master.

The tradition that when Derwentwater left France for England in 1733 (not as Thory erroneously states in 1735), he appointed Lord Harnouester as his Deputy and Representative during his absence, is therefore a mere fiction. He could not delegate a position and powers which he did not possess. But it is reason able to suppose that on the departure of Derwentwater, Lord Harnouester as of high rank, influence, and popularity among the English exiles who were Masons, assumed the position of a leader, which Derwentwater had previously occupied.

After a temporary absence in England, where, notwithstanding the sentence of death which had been adjudged against him in 1715, he was not arrested, the government exercising a merciful forbearance, he returned to the Continent, but we find no evidence of him having taken any further active interest in Masonic affairs.

The French writers all agree in saying that in 1736 Lord Harnouester was elected Grand Master. But we have no record of the circumstances attending his election. Rebold's statement that he was elected by the lodges then existing in Paris, may or may not be truth. There is not sufficient historical testimony of the fact to remove it out of the realm of tradition.

Thory simply says, " Lord Harnouester was elected Grand Master, after Lord Derwentwater, in 1736."[45] of Harnouester we know so little that we have not been able to identify him with any of the public personages of the period, or to find any record of him in the contemporary lists of the English peerage.

If, however, we accept, on the mere dictum of the French historians, the truth of the statement that Harnouester was the first Grand Master of Masons in France, we must also accept the statement, equally authentic or unauthentic, that his Grand Mastership was a brief one and unattended with any events that it has been deemed worthy to record.

Thory merely says that the Duke d'Antin succeeded Harnouester in 1738.[46]

Rebold indulges in more details, which, however, we must take on his sole authority. He says that "in 1737 Lord Harnouester, the second Provincial Grand Master of France, wishing to return to England, requested that his successor should be appointed, and having expressed the desire that he should be a Frenchman, the Duke d'Antin, a zealous Mason, was chosen to succeed him in the month of June, 1738."[47]

The account given by French writers of the character of the Duke is a very favorable one. It is said that he was selected by the Freemasons for their presiding officer from among those of the nobility who had shown the most zeal for the Order.

Of his own attachment to it, he had shown a striking proof by disobeying the express command of the King, Louis XV., who had forbidden his courtiers to unite with the society, and especially in daring to accept the Grand Mastership, notwithstanding that the monarch had declared, when he was informed that the Masons were about to elect

---

[45] "Histoire de la Fondation du Grand Orient," p. 14
[46] Ibid.
[47] "Histoire des Trois Grandes Loges," p. 45.

such an officer, that if the choice fell on a Frenchman who should consent to serve he would immediately send him, by a lettre de cachet, to the Bastille. But the threat was not carried into execution.[48]

We are now about to pass out of the realm of what, borrowing a term of science from the anthropologists, may be called the pre-historic age of French Freemasonry. Henceforth we shall have something authentic from contemporary authorities on which to lean. The myths and mere traditions which mark the story of the second decade of the 18th century will be succeeded by historical facts, though we must still be guarded in accepting all the speculations which the writers of France have been prone to blend with them so as in many instances to give us a mingled web of romance and history.

Before continuing the history of the Grand Lodge from the accession of the Duke d'Antin, it will not be uninteresting nor unprofitable to suspend the narrative and to take a view of the condition of Freemasonry in France, and especially in Paris, at the period of time embracing a few years before and a few years after his accession to the Masonic throne.

At so early a period as 1737, the institution, though apparently very popular among the noblesse and the bourgeoisie - the lords and the citizens - had become distasteful to the King, Louis XV., whom we have already seen threatening to imprison its Grand Master if he was a Frenchman.

This fact is confirmed by a statement made in the Gentleman's Magazine for March, 1737. The statement is in a letter from Paris and is in the following words:

"The sudden increase of the Society of Free Masons in France had given such offense that the King forbid their meetings at any of their lodges."

This was the cause of an apologetic letter which was published in Paris and a part of it copied into the Gentleman's Magazine for the following month.[49]

---

[48] Ibid., p. 49, note.

[49] This expression is found in some of the early French rituals as a definition of the object of Freemasonry. The English Masonic borrowed and made use of it. In a Pro Vogue spoken at Exeter, in 1771, are the following lines:
"The Lodge, the social virtues fondly love:
There Wisdom's rules we trace and so improve:
There we (in moral architecture skill'd)
Dungeons for Vice - for Virtue temples build."

Portions of this letter are worth copying, because of the principles which the French Masons, at least, professed at the time.

"The views the Free Masons propose to themselves," says this apology, "are the most pure and inoffensive and tend to promote such qualities in them as may form good citizens and zealous subjects; faithful to their prince, to their country and to their friends.

The duty it prescribes to those who bear it is to endeavor to erect temples for virtue and dungeons for vice. . . . Their principal design is to restore to the earth the reign of Astrea and to revive the time of Rhea."

From Kloss and from all the French writers we have the record of other instances of the persecution to which the Freemasons in Paris were subjected at this period by the municipal authorities, whose actions were undoubtedly in accord with the sentiments of the king. One of these is worth a relation.

On the 10th of September, 1787, the police surprised a lodge of Freemasons which was being held in the house of one Chapelot. He had for safety bricked up the door of his public and secretly opened another to the room of meeting. Notwithstanding these precautions, the police obtained an entrance and dispersed the assembly. Chapelot was condemned to pay a fine of a thousand livres and was deprived of his license as a tavern-keeper for six months.

On April 27, 1738, Pope Clement XII. fulminated his celebrated bull in eminenti, in which all the faithful were forbidden to attend the meetings of the Masonic lodges, or in any way to consort with the Freemasons under the penalty of ipso facto excommunication, absolution from which, except at the point of death, was reserved to the Supreme Pontiff.

This condemnation by the Church gave an increased vigor and vigilance to the attacks of the police. On St. John the Evangelist's day, 1738, the Freemasons having assembled at the room of the lodge in the Rue des Deux-Ecus to celebrate the feast of the Order, were arrested and several of them imprisoned.

But notwithstanding these efforts to suppress the Order in France, it grew apace, and was not without an acknowledged standing outside of the Order, and of a recognition of its independence and regularity by the Grand Lodge at London.

See Jones's Masonic Miscellanies, p. 164.

This we learn from Anderson, who, in his second edition of the Book of Constitutions, published by authority of the Grand Lodge of England, in 1738, says:

"But the old lodge at York City and the lodges of Scotland, Ireland, France, and Italy, affecting independence, are under their own Grand Masters, though they have the same Constitutions, Charges, Regulations, etc., in substance, with their brethren of England and are equally zealous for the Augustan style, and the secrets of the ancient and honorable fraternity."[50]

Anderson was right in his statement that the usages of the Craft in the two countries were similar. The ritual of the French Freemasons, at that early period, has not been altogether lost. An interesting description of it was published in a contemporary journal of London, and as the volume which contains it is not generally accessible except in large public libraries, it is here copied in full. The reader will be pleased to compare the ceremonies of admission to the Society, as practiced in the year 1737, in Paris, with those of the London Masons at about the same period, which appear in a preceding part of this work.

In the Gentleman's Magazine, published at London, in March, 1737, is the following letter, which bears the date of "Paris, January 13:"

"THE SECRET OF THE ORDER OF FREE MASONS AND THE CEREMONIES OBSERVED AT THE RECEPTION OF MEMBERS INTO IT.

"First of all, persons must be proposed in one of the Lodges by a Brother of the Society as a good Subject; and when the latter obtains his request, the Recipiendary is conducted by the Proposer, who becomes his Godfather, into one of the Chambers of the lodge where there is no light, and there they ask him whether he has a calling to be received: He answers, Yes. After which they ask him his Name, Sirname, and Quality, take from him all Metals or Jewels which he may have about him, as Buckles, Buttons, Rings, Boxes, etc., his Right knee is uncovered, he wears his left shoe as a slipper, then they blindfold him and keep him in that condition about an hour delivered up to his reflections; after this the Godfather goes and knocks three times at the Door of the Reception room, in which the venerable Grand Master of the Lodge[51] is, who answers by three knocks from within and orders the

---

[50] Anderson's " Constitutions," second edition, 1738, p. 196.
[51] Kloss, in his Geschichte, infers from a contemporary document which he quotes that at this time the title of Grand Master was equivalent in France to that of Worshipful Master of a lodge. The use of the title in this account of the ritual leaves no doubt of the truth of that fact. To this undiscriminating use of

door to be opened; then the Godfather says that a Gentleman by name ……. presents himself in order to be received. (Note, That both on the outside and within this chamber several Brothers stand with their swords drawn in order to keep off profane people.) The Grand Master who has about his neck a blue ribband cut in a triangle says, Ask him whether he has the calling ? The Godfather puts him the question and the Recipiendary, having answered in the affirmative, the Grand Master orders him to be brought in: Then they introduce him and make him take three turns in the room round a sort of ring on the floor in which they draw with a pencil upon two Columns a sort of representation of the ruins of Solomon's Temple, on each side of that space, they also make with the pencil a great I and a great B. which they don't explain till after the Reception. In the middle there are three lighted wax candles laid in a Triangle upon which they throw gunpowder and rosin at the Novice's arrival, in order to frighten him by the effect of these matters The three turns being made, the Recipiendary is brought into the middle of the writing above mentioned in three pauses over against the Grand Master, who is at the upper end behind an armchair on which is the Book of St. John's Gospel and asks him: Do you feel a Calling? Upon his answering, Yes, the Grand Master says.

Shew him the Light, he has been long enough deprived of it. In that instant they take off the cloth from before his eyes and all the Brothers standing in a circle, draw their swords; they cause the Recipiendary to advance on three pauses up to a stool which is at the foot of the arm-chair; The Brother Orator addresses him in these terms: You are going to embrace a respectable Order which is more serious than you imagine; there is nothing in it against the Law, against Religion, against the State, against the King, nor against Manners:

"The venerable Grand Master will tell you the rest. At the same time they make him kneel on the stool with his Right knee which is bare and hold his Left Foot in the air: Then the Grand Master says to him, 'You promise never to trace, write, or reveal the secrets of Free Masons or Free Masonry but to a Brother in the lodge or in the Grand Master's presence.' Then they uncover his Breast to see if he is not a Woman and put a pair of Compasses on his left pap, which he holds himself; he puts his Right Hand on the Gospel and pronounces his Oath in these terms: 'I consent that my Tongue may be pulled out, my heart torn to pieces,

---

the two titles are we to attribute much of the confusion and uncertainty that exists in reference to the leadership in French Freemasonry, at this early period of its history.

my Body burnt, and my Ashes scattered, that there may be no more mention made of me amongst mankind if, etc.,' after which he kisses the Book. Then the Grand Master makes him stand by him; they give the Free Mason's Apron which is a white skin, a pair of men's gloves for himself and a pair of women's gloves for the person of that sex, for whom he has the most esteem. They also explain to him the I and B traced on the floor which are the type of the Sign by which Brothers know one another. The I signifies Jahkin and the B. Boiaes. In the Signs which the Free Masons make amongst one another they represent these two words by putting the Right Hand to the Left side of the Chin, from whence they draw it back upon the same line to the Right Side; then they strike the skirt of their coat on the Right Side and also stretch out their hands to each other, laying the Right Thumb upon the great joint of his comrade's first finger which is accompanied with the word Jahkin, they strike their breasts with the Right Hand and take each other by the hand again by reciprocally touching with the Right Thumb the first and great joint of the middle finger which is accompanied with the word Boiaes. This ceremony being performed and explained, the Recipiendary is called Brother, after which they sit down and, with the Grand Master's leave, drink the new Brother's health. Every body has his bottle. When they have a mind to drink they say, Give some powder, viz: Fill your glass. The Grand Master says, Lay your hands to your firelocks; then they drink the Brother's health and the glass is carried in three different motions to the mouth; before they set it down on the table they lay it to their Left pap, then to the Right and then forwards and in three other pauses they lay the glass perpendicular upon the table, clap their hands three times and cry three times Vivat. They observe to have three wax candles disposed in a triangle on the table. If they perceive or suspect that some suspicious person has introduced himself amongst them, they declare it by saying it rains, which signifies that they must say nothing.

As some people might have discovered the Signs which denote the terms Jahkin and Boiaes, a Free Mason may be known by taking him by the hand as above mentioned and pronouncing I, to which the other answers A, the first says K, the second replies H. the first ends with I, and the other with N. which makes Jahkin: It is the same in regard to Boiaes."

The administration of the Duke d'Antin was not, so far as respects the institution and the successful carrying out of reforms, a success. The anarchy and independence of the lodges which had hitherto prevailed did not altogether cease. The claim of a personal possession and an immovable tenure of office made by many Masters, especially tavern-keepers, who had organized lodges at their places of public entertainment, was not altogether abandoned.

Warrants of Constitution were frequently issued by private lodges, which should have emanated from the Grand Lodge, had there really been such a body in existence, of which fact there is much doubt.

Thory admits that there was in 1742, the year before d'Antin's death, no Grand Lodge organized like that of England, and an English writer having stated that in the year mentioned there were twenty-two lodges in Paris and more than two hundred in all France, he confesses his inability to verify the statement because French Freemasonry was at that time in such a disordered condition that there were no registers or official reports of lodge meetings.[52]

The persecutions of the Church, of the Court, and the police were unabated, and if the Masonic reign of the Duke d'Antin was eventful in nothing else, it certainly was in the continual contests of the enemies and the friends of Masonry, the one seeking to crush and the other to sustain it. That the latter often were placed in danger, and sometimes endured a sort of martyrdom when their meetings were detected, is well known. And for their zeal and their perseverance under all these difficulties and dangers in preserving the existence, however feeble, of the institution and in delivering to their successors for better growth and greater strength, the Freemasons owe them a debt of gratitude.

The ritual, too, of the order in France was, as we have seen, derived from that of the English system, though changes and innovations were already beginning to appear. The extract given above shows that the ceremony of the table lodge and the peculiar language accompanying it were the pure invention of French ingenuity, wholly unknown then and since to English-speaking Masons.

In 1743 the Duke d'Antin died and he was succeeded in the Grand Mastership by the Count of Clermont. There were other candidates, and the Prince of Conti and Marshal Saxe received some votes during the election. This shows that French Masonry, whatever were its faults of irregularity, had not fallen in the social scale.

The Count of Clermont was higher in rank than the Duke d'Antin. He belonged to the royal family of Orleans and was the uncle of the infamous Duke of Chartres, afterward Duke of Orleans (who succeeded him in the Grand Mastership), and was the father of Louis Philippe, subsequently the popular King of France.

---

[52] "Fondation du Grand Orient," p. 13.

But the French Masons were disappointed in the advantageous results which they anticipated would follow the choice of one so illustrious in rank as their leader. This will be seen hereafter.

His election, if we may believe the French authorities on the subject, was accomplished by forms that made it regular and legal, the Masters of the Parisian lodges having for that purpose united in a General Assembly on December 11, 1743.

Hence Thory[53] says that it is from this epoch that we are to regard the existence of the Grand Lodge of France as legal and authentic, because it was founded at Paris with the consent of the Masters of the lodges in the Provinces.

He says that it assumed the title of the "English Grand Lodge of France." Whether it did so at the time of its organization or at a subsequent period is uncertain, but it is proved that it bore that title in 1754, for Thory says that he had seen a print engraved in that year by Jean de la Cruz on which were the words - "Grange loge Anglaise de France."

But the assertion made by some writers that the use of the title was authorized by the Grand Lodge at London, with whom the Freemasons of Paris had, about that time, been in successful negotiation for recognition and patronage, is undoubtedly a fiction. There is not a particle of evidence in the contemporary records of the Grand Lodge of England that any such negotiations had taken place. It has, however, been seen heretofore that Anderson, in 1738, acknowledged that the independent authority of the Grand Master of the French Masons was recognized in England, and that the brethren in Scotland, Ireland, and France were placed upon the same footing of autonomy.

Very soon after his election as Grand Master the Count of Clermont ceased to pay much attention to the administration of the affairs of the Fraternity, whose interests were thus materially affected by his indifference.

One of the greatest difficulties with which the Grand Lodge had to contend in its efforts to secure harmony and to preserve discipline arose from the practice which it pursued of granting Charters to lodges, the Masters of which held their offices for life. They were called "Maitres inamovibles" - unremovable or perpetual Masters. A great many of these were already in existence, having been created under the irregular system of the preceding times, and the new Grand Lodge unfortunately increased the number.

---

[53] "Histoire de la Fondation du Grand Orient." p. 14.

Then "unremovable Masters" organized local administrations under the denomination of "Provincial Grand Lodges," which were governed by the presiding officers of the lodges which had created them.

Thory speaks of these early days of the English Grand Lodge of France as the period of illegal constitutions, of false titles, of antedated charters delivered by pretended Masters of lodges or fabricated by the lodges themselves, some of which claimed a fictitious origin which went back to the year 1500.[54]

Another evil to which French Freemasonry was subjected at the beginning of its legal and constitutional career was the inundation of high degrees and the establishment of Chapters and Councils which became the rivals of the Grand Lodge.

It is to the Chevalier Ramsay that the Order is indebted for the doubtful gift of these high degrees which began to overshadow primitive, symbolic Freemasonry, and for the invention of new theories as to the origin of the Institution, which wholly rejecting the Operative element, on which the true symbolism of Freemasonry so much depends, sought to trace its existence as a Speculative Organization to the era of the Crusades and to the work of the Christian Knights.

The Grand Lodge of France, like that of England, recognized and practiced only the three symbolic degrees. Its charters to the lodges which it instituted authorized them to confer only these three degrees. It claimed that the complete cycle of Speculative Freemasonry was embraced within these prescribed limits. They denied that there was or could be any mystical knowledge above and beyond that which was taught in the Master's initiation. And it emphatically refused to concede that there existed any higher authority than itself from which the power to impart this knowledge could be derived.

Now when Ramsay's Rite of six or seven degrees was rapidly developed into other Rites professing a still greater number - when both at Paris and in the Provinces, other bodies began to be established by the illegal acts of some of the lodges, which, with the lofty titles of Colleges, Chapters, Councils and Tribunals, assumed an authority equal to that of the Grand Lodge in respect to the primitive degrees and one superior to it in respect to the new systems - when these self-constituted or illegally constituted bodies, looked with contempt on the meager initiations and the scanty instructions of the simple system of the lodges, and claimed a more elevated, more philosophic, more splendid system of their own - it is not surprising that hundreds should have been attracted by their false

---

[54] "Acta Latomorum," Tome i., p. 56.

theories, their grandiloquent pretensions, and the glamour which they created by their high titles, their glittering jewels, and their splendid decorations, so that pure and simple Masonry was beginning to lose its attractions and the Grand Lodge its prestige.

Nor is it less surprising that, as Thory has said, the result of all these disorders was such a complication, that at that epoch and for a long time afterward a stranger and even a Frenchman could not positively determine which was the true constitutional authority of Freemasonry in the kingdom, in what body it was vested or by what it was justly exercised.

Harassed by these conflicts for authority, these incessant assumptions of jurisdiction, which were debasing its position, the Grand Lodge resolved to take a higher stand, which it was supposed, or hoped, would secure for it a stronger hold upon the obedience of the Fraternity.

In 1743 it had adopted, as has been shown, the title of "The English Grand Lodge of France." This title had been assumed, not with the authority of the Grand Lodge at London, nor because there was any official connection with the two organizations, for there is not the slightest evidence of any historical value to that effect, but rather as an indication, as we may suppose, that the Freemasonry of France had originally come from England.

But there must have prevailed an idea that the English Grand Lodge of France was in some way a dependence on the London body, which would of course impair its claim to absolute sovereignty.

Accordingly, the French Grand Lodge asserted its thorough independence in the year 1756 by omitting the word English from its title and assuming the name of "The National Grand Lodge of France."

Thory, and all the other French writers who followed him, has said that "it shook off the yoke of the Grand Lodge at London," a phrase that is altogether inaccurate, as no such "yoke" had ever existed.

The effect, however, of this apparent declaration of independence was not such as had been expected. Chapters of High Degrees persisted in their rivalry of jurisdiction, and irregular and illegal chapters were still issued by the perpetual or irremovable Masters of many of the lodges. French Freemasonry was yet in a sort of chaotic condition.

To add to these annoyances and to still further embarrass the efforts for the establishment of a constitutional authority, the Count of Clermont withdrew from all participation in the administration of affairs as Grand Master, and confided the discharge of his functions to a substitute or Deputy, in the selection of whom he was by no means judicious.

The first appointment of a Substitute was one Baure, a banker. This selection was a most unfortunate one for the Craft. Baure, instead of devoting himself to the affairs of the Order, neglected to assemble the Grand Lodge. This inactivity was very disastrous, inasmuch as it encouraged the continuance of old irregularities and the introduction of many new ones.

A contemporary writer mentions among these that certain tavern- keepers who had on former occasions prepared their houses for the meetings of lodges to which they had been admitted as serving brothers, wishing to revive the banquets from which they had derived so much profit, now assumed the functions of Masters and conferred the degrees on candidates regardless of their proper qualifications. Warrants became, like the initiations, objects of traffic, and lodges whose constitutions were purchased, opened their doors to the lowest classes, and celebrated their indecent orgies in disreputable eating houses. [55]Freemasonry under this Baure was falling into a deplorable condition.

At last, but by no means too soon, he was dismissed by the Grand Master, whose next selection was one Lacorne, a dancing master. His social position was inferior to that of his predecessor, and his character not as good. In vain the old and respectable members of the Fraternity protested against the appointment of Lacorne, who had by some services to the Grand Master secured his favor, and in reward he received the title of Particular Substitute, with a power to execute all the functions of his superior.

If the fault of Baure had been a supine inactivity, that of Lacorne was too much activity employed in a wrong direction. The Craft had exchanged King Log for King Stork. The history of the Grand Lodge for many succeeding years is a history of agitations, dissensions, and schisms fomented by Lacorne to suit his own private ends.

Lacorne hastened to hold a meeting of the Grand Lodge, which was followed by several others, in the course of which he succeeded in effecting a reorganization of the body, which had almost ceased to exist under the indifference of his predecessor. He admitted a great many Masons of all conditions and professions, and consulted his own caprice in the selection of officers.[56]

---

[55] La Chaussie, in a Memoire Justicatif, quoted by Thory, "Fondation du Grand Orient," p. 20.
[56] Thory, "Fondation de la Grand Orient," p. 21.

The first signs of a coming schism began now to make their appearance. The old members of the Fraternity, who had refused to recognize the new Substitute, refrained from any participation in these acts, more especially as, in the appointment of his officers, he had selected illiterate men.

The Grand Lodge was soon divided into two factions, the one the adherents, the other the opponents, of Lacorne. Both claimed to represent the constitutional authority, and each arrogated the titles and the functions of a Grand Lodge, so that two pretended Grand Lodges were in active existence at the same time.

These dissensions lasted for several years. Finally some zealous brethren, who foresaw the threatened destruction of the Order, or at least its reduction to a state of anarchy, offered their services to effect a reconciliation. The offer was accepted.

Representations were made to the Count of Clermont, who was prevailed upon to divest Lacorne of the powers which he had so much abused, and to appoint as his successor M. Chaillon de Joinville.

Peace and harmony seemed to be about to be restored. The two contending parties came together. All the Masters in Paris hastened to assist in the reconciliation. The Grand Lodge was reestablished and a circular was issued on June 24, 1762, which announced the auspicious event to the Freemasons of France.[57]

But the promise of peace proved too soon to be fallacious. The two rival Grand Lodges, which had existed under the administration of Lacorne, were apparently dissolved and a United Grand Lodge was organized; but the elements which composed it were so different in character that it is not surprising that new and still more bitter factions arose in a short time to disturb its harmony and to seriously affect its usefulness.

The cause which led to the birth of these new factions was a very natural one, and is to be found in the uncongeniality of the two parties who had united in the reestablishment of the Grand Lodge, arising from the great difference in the character, habits of life, and social condition of the individuals.

The old Masters and Past Masters who had contributed to the support of the institution in the earlier years of the Grand Mastership of the Count de Clermont, were members of the nobility, the bar, and the better class of citizens. They mingled with reluctance with the newcomers and the partisans of Lacorne, who for the most part were

---

[57] Ibid.

workmen without education or men of bad reputations, wholly incapable, from their want of culture and refinements to conduct the labors of the Grand Lodge.[58]

The old Masters would willingly have expelled them, and in so doing they would undoubtedly have improved the moral and intellectual tone of the Grand Lodge; but the objectionable members had legal and Masonic rights, which made them in one sense the equals of their adversaries, and it was well considered by the latter that any violent coercive measures would expose the Order to the danger of new and perhaps fatal convulsions.

Accordingly, the old brethren resolved to temporize. The regulations of the Grand Lodge prescribed a triennial election of officers. The time having arrived, very few of the new members and the partisans of Lacorne were elected to any of the offices. These, feeling assured that this act had been preconcerted, declared the election to be illegal and protested against it.

They caused defamatory libels to be printed, and scattered them with profusion among the Fraternity. In these the Grand Lodge and its officers were bitterly abused.

Under these circumstances, the older brethren who formed the most numerous as well as the most respectable part of the Grand Lodge, could do no less than vindicate its authority by expelling the malcontents from it and from all their Masonic rights and privileges.

The expelled members encountered the decree of expulsion with renewed libels, insults, and personalities, to which the other side responded by publications of a similar character. The war of words became so vigorous and offensive even to public decency that the government thought it necessary to interfere and to issue, in 1767, an order prohibiting any further assemblies of the Grand Lodge.

It must have been previous to this suspension of its meetings by the government and when the Grand Lodge had hoped that its union of the discordant elements would effect a permanent and a happy reconciliation, that it announced its existence to the Grand Lodge of England and sought to establish a fraternal interchange of courtesies between the two bodies.

Northouck tells us that on January 27, 1768, the Grand Master of the Grand Lodge of England informed the brethren that he had received from the Grand Lodge of France letters expressing a desire of opening a regular correspondence with the Grand Lodge of England.

---

[58] Thory, " Fondation de la Grand Orient," p. 22.

These letters having been read, it was resolved "that a mutual correspondence be kept up, and that a Book of Constitutions, a list of lodges, and a form of a deputation, bound in an elegant manner, be presented to the Grand Lodge of France."[59]

This, it must be remarked, is the first official recognition, by the Grand Lodge of England, of the existence and legality of such a body in France. But the ready willingness of the English Masons to cement a union with their brethren of the neighboring Grand Lodge appears to have led to no active results.

At the very time that this friendly act of the English Grand Lodge was recorded the Grand Lodge of France had suspended its labors.

The body was temporarily dissolved and its members dispersed.

The expelled members availed themselves of this favorable opportunity to renew their efforts to obtain a supremacy of the Order. They held clandestine meetings in the faubourg St. Antoine, and notwithstanding the vigilance of the magistrates, they resumed the ordinary labors of Freemasonry, and even went so far as to grant several charters to new lodges. They sent to the lodges in the country circulars in which they stated that the Grand Lodge having, in obedience to superior authority, ceased its labors, had delegated to three Brethren, Peny, Duret, and L'Eveille, the exercise, during the continuance of the persecution, of all its rights and powers.

But they did not succeed in this bold effort at deception. The provincial lodges on examining the lists of expelled Masons which had long before been sent to them by the Grand Lodge, saw that among them were the names of those persons who had signed the circular as well as of those who were said to have been appointed as commissioners to exercise the functions of the Grand Lodge during its enforced abeyance. They therefore wrote to the Substitute of the Grand Master, M. Chaillon de Joinville, for an explanation, which was readily given He denounced the encyclical letter as a false document and declared its signers to be rebels.

In consequence the provincial lodges declined the correspondence which had been offered to them and refused to take a part in the conspiracy against the Grand Lodge.

This illegal faction was led by Lacorne, who had been deposed from his office as Substitute of the Grand Master. The legal faction, for

---

[59] Northouck, " Book of Constitutions," p. 291.

the Grand Lodge was thus divided, was headed by Chaillon de Joinville, the successor of Lacorne in the office of Substitute General.

This body also held its secret meetings and also issued Charters, which, however, to avoid the appearance of violating the suspensory decree of the Magistrates, were all dated anterior to the issuing of that decree.

The object of the Lacorne faction was to abolish the Grand Lodge and to replace it by a new power from which all the respectable members should be removed and all authority be vested in the hands of the conspirators. As a preliminary step, they sought, but without success, to obtain from the lieutenant of police a revocation of the edict of suspension.

At length the death of the Grand Master, the Count of Clermont, which event occurred in 1771, gave a renewal of their hopes of seizing the supreme power. France presented, at this time, the spectacle of two Grand Lodges, or rather of two discordant and rival factions, each pretending to represent a Grand Lodge and each exercising the functions of a Supreme authority.

One of these was the National Grand Lodge, which had existed under the Count of Clermont and which, though interdicted by the government in 1767, still continued, though it held no meetings openly to exercise its prerogatives through its acknowledged officers.

The other body was a fragment, consisting of the adherents of Lacorne, all of whom had been expelled by the legal Grand Lodge, but who in violation both of the law of Masonry and the Municipal decree of interdiction, persisted in holding clandestine meetings, granting constitutions to new lodges, and in short exercising, without the least semblance of legal authority, all the functions of a Grand Lodge.

It is very clear that on the death of the Count of Clermont the National Grand Lodge, the only body in which the supreme authority of Freemasonry was at the time vested, had but one course to adopt.

It should have assembled in open session, and duly elected a successor.

Unfortunately for its own interests and for those of the institution over which it held so loose a control, it did no such thing.

Discouraged by the useless efforts it had made to obtain, from the government, a revocation of the decree of suspension, it supposed that the time was not propitious for an attempt to revive its dormant existence. Its hesitancy and its timidity were eventually the causes of its destruction.

On the contrary, the Lacorne faction, consisting, as has been said, wholly of expelled Masons, who had previously formed the disreputable part of the Grand Lodge, were more politic and more bold.

Proclaiming themselves as the nucleus of the old Grand Lodge, the labors of which had been suspended in 1767, they approached the Duke of Luxembourg, with the design of securing his influence in getting the Duke of Chartres to accept the Grand Mastership as the successor of the Count of Clermont.

Their application was successful. The Duke of Chartres consented to accept the position.

The expelled faction, elated with the success of their plan, convoked a general assembly of all the Masters in Paris, including even the members of the Grand Lodge which had formerly expelled them.

The acceptance of the Grand Mastership by one who was closely related to the sovereign, but whose infamous character had not yet been developed, had produced much enthusiasm among the Craft. The Grand Lodge was willing to be indulgent. The expelled members were restored to all their Masonic rights. On June 24, 1771, the nomination of the Duke of Chartres as Grand Master was confirmed and announced to all the lodges of Paris and the provinces The submission of the Grand Lodge to what it supposed to be the inevitable force of events, did not have the effect it had hoped of securing harmony in the Craft. The expelled members, though now restored, do not appear to have forgotten or forgiven the wrongs which they thought had been inflicted on them. The old members were still in their view their enemies. They resolved to maintain a factious rivalry, with the ulterior purpose of abolishing the old Grand Lodge and establishing a new body on its ruin" Carthage must be destroyed."

A new element of discord was now introduced, the tendency of which was favorable to the execution of these views - an element not new in French Masonry, but which had not before been introduced into the internal government of the Order. This element was found in the cultivation of the Hautes grades, or High Degrees.

It is well known that we are to attribute this innovation, wholly unknown to the ancient Operative or to the modern Speculative system, to the inventive genius of the Chevalier Ramsay. He was the first to devise these supplements to Craft Masonry and to endeavor to develop the instructions of the Third degree by the establishment of higher initiations, to which the initiation of the Master Mason was to be deemed subordinate. Ramsay's system of seven degrees was, however, simple in comparison with those subsequently introduced into France by his followers and disciples.

France was soon inundated by these "high degrees," combined in various series forming what were called "Rites," and thrusting themselves into rivalry and competition with the legal authorities which professed to know nothing about them.

The Grand Lodge of France, like its sister of England, had always remained true to the simplicity of the Speculative system, founded as it was on the traditions of the old Operative Craft, who had recognized only three classes of workmen. It had more than once authoritatively declared that Ancient Craft or Speculative Freemasonry consisted only of three degrees. This was a fundamental point in its organic law, and it had never as a body violated it.

Not so, however, was it with its leaders, many of whom had been attracted by the glimmer of imposing titles and brilliant decorations. Chaillon de Joinville, who was then the Substitute Grand Master under the Count of Clermont, had, as far back as 1761, proclaimed himself the "chief of the high degrees and a Sublime Prince of the Royal Secret." As such he had issued a commission authorizing Stephen Morin to disseminate these high degrees in America.

That fact is, itself, enough to show how far the influence of this advanced Masonry had already extended when it had been enabled to secure as its chief the actual head of the legitimate Grand Lodge.

But we also find that, from an early date, there existed at Paris and in other places in France, Colleges, Councils, and Chapters which were engaged in the cultivation and in the conferring of these high degrees, but which were always without the official recognition of the Grand Lodge.

But this recognition they greatly desired, and when the dissidents began to conspire for the abolition of the Grand Lodge and the establishment of a new body, they readily lent their assistance, because they anticipated, as was really the case, that these high degrees would receive some sort of recognition from it.

And in this hope they were encouraged by the fact that on June 24, 1771, when the Duke of Chartres was elected and proclaimed as "Grand Master of the Grand Lodge," he was also proclaimed by the additional title of " Sovereign Grand Master of all Scottish Councils, Chapters, and Lodges of France."[60]

---

[60] See Thory, " Histoire de la Fondation du Grand Orient," p. 27.

Thus, for the first time the symbolic Freemasonry of the primitive Speculative lodges and the Scottish Masonry of the High Degrees were reunited under one Grand Master by those who had formerly opposed the fusion of the two systems, and now accepted it without opposition but not without regret. The presence of the Duke of Luxembourg, who presided over the meeting in which the Grand Master was proclaimed, was an influence which closed the mouths of the discontented, who might under more auspicious circumstances have been less reticent, and less complaisant.

We can not doubt that the object of the dissidents or schismatics (which are the titles bestowed by Thory on the Lacorne or less reputable faction of the Grand Lodge) was to entirely change the features of the system of Freemasonry which had existed in France since the establishment of the first lodge and to substitute for it another less primitive and more complicated one. This they could only expect to do by the total dissolution of the old Grand Lodge and the organization of some other Masonic authority on its ruins.

Hence, Thory is led to say that at this meeting when the Duke of Chartres was elected, there was the first appearance of the symptoms which threatened the destruction of the Grand Lodge. The assembly was entirely influenced by the dissident brethren. The old controversy as to amendments of the statutes was revived, the necessity of correcting existing abuses was vehemently insisted on and the old members saw too late to successfully oppose them the aims of their rivals. Eight commissioners were appointed to report to the Grand Master some method for effecting the proposed reforms.

The history of the proceedings of these eight commissioners, in carrying out the reforms contemplated by the dissidents, has been given by a contemporary writer,[61] and it proves that they arrogated powers which the Grand Lodge had never intended to entrust to them, and exercised them with an energy that crushed by its own force all opposition.

Encouraged by the protection of the Duke of Luxembourg, who had been appointed by the Duke of Chartres as his Substitute, they held meetings at the Hotel de Chaulnes, where they exercised the functions of a General Assembly or Grand Lodge. They were joined by several Masters of the Parisian lodges and deputies from some of the lodges in

---

[61] Le Frere de la Chaussee, a man of letters, who took an active part in the Masonic discussions of the day, was a member of the old Grand Lodge and wrote a "Memoire justificatif," whence Thory has derived many of the facts on which he has based his "History of the Grand Orient."

the Provinces, their professed design being to abolish the old Grand Lodge. Some of the changes which were calculated to produce that effect were opposed by a few of the Masters and delegates. But their opposition was overruled and they were compelled to withdraw from the future meetings of the commissioners.

After much noisy discussion a plan was at length presented of a new constitution. This was adopted by the eight commissioners, without having submitted it to the Grand Lodge for its approval or even for its consideration.

On December 24, 1772, the old Grand Lodge of France was declared to have ceased to exist, and for it was substituted a National Grand Lodge, which was to constitute an integral part of a new power which should administer the affairs of the Order under the title of the GRAND ORIENT OF FRANCE.

The progress of this body, its controversies with the old Grand Lodge, whose members would not consent that it should be thus summarily abolished, and its final triumph and recognition as the head of Freemasonry in France, a position which it holds at the present day, must be the subject of another chapter.

CHAPTER XLV

ORIGIN OF THE GRAND ORIENT OF FRANCE

THE truth of history compels us to acknowledge the fact that the Grand Orient, now and for a century past the supreme Masonic authority in France, was, in its inception, a schismatic body.

Those principles of law, then recognized, as they still are, as directing the organization of Grand Lodges, appear to have been violated in almost every point by the dissidents who broke off from the old Grand Lodge and conspired to establish its rival.

The Grand Lodge was still in existence; it is true it was not energetic in action, but it was not asleep; its consent had neither been asked nor obtained for this radical change in its constitution; the lodges had not been invited to meet in general assembly nor to give their sanction to the dissolution of the old body and to the creation of the new one; everything had been done by the irresponsible authority of the eight commissioners, who were merely a committee appointed to make a report on the condition of the Order and to suggest reforms to the Grand Lodge. But they exceeded their powers; made no report, and proceeded in secret sessions, to which none but their friends and co-conspirators were admitted, to the inauguration of a new system, the adoption of which was to result in the abolition of the body which had appointed them and the creation of a new one, of which not the remotest idea was entertained by the authority from which they derived their powers.

But if ever a violation of law could be defended by the necessity of a reform of abuses, which could not be effected in a more legal manner, such defense might surely be found in the corrupt condition to which Freemasonry had been reduced by the mal-administration of affairs through the neglect of the Grand Lodge, the indifference of the Grand Masters, and the usurpations of their Substitutes.

Under the constitution of the old Grand Lodge it will be shown that there were many abuses and corruptions of the pure and primitive principles on which Speculative Freemasonry had been founded at the beginning of the century. A reformation of these abuses was undoubtedly necessary, if the existence of the Order was to be preserved. There ought not to have been any objection to the reform, it is only the method in which it was effected that is to be condemned.

A comparison of the old constitution of the Grand Lodge with that of the Grand Orient presents us with the abuses of the one and the reforms proposed by the other.

The Grand Lodge of France was composed only of the Masters of the lodges of Paris. Hence the Masons and the lodges of the Provinces had no voice in the government of the Order, though they were required to contribute to the revenues of the Grand Lodge and pay implicit obedience to its decree. It was simply the old tyrannic principle of taxation without representation, and was in direct violation of the organic law on which the Mother Grand Lodge at London had been instituted.

The Quarterly Communications, on which the supreme authority rested, was composed of thirty officers who were elected triennially.

There was also a Council consisting of nine officers and nine Masters of Paris lodges, whose decisions were, however, only provisionary and required to be confirmed by the Quarterly Communication to which they were reported.

The power of punishing offending members was vested in the Masters of lodges, but there lay an appeal to the Grand Lodge.

The Masters of lodges were in general chosen for life, and were not removable by the lodges over which they presided, and which in fact were merely, in many instances, instruments provided for the pecuniary interests of their Masters.

Thory, very strangely, calls the constitution of which these are the principal points "simple, uncomplicated, and conformable to the regulations of foreign Grand Lodges." The reader will be able to give to these two favorable views their proper value.

He admits that there were abuses, but he attributes them to the factions which agitated the Grand Lodge after the death of the Duke d'Antin, and to the state of anarchy which supervened on the suspension of the labors of the Grand Lodge by the order of government.

Doubtless, these circumstances exerted an unfavorable influence on the purity of the administration of the law, but whatever were the causes, the abuses existed, and, of course, their reformation was urgently demanded.

In all these points the new constitution of the Grand Orient provided a remedy and presented the desired reform, as may be seen from the following brief view of its principal features.

"The Statutes of the Royal Order of Freemasonry in France," for such was the imposing title of the new constitution, provided in the initial article that the "Masonic Body of France," that is, the Grand Orient, should be composed, as its only members, of regular Masons, meaning thereby the members of lodges which had received Warrants from or had them renewed by the Grand Orient.

In this way, while all regular Masons were recognized as constituting a part of the great Masonic family of France, those who still retained their allegiance to the old and rival Grand Lodge were excluded from recognition.

This was a defensive act, the necessity of which excused its severity.

Again: It was declared that the Grand Orient should be composed of all the actual Masters or the deputies of lodges not only of Paris but also of the Provinces.

The Grand Lodge had never recognized the Provincial lodges as forming any part of its constituency. Their recognition by the Grand Orient as entitled to participate in its labors was the removal of a very flagrant abuse of the Masonic law of equality.

Again: All the Warrants of constitution which had been granted by the old Grand Lodge to irremovable Masters, that is, to Masters elected for life, were suppressed by the Grand Orient, which recognized as Masters only those who were elected from time to time by the lodges.

These were the most important points of difference between the Grand Lodge and the Grand Orient; but they were so important as to make the old Masonic form of government, as Thory expresses it, an oligarchical government by an irresponsible few, while that of the new one was representative, the only form that was recognized by the founders of the Speculative system of Freemasonry.

In a Society based on the principle of equality it is very endent that the administration of affairs should not be confided to a privileged class, to the exclusion of many of its members.

Hence, though the Grand Orient of France originated in a schismatic usurpation of power, and was therefore irregular and illegal in its methods of organization, the end would seem to have justified the means. It can not be doubted that at that important epoch, the Masonic Order in France was indebted for its salvation from impending dissolution to the establishment of the Grand Orient.

The "Grand Orient" was, as it were, the generic title assumed for the whole Masonic Order; within its bosom was the body called "The National Grand Lodge." The distinctive titles were, how ever, more shadowy than real. The "Grand Orient" is the name by which the Supreme authority of Freemasonry is always described by French as well as other writers.

The title was a novel one, first invented in France at that time.

It had never before been heard of in Masonic language, though it has long since become quite common on the Continent of Europe and in South America. It has, however, never been adopted by the Freemasons of any of the English-speaking nations, who adhere to the primitive and better phrase, " Grand Lodge," as the title of the Supreme Masonic authority.

The first meeting of the Grand Orient as a National Grand Lodge was held on March 5, 1773. Other meetings succeeded, until June 24th, when the new Constitution was adopted, and the nomination of the Duke of Chartres as Grand Master, which had been made by the old Grand Lodge, was confirmed. The amovability of the Masters of lodges, and the right of the Provincial lodges to base represented in the Grand Orient were again proclaimed, and the choice of fifteen officers of honor as well as the nomination of the ordinary officers was referred to the Duke of Luxembourg.

But though the Duke of Chartres had been nominated as Grand Master, he had not yet formally accepted the nomination, an act which the members of the new Grand Orient felt to be imperatively necessary to the success of their designs. Having been previously elected to the same office by the old Grand Lodge, the founders of the Grand Orient recognized the policy of withdrawing him from all connection with the rival organization and of securing the adhesion to their cause of a prince of the royal blood.

Morally considered, no man in France was more unfit to be called to the head of the Masonic institution than the Duke of Chartres. From his early youth he had exhibited a depraved disposition, and passed amid companions, almost as wicked as himself, a life of vice and in the indulgence of the most licentious practices. When on the death of his father he became the Duke of Orleans, he developed a hatred for the king, who had refused to elevate him to posts to which his high birth entitled him to aspire, but from which he was excluded by his blackened reputation. Inspired with his hatred for the king, and the court, and moved by his personal ambition, he fomented the discontents which were already springing up among the people. On the breaking out of the revolution he became a seeker for popular favor; rivalled the bitterness of the most fanatical Jacobins, renounced his rank and title and assumed as a French citizen the name of Philip Egalite, repudiated Freemasonry as opposed to republican ideas, such as were then the fashion, threw up his office as Grand Master, was elected to the National Assembly, voted for the death of his cousin Louis the Sixteenth, and finally, as a fitting close to his life of infamy, expired on the guillotine, one of the many victims of the reign of terror.

At the period of his election as Grand Master, the Duke of Chartres had, though very young,[62] already exhibited a foreshadowing of his future career of infamy. Enough certainly was known of his vicious character to have made him an unfit leader of a virtuous society. But motives of policy overcame all other considerations.

The Duke himself was reluctant to accept the position which was tendered to him. Some jests made by the wits of the court, who perhaps saw the unfitness of the appointment, are said to have been the cause of the coldness with which he viewed the dignity tendered to him.[63]

A deputation consisting of four members of the Grand Orient, all men of rank, waited on the Duke to obtain his consent to the adoption of the new constitution, which would of course have been the recognition of the new body which had enacted it. But he refused to see the deputation.

The joyful event of the birth of a son[64] and heir presented it was supposed a more favorable opportunity for obtaining his consent to their proceedings. The expectation was gratified. The Duke of Luxembourg, who took an earnest interest in the success of the Grand Orient and who exercised much influence over the mind of the prince,

---

[62] He was born in 1747, and was therefore only twenty-six when elected Grand Master.

[63] This was the cause assigned by contemporary writers for the reluctance with which he gave his consent. See Thory, "Fondation de la Grand Orient," p. 39.

[64] This was the Duke of Valois, afterward Duke of Chartres, then Duke of Orleans, and finally King Louis Philippe of France.

repaired to his residence long before the appearance of the deputation and succeeded in obtaining his consent to grant an interview.

Having been admitted to his presence, his approval of the proceedings by which the Grand Orient was organized was obtained, and he consented that his installation as Grand Master should take place soon after his return from a visit to Fontainebleau which he was obliged to make.

Accordingly, he was installed in his own house, called la Folie Titon, in the Rue de Montreuil, on October 28, 1773. The Grand Orient was thus legalized, so far as his patronage could make it so, as the supreme legislative authority of the Masonic Order in France. Hence, this installation by its rival of the same Grand Master whom it had itself elected in 1771, and who still retained that position, was a cause of great annoyance to the old Grand Lodge. The old Grand Lodge did not, however, cease at once to exist, but continued its labors, exercising a warfare with the Grand Orient for several years.

It held a session on June 17, 1773, at which were present those Masters of the Paris lodges who were still faithful to it and some deserters from the Grand Orient, who had abandoned that body when it suppressed the law of immovability.

At this session the Grand Lodge fulminated its decrees against the Grand Orient, which it declared to be a schismatic body, surreptitiously formed - a mere faction.

On September 10th it declared the eight commissioners deprived of all Masonic rights, and forbade their admission to any of the lodges.

Though fully recognizing the embarrassment which resulted from the installation of the Duke of Chartres, it determined to maintain its independence and to continue its labors with the assistance of the few lodges which still adhered to it. For this purpose it continued its denunciations of the Grand Orient and revoked all its decrees as fast as they were passed. It had among its adherents some able men, who employed their talents in the composition and publication of circulars and even books in which the Grand Orient and all its proceedings were denounced.

Responses were not wanting on the part of the Grand Orient, among whose most able and energetic defenders was the Duke of Luxembourg, while M. Gouilliard, a Doctor of Laws and the Grand Orator of the Grand Lodge, was the most conspicuous writer on behalf of that body.

It would be tedious to follow in all its details this internecine war of "paper pellets," which lasted with equal acrimony on either side for many years. It will be sufficient to pursue, with rapid sketch, the progress of each of the rival bodies until the close of the century, when a union was finally accomplished.

In 1774 the Grand Lodge assumed the title of the "Sole and only Grand Orient of France,"[65] and proceeded to the election of its Grand Officers under the auspices of the Duke of Chartres, whom it recognized as "Grand Master of all the lodges of France." It again decreed that the so-called Grand Orient of France was irregular, and its members and partisans were clandestine Masons; it forbade its lodges to admit them as visitors unless they abjured their errors and promised submission to the Grand Lodge; it also interdicted the members of its own lodges from visiting the Grand Orient.

In 1775 the Grand Lodge granted Warrants to eight lodges in Paris and to still more in the Provinces, and continued to increase the number of lodges under its obedience for many successive years, so that its existence was not merely a formal one. On the contrary, it appears to have been a troublesome though not eventually a successful rival of the Grand Orient.

In 1780 it must at last have felt the inconvenience of having a Grand Master only in name, for there is no record that the Duke of Chartres, or his Substitute, the Duke of Luxembourg, ever attended its communications. To remedy this evil, the Grand Lodge in 1780 appointed three honorary Presidents, who were to supply the place of the Grand Master in his absence from the meetings.

That the old Grand Lodge was not yet moribund notwithstanding the greater activity of its rival, the Grand Orient, is evident from the fact that in its Tableau issued in 1783, it reports the number of lodges under its jurisdiction in Paris as well as the Provinces as amounting to the respectable number of 352. In the same yeas the English printed lists enumerate 453 lodges, but many of these were extinct and 123 were situated in foreign countries, so that there were actually at that time more lodges in France under obedience to the old Grand Lodge than there were in England under the jurisdiction of the constitutional Grand Lodge.[66]

But in 1789 the political troubles which then began to agitate the kingdom, and which soon after resulted in the French Revolution, had a very serious effect on the condition of Freemasonry. The

---

[65] Seul et Unique Grand Orient de France.
[66] See List No. 16 in Gould's " Four Old Lodges," p. 68

attendance on the lodges was very infrequent, and finally, in 1792, the Grand Lodge suspended its labors and the members were dispersed.

From the time of its organization in 1773, the Grand Orient had maintained a successful existence; it was patronized by a better class of Masons than that of which the Grand Lodge was composed, and had the support of the Grand Master of both bodies, his substitute, the Duke of Luxembourg, showing a very evident partiality for the Grand Orient, and not only never attending the meetings but actually denouncing the authority of the Grand Lodge.

The record of its transactions for these sixteen years supply us with more interesting incidents than those which marked the quiet progress of the Grand Lodge during the same period.

Its contests with the Grand Lodge for supremacy were unremittingly maintained. The mutual recriminations of both bodies did not tend to cultivate a spirit of fraternity. Finding itself embarrassed for the want of the registers and other archives which were retained by the Grand Lodge, the Grand Orient went so far as to apply to the Lieutenant of Police and cause the arrest and imprisonment of the keeper of the Seals and some other members of the Grand Lodge. But the effort to obtain possession of the documents, even by this harsh means was unsuccessful.

It was found impossible for want of the registers to discover the number and names of the country lodges, most of which, having been established under the old, corrupt system of immovable Masters or Masters for life, retained their allegiance to the Grand Lodge, which still preserved the usage.

The Grand Orient, therefore, that the knowledge of its existence and its authority might be brought nearer these country lodges, established Provincial Grand Lodges, as another of the important changes which it was making in the usages of French Freemasonry.

These Provincial Grand Lodges were not, however, established on the same plan as those of England. Their design was, as has been said, to relieve the Grand Orient of the embarrassment of governing lodges at a distance. A provincial Grand Lodge was to be established not in a Province only, but in any town or place where there were not less than three lodges; it was to have a superintendence over them; its decrees were to be subject only to appeal to the Grand Orient, it was to collect and transmit all dues; and was to be the medium of all correspondence between the lodges and the Grand Orient.

The Grand Orient became rather aristocratic in its ideas and refused to recognize as members of the Order persons who were attached to the public theatres and to all artisans who were not Master workmen in their trades. Subsequently it forbade the lodges to meet in public taverns, a reformation which their English brethren had not yet reached.

In 1774 the title of "Royal Order," by which Freemasonry had hitherto been designated in France, was exchanged for that of the "Masonic Order," certainly a more appropriate name.

In 1775 the Grand Orient was occupied in determining the form of the Masonic government in the kingdom, and several decrees were made for the regulation of the deputies and representatives of lodges. It expressed its intention to purify the Order and the lodges which were profaned by the presence of corrupt men, and a commission was appointed to carry these views into effect.

The Duke of Chartres presided at a meeting of the Grand Orient in July, 1776, being the first time that he had been present since his installation in 1773.

The prevalence of "high degrees" and of Councils and Chapters which conferred them independently of the Grand Orient, had led the members of that body to take into consideration the expediency of following what had now become the fashion on the Continent and more especially in France, and of developing within its own bosom a rite which should be founded on the three symbolic degrees which had hitherto been practiced by it and by the Grand Lodge. A chamber of degrees or committee to regulate this matter was accordingly appointed in 1782. Two years after this chamber reported four degrees, which, with the three symbolic as a foundation, were to constitute the " Rise Francaise."

These degrees were entitled Elu, Ecossais, Chevalier d'Orient, and Chevalier Rose Croix, or, as they may be translated, Elect Mason, Scottish Mason, Knight of the East and Knight Rose Croix. Though there were some modifications of the rituals, the degrees were not an original conception of the Committee, but were borrowed substantially from those systems which had been practiced in France since the time of the Chevalier Ramsay.

The degrees having been adopted by the Grand Orient, it decreed that they should henceforth be the only ones recognized and practiced in the several chapters which were attached to the lodges under its jurisdiction.

Undoubtedly the adoption of these new degrees was a manifest innovation on the pure system of primitive Speculative Freemasonry, an innovation which the more conservative spirits of the English- speaking Grand Lodges had always resisted.

But under the peculiar character which Continental Masonry had long assumed, it was far better that the Grand Orient should adopt a system of development comparatively simple and consisting of only four additional degrees, and confine its lodges within those limits, than to permit them to become the victims of the numerous and extravagant systems by which they were surrounded and which were practiced by irresponsible Chapters and Councils.

The French lodges of the Grand Orient were thus provided with a uniform system of their own, far better than the many diverse ones, which bid defiance to all homogeneity of Speculative Freemasonry.

In 1791 the lodges under the Grand Orient, like those under the Grand Lodge, suspended their labors and closed their doors in consequence of the existing political agitations. Still the Grand Orient, even in that year, constituted two or three lodges, but Freemasonry had really assumed a dormant condition throughout the kingdom.

But notwithstanding the dissolution of the lodges, several of the officers of the Grand Orient boldly sustained its activity so far as circumstances would permit. In France, in this day of trial, there were, as there were in America in a long subsequent period of persecution, some Masons who were willing to become Martyrs to their convictions of the purity of the Institution, and to the love which they bore for it.

But no such sentiments animated the bosom of the recreant Grand Master, the Duke of Chartres, who by the death of his father had become Duke of Orleans, and who, having abandoned his family and his class, had repudiated his hereditary title and assumed, according to the fashion of the sans culottes, the name of Citizen Equality - le citoyen Egalite.

The Secretary of the Grand Orient having in December, 1792, addressed him an official note relative to the labors of the Grand Orient, the Duke made a reply in the following words, on May 15, 1793:

"As I do not know how the Grand Orient is constituted, and as I moreover, do not think that there should be any mystery or secret society in a republic, especially at the beginning of its establishment, I no longer wish to have anything to do with the Grand Orient or with the meetings of Masons."

This peremptory, and in its terms insulting, withdrawal was received, as it may be supposed, by the members of the Grand Orient with expressions of the utmost indignation. It is said that the sword of the Order, one of the insignia of the Grand Master, was broken by the presiding officer and cast into the midst of the Assembly, and the Grand Mastership was declared vacant.

In 1795 a few of the lodges resumed their labors, and M. Rotiers de Montaleau was elected Grand Master. He, however, refused to take the title, and assumed that of "Grand Venerable," with, however, all the prerogatives and functions of a Grand Master.

The progress of Masonic restoration to activity was, however, very slow. In 1796 there were but eighteen lodges in active operation in the whole of France, namely, three at Paris, and the remaining fifteen in the Provinces.

In May, 1799, commissioners who had been appointed by the Grand Lodge and the Grand Orient concluded a treaty of union between the two rival bodies. The Grand Lodge in this treaty agreed to the abolition of the usage it had always hitherto maintained of the irremovability of Masters, and accepted the doctrine of the Grand Orient, that they should hereafter be elected by the members of the lodges.

On June 22, 1799, the two hitherto rivals met in a United Assembly, and the union of all the Freemasons of France was consummated, the title of Grand Orient being continued, to designate the supreme Masonic authority, and the Grand Lodge ceased to exist

Thus the rivalry which had existed in France for twenty-six years between two bodies, each claiming to be the head of the Order, was terminated by an amicable union.

In England the same sort of rivalry had existed between the Grand Lodge of the "Moderns " and that of the "Ancients" for a much longer time, and was terminated at a later period by a similar union.

But in the circumstances connected with this internecine war there were some singular coincidences which are worthy of remark.

In the first place, the original disruption was based in each kingdom on a single fundamental point of difference.

In England it was on the recognition of a Fourth degree in the ritual. The "Moderns" contended that there were in Speculative Freemasonry no more than the three primitive degrees of Apprentice, Fellow-Craft, and Master. The "Ancients" affirmed that for the completion of the ritual a Fourth degree, which they called the "Royal Arch," was essentially necessary, and that without it as a development of the Third degree, the system of Speculative Masonry was imperfect and worthless.

In France the single point of difference between the two bodies was that of the irremovability of the Masters, of lodges. The Grand Lodge had from the very beginning of its authentic history granted constitutions to certain Masters for the establishment of lodges over which they were to preside by a perpetual tenure of office, that is, they were Masters for life. Now as these "irremovable Masters" were often, nay almost always, appointed through corrupt motives, and as the lodges thus became, in a way, their personal property, the attempt was made to abolish them and to make the presidency of the lodges elective.

This reform, for it was evidently a reform, was opposed by the Grand Lodge, and hence those who were in favor of it established the Grand Orient, for the purpose of carrying out their views, and hence one of its first acts was to pass a decree abolishing the usage and suppressing the irremovable Masters.

There were, of course, supplementary motives for the schism, but this was undoubtedly the leading one.

So in England and in France there was a schism founded on a single difference of opinion, but this difference as it existed in each country never extended into the other. The English lodges never entertained the question of Masters for life, because from the organization of the Grand Lodge at London, those officers had always been annually elected, and this doctrine was held by both Grand Lodges.

The French lodges were never embarrassed by the question of a Fourth degree, which was the bone of contention in England. Though there were Chapters and Councils in which a Royal Arch degree under various modifications had existed from the time of the Chevalier Ramsay, these bodies had no legal connection with or recognition by either the Grand Lodge or the Grand Orient, both of which maintained the doctrine that pure Freemasonry consisted of only three degrees.

Another point of very interesting coincidence in the contention in the two countries was the following.

As both in England and France there were, during the contest, two bodies, each claiming Masonic sovereignty, it is evident that in each, one of the bodies must have been irregular, illegal, and schismatic, for it is the law of Freemasonry that the sovereignty can not be divided.

In England the schismatic and illegal body was the Grand Lodge of the "Ancients," the legal and constitutional one was the Grand Lodge of the "Moderns."

In France the schismatic and illegal body was the Grand Orient, which had been surreptitiously and irregularly formed; the legal and constitutional body was the Grand Lodge. Now it is very remarkable that when in each country the dissensions which had so long existed were brought to an amicable end and a union effected in the settlement of the principal question upon which the schism had been founded, the irregular and schismatic gained the victory, and the regular body was compelled to accept the doctrine which it had so long and so pertinaciously resisted.

Thus in England the Grand Lodge of "Moderns" recognized the Royal Arch, which it had always repudiated as an innovation, as one of the regular degrees of ancient Craft Masonry.

In France the Grand Lodge abandoned the doctrine of the irremovability of Masters, for which it had always strenuously contended, and accepted the theory and usage of the Grand Orient that the office of Master should be elective.

But though the Grand Lodge and the Grand Orient had been merged into one governing body of the French Masons, there were still difficulties presenting themselves in the effort to establish a unification of the Masonic system in the kingdom.

The abundance of high degrees, which from a very early period had been introduced into France, had been conferred in Councils and Chapters, which had never been recognized by either the Grand Lodge or the Grand Orient, but which had always acted independently of either authority.

Such were the Council of Emperors of the East and West, the General Grand Chapter, and finally the Supreme Council which had been organized by Count de Grasse Tily in 1804, under the authority of the Supreme Council at Charleston in the State of South Carolina.

In 1802 the Grand Orient had forbidden its lodges to confer any degrees which were not recognized by it. This caused the Scottish lodges, or those conferring these degrees, to establish a separate locality in the boulevard Poissonniere. Here they continued in defiance of the decree of the Grand Orient to practice the Scottish Rite. Finally, they established the "General Scottish Grand Lodge of France." The existence of this body was but an ephemeral one, for in two years it united with the Grand Orient.

Seeing the infatuation of the French Masons for the decorations and the mysteries of these high degrees, the Grand Orient, through the prudent counsels of Rotiers de Montaleau, the Grand Master, that it might put an end to all divisions in reference to Masonic Rites, declared that it would unite in its own bosom and recognize all Rites and Degrees whose dogmas and principles were in harmony with the general system of the Order.

Hence, at the present day the Grand Orient assumes jurisdiction over all the degrees of Freemasonry from the First to the Thirty third.

After an abortive attempt to effect a union between the Grand Orient and the Supreme Council of the Ancient and Accepted Rite, the latter body assumed and still maintains jurisdiction over the Rite on which it is founded, and grants constitutions to lodges of the Symbolic degrees.

Hence, at the present day there are in France two independent authorities in Freemasonry - the Grand Orient, which claims jurisdiction over all Rites, and the Supreme Council, which confines its jurisdiction to the Ancient and Accepted Rite.

Very recently out of this body has sprung an independent Scottish Grand Lodge, whose existence as permanent or ephemeral is yet to be determined.

But these matters belong to the contemporary history of the present day, and as our investigations are properly restricted to the Origin of the Grand Orient, which subject has been fully discussed, an end may now properly be given to the present chapter.

CHAPTER XLVI

INTRODUCTION OF FREEMASONRY INTO THE NORTH AMERICAN COLONIES

THE intercourse of the English colonies with the mother country was continuous, and, considering the condition of navigation, conducted entirely by sailing-vessels, was frequent. The colonists brought with them, in their immigration to the new country, the language, the laws, and the customs of their ancestors. The personal and political relations existing between the people on either side of the Atlantic were very intimate, and the wide ocean formed no sufficient barrier to the introduction among the Americans of new discoveries and inventions, of new styles of living or of new trains of thought which, springing up in England, were in a brief course of time brought over by visitors or by new settlers to the growing colonies.

It is not, therefore, to be doubted that very soon after the establishment of Speculative Freemasonry in London, by the organization of a Grand Lodge, in 1717, persons who had been initiated in the London lodges came over to America and brought with them the principles of the new system as it was just beginning to be taught at home.

At whatever precise date we may place the legal establishment of the first lodge in America, it is very certain, from the testimony of authentic public documents, that there was no lack of Freemasons in America not very long after the establishment of the system in England and anterior to the known legal organization of any lodge in the country.

Of course, it is understood that many of these Freemasons had been initiated in England, either while on a temporary visit to that country, if they were residents of the colonies, or, if they were recent immigrants, then before they left their old home for their new one.

This is very plain; nothing could be more natural than that a colonist going "home," as England was affectionately styled, should have availed himself of the opportunity afforded by his visit, to unite with a society enticing by its mystic character and its great popularity, and that among the emigrants who were daily crossing the ocean, to make their homes in the new country, there should have been many who were members of that society.

But the question has never yet been mooted whether some persons had not been initiated in America before any deputation had been insured by a Grand Master of England for the organization of a regular lodge, under the constitutions adopted at London in 1723.

Yet this is a very interesting question, and the fact that it is a novel one never having before been entertained, makes it still more interesting.

I may premise the investigation into which I am about to enter, by saying that whether the fact be proved or not, its occurrence is by no means impossible.

We have seen that lodges were established in France as early as 1721, eleven years before the constitution of a regular lodge by the Grand Lodge at London. I have already said that these lodges were organized without a Warrant, by certain Freemasons from England, who had exercised the ancient privilege of the Operatives to open lodges and make Masons without a Warrant, whenever a competent number were present. This privilege had been surrendered its 1717 by the four London Lodges to the newly erected Grand Lodge, but it was for some time after asserted occasionally It was in France, may it not also have been in America ?

The first Deputation granted from England for the colonies was granted by the Duke of Norfolk to Daniel Coxe, Esq., of New Jersey.

The date of this Deputation is June 5, 1730. It appoints him Provincial Grand Master of New York, New Jersey, and Pennsylvania, and it empowers him to constitute lodges.

While there is the indisputable evidence of the original Deputation still preserved in the Archives of the Grand Lodge of England, as well as the printed List of Deputations published by Anderson in the Second edition of the Book of Constitutions, and many other irrefragable proofs that the Deputation was granted to Coxe in June, 1730, there is not the slightest testimony of any kind, even traditional, that any similar Deputation can have been previously granted to any person residing in the American Colonies.

In other words, the proof is very satisfactory that previous to the latter half of the year 1730[67] there was no legal authority in the colonies to constitute lodges according to the English regulation adopted in 1717.

If, then, there were any lodges which met in the colonies previous to that date, they must have been lodges which derived their authority for meeting from the old Operative usage, which was that a sufficient number of Masons met together were empowered to make Masons and to practice the rites of Masonry without a Warrant of Constitution.

It has now been conceded that the first constitutional lodge of Freemasons acting under the authority of a Warrant was established in Philadelphia in the latter part of the year 1730. The evidence of this will be hereafter given in its proper place.

But there are also proofs that one or more lodges were in existence in Philadelphia before the time of the reception by Coxe of the Deputation which had been granted to him by the Duke of Norfolk.

The first of these proofs is furnished by the celebrated Dr. Benjamin Franklin, who was in 1730 the Printer and also the Editor of a paper published in Philadelphia with the title of the Pennsylvania Gazette.

In No. 108 of that paper, published on December 8, 1730, is the following article: "As there are several lodges of FREE MASONS erected in this Province, and people have lately been much amused with conjectures concerning them, we think the following account of Free Masonry, from London, will not be unacceptable to our readers."

Now Coxe's Deputation was only issued in June of that year, It could hardly have taken less than two or three months for it to pass from the Grand Secretary's office in London into the hands of Bro. Coxe in New Jersey. Between the time of his receiving it and the publication of the article just cited from Franklin's Gazette, the interval would be hardly long enough to enable Coxe to organize and constitute several lodges.

We know from the records that there was one lodge constituted in 1730, but we have no evidence of the constitution in that year of any others, either by Coxe as Provincial Grand Master or by any brother appointed by him as his Deputy.

---

[67] The Deputation having been issued at London, June 5, 1730, allowing for necessary delays and the length of the passage across the ocean at that time, it could hardly have reached Philadelphia before the end of August or more probably September in the same year.

And yet Franklin says (and he was neither a truthless nor a careless writer) that there were several lodges at that time in the Province of Pennsylvania.

But as several includes more than one, where did the additional lodges come from? They were not constituted by Coxe nor by his authority, at least we have no knowledge of any such constitution.

It is therefore not unlikely that these lodges were like the first lodges in France, formed by what the Freemasons had been taught was their prescriptive right, and who, without a Warrant, had before the coming of the Deputation assembled together in competent number and practiced the rites of Masonry.

But there is something more than probable conjecture to support this theory. A letter was written in 1754 by Henry Bell, at that time residing in the town of Lancaster (Pennsylvania), to Dr. Thomas Cadwallader of Philadelphia, in which he makes the positive statement from his own knowledge and participation in the circumstance that there actually was in 1730, perhaps before, at least one lodge formed by prescriptive right without a Warrant.

Bro. Bell's letter, containing this important historical statement, was exhibited in the office of the Grand Secretary of the Grand Lodge of Pennsylvania in the year 1172. A copy of it made at that time was published in the Early History and Constitutions of the Grand Lodge and is as follows:

"As you well know, I was one of the originators of the first Masonic lodge in Philadelphia. A party of us used to meet at the Tun Tavern, in Water street, and sometimes opened a lodge there.

Once in the fall of 1730 we formed a design of obtaining a charter for a regular lodge, and made application to the Grand Lodge of England for one, but before receiving it, we heard that Daniel Coxe of New Jersey had been appointed by that Grand Lodge as Provincial Grand Master of New York, New Jersey, and Pennsylvania. We therefore made application to him, and our request was granted."

It thus appears from the testimony of one engaged in the transit action that for some time previous to any authority existing in America for granting Warrants, a lodge had been opened in Philadelphia, without the sanction of such Warrant and of course by the old prescriptive right, which had always prevailed as the law of Freemasonry, until the right was surrendered in 1717 by the four Lodges which united in forming the Grand Lodge at London.

Bro. Clifford P. MacCalla, who has been a most indefatigable and successful explorer of old documents connected with the early history of Freemasonry in Pennsylvania, published in his valuable paper, the Key Stone (December 22, 1877), an important and interesting letter which furnishes the evidence that there were Freemasons in Philadelphia one year at least before the severance of the Speculative from the Operative element, and the organization of the Grand Lodge at London.

This letter is dated "March 10, 1715,"[68] and was written by John Moore, the King's collector at the port of Philadelphia, and addressed to James Sandilands, Esq., of Chester, Penn.

The letter is an official one, communicating the fact that he had received from England a bell and some altar furniture, intended for a church at Chester, and requesting to know how they were to be delivered. But this business matter having been dismissed, the letter concludes with the following remarkable passage:

"Ye winter has been very long and dull, and we have had no mirth or pleasure except a few evenings spent in festivity with my Masonic Brethren."

Since the authenticity of this letter is indisputable,[69] it is of great historical importance. It shows without a doubt that in America, as in England and in Scotland, there were Freemasons, who lived under the old partly Operative and partly Speculative regime anterior to what has been called the " Revival." which took place in London in 1717, when the Speculative began to be wholly dissevered from the Operative system.

In England and Scotland we know that these Freemasons were united in lodges, which worked without the sanction of a Warrant of Constitution, which was a new regulation adopted for the first time at the time of the so-called Revival. They were organized, as has been already said, by a prescriptive right by which a competent number of Freemasons were always authorized to assemble and perform the rites of Masonry.

---

[68] Although the double reference, as 1715-16, was generally affixed to dates in the first three months of the year, to indicate the old and the new styles, it is very probable that by "March 10, 1715," the writer meant what we should now write as "March 10, 1716."

[69] Bro. MacCalla states that at the time of publication the letter was in the possession of Bro. Horace W. Smith, the great-grandson of the Rev. Dr. William Smith, the Secretary of the Grand Lodge of Pennsylvania; the grandson of Bro. William Moore Smith, Grand Master of Pennsylvania, and the son of Richard Penn Smith of Lodge No. 72 in Philadelphia, and that the granddaughter of John Moore, the writer of the latter, intermarried with the Rev. Dr. Smith, the great-grandfather of its present custodian. The letter is thus traced through a reputable descent, which gives it all needful color of authenticity.

There is, it is true, no direct evidence that the Freemasons referred to in the letter of Bro. Moore pursued the same plan in 1715, and "spent their evenings in festivity" in an organized lodge. But it is very probable that such was the fact. There is no reason why, if there were a sufficient number of Freemasons then living in Philadelphia, and who were in the habit, as the letter indicates, of meeting for festive purposes, they should not have followed the custom which prevailed "at home," and for better regularity and discipline in their meetings have formed themselves into a lodge.

At all events, we have the positive proof that fifteen years later there was a lodge which met in Philadelphia in 1730 and for some time before, which acted without a Warrant, until the latter part of that year, when it asked for and received one from Coxe, the Provincial Grand Master.

We have no such direct proof of the existence in other parts of the continent of lodges held by "prescriptive right," but there are some circumstances that lead us to believe that such was sometimes the case.

In 1736 the brethren of Portsmouth in New Hampshire applied to Henry Price for a charter. The petition is at least singular in its phraseology. It is subscribed by "persons of the holy and exquisite Lodge of St. John," as if there were already a lodge existing under that title, and in asking for a "Deputation and power to hold a lodge according to order as is and has been granted to faithful Brothers in all parts of the World;" and in asking for the Deputation, they say, "we have our constitutions, both in print and manu script, as good and as ancient as any that England can afford." [70]

Now, this may mean either that the Portsmouth brethren were in possession of rituals and other necessary books to use in forming a lodge; or it may mean that they were already working and had been working as a lodge by prescriptive right and now wanted to be duly regularized under the new system which Price had just received from England. It is an open question.

The colonies into which Freemasonry under the new system of the Revival was first introduced were Pennsylvania, Massachusetts, South Carolina, and Georgia.

There is no positive evidence that any lodges existed under the old Operative System, in either Massachusetts or South Carolina In the former Price opened his Provincial Grand Lodge in 1733, and in such of

---

[70] See the petition in Bro. Gardiner's able report in the "Transactions of the Grand Lodge of Massachusetts," anno 1871, D.307.

the records as have come to light there is no reference to any previous meeting of the Masons.

In South Carolina Hammerton opened a lodge at Charleston in October, 1736, under a Warrant granted by the Grand Master, Lord Weymouth. There is no traditional or other evidence that any lodge of Masons had ever met in the Province before that date.

In Georgia regular Freemasonry under the Grand Lodge of 1717 was introduced in 1736 when Solomon's Lodge at Savannah was opened under sanction of a Warrant from Lord Weymouth. But the late Bro.

W. S. Rockwell, in his Ahiman Rezon of Georgia, published in 1859, says that "many still living in Savannah have heard from older Brethren who have passed to that Undiscovered country from whose bourne no traveller returns,' that a Lodge was at work in that city before Solomon's Lodge No. I had an existence."[71]

If there were any such lodge, it must have been one which worked under the "prescriptive right" or "immemorial usage" of the olden time.

In Pennsylvania we have already seen that at least one such lodge was in existence in 1730 before Coxe had received his authority as Provincial Grand Master. And there is also evidence that Freemasons were in the habit of meeting in Philadelphia for convivial purposes at least two years before the organization of the Grand Lodge at London.

Now It is true that we have no evidence of the existence of these independent lodges anywhere in the colonies outside of Pennsylvania, nor any intimation of their existence, except the traditional report, mentioned by Rockwell, that a lodge had been in operation in Savannah before the Constitution of Solomon's Lodge and the suspicious phraseology of the petition for a lodge at Portsmouth, N. H., which might have emanated from a number of Masons who either were desirous of forming a new lodge, or who already working as a lodge by the old prescriptive right, wished to be regularized under the new system.

But notwithstanding this deficiency of positive evidence, does not all this show that there were lodges of this character in various parts of the colonies long before the issuing of Warrants by the London Grand Lodge ? That is to say, we have a right to suppose that Freemasonry was first established in this country by the voluntary association of a certain number of Masons together without the sanction

---

[71] Rockwells "Ahiman Rezon of Georgia," 1859, 4th edition, p. 323.

of a Warrant. This was the rule in England previous to the year 1717, when this right of meeting by what was termed " immemorial usage" was surrendered to the Grand Lodge by the four Lodges in London.

But the right and the practice was not at once abandoned everywhere. Some lodges in the rural districts of England continued to act without Warrants for a few years, and lodges under the old privileges were established in France, apparently by the Jacobites or adherents of the House of Stuart.

There is no reason therefore to doubt that the same custom prevailed to some extent in the American Colonies. During the constant intercourse which was maintained between the Mother- country and its colonies, many Freemasons would be constantly repairing to them, either as visitors, as emigrants, or as officers of the parent government.

The Freemasonry that they brought with them they would naturally desire to practice in the new country into which they had come.

Hence it is probable that they voluntarily associated in lodges and practiced the rites of the Institution in other parts of the colonies, as we now know that they did in Philadelphia in 1715.

The negative evidence that there are no minutes or records extant of the meetings of such lodges is not of the least value. It is not certain that they kept any records, or if they did, it is natural that in the lapse of time and with the intervention of so many stirring events, these records may have been lost. There are very few lodges of any antiquity, now existing in this country, whose earliest records have been preserved.

So the absence of records is no proof that such unwarranted lodges did not exist at an early period in this country, and the indisputable fact attested by documentary proof that one or more did exist at that early period in Pennsylvania, gives strong presumption to the hypothesis that similar lodges existed in some of the other colonies.

I advance therefore the following theory in reference to the introduction of Freemasonry into the American Colonies. I do not deny that it is, with the exception of the colony of Pennsylvania, a mere hypothesis, but an hypothesis is not necessarily false nor untenable because the proofs of it are not as strong as the enquirer might desire.

It can not be doubted or denied that the Masonic spirit which was prevailing in England in the early part of the 18th century, and which led in 1717 to the establishment of a Speculative Grand Lodge in London was carried into the remotest part of the British empire by emigrants and settlers in the colonies who preserved in their new home the manners and customs, the habits and associations, which had distinguished them in their old one.

Now as lodges existed in London and other parts of England and had long existed, organized under the old law of the Craft which authorized the congregation of Masons for Masonic purposes, without the sanction of a Warrant, we may reasonably suppose that Freemasons coming from England into the colonies, some of whom had probably been members of such lodges at home, would continue the custom in the new country into which they had come and there institute similar lodges.

At first the brethren may have met together for the purpose of preserving their Masonic recollections and of renewing the pleasures of their Masonic re-unions at home. Such appears to have been the case with the brethren referred to by Bro. Moore, who met in Philadelphia in 1715. As the Speculative Grand Lodge was not organized in London until two years afterward, these Masons must have come out of the old Operative lodges.

At first, these Masons may have been content to meet together without proceeding to make initiations. But there was no law to prevent their doing so, and I see no reason why they should not have proceeded to secure the prosperity of the Institution by an increase of its numbers.

Hence, I think that lodges must have been in existence in the colonies long before the granting of a Deputation to Coxe. There are no records now extant of the meetings of any such lodges, but as I have already said, this was not to be expected, and the fact that no such records can now be found, is not the slightest evidence that they never existed.

Certainly we know from authentic testimony, which has already been cited, that such a lodge was in existence and in operation in Philadelphia in 1730, and we know not how many years before, which applied to Daniel Coxe, when his Deputation as Provincial Grand Master arrived, and received from him authority to continue their labors as a regular lodge.

If this occurred in Pennsylvania, why should not the like have occurred in other colonies ? Why should not there have been lodges thus voluntarily formed, in Massachusetts before the Deputation of Price, in South Carolina before that of Hammerton, or in Georgia before that of Lacy ?

To say that there are no records of any such lodges is no answer to the question. The early records of Freemasonry, everywhere, have been too poorly kept and too illy preserved to authorize us to found any argument on their absence. Horace wisely tells us that many heroes perished before Agamemnon, unwept and unsung, because there was no poet to record their deeds.

The conclusion to which I arrive by this course of reasoning is, then, that Freemasonry was introduced into the colonies of North America at a very early period in the 18th century, by means of officers of the parent government, or emigrants intending to be future permanent residents.

These Freemasons soon established lodges in various places, which they worked without the sanction of Warrants, and under the regulation which existed in England at the time when they left it.

At this period Warrants were unknown and lodges met whenever and wherever a competent number of brethren thought proper to establish one.

It was in this way that the love of Freemasonrywas preserved in these distant regions, and when at length the new system of warranting lodges which had been inaugurated in 1717 by the foul old Lodges in London began to be understood and Deputations for Provincial Grand Lodges and Provincial Grand Masterships began to be sent over from the parent country, these primitive, unwarranted lodges ceased to exist and their members took out Warrants which regularized them.

They had performed their mission. They had introduced Freemasonry into America. They had fostered it, with the best of their feeble rneans. They had planted the seed, and the nursing of the plant and the gathering of the crop they were willing should be left to those who came after them.

The new system brought by the various Deputations from England resulted in the introduction of the regulations which had been adopted by the English Grand Lodge. Provincial Grand Lodges were organized and no lodge was instituted except under the sanction of a Warrant.

From this time Freemasonry in the colonies begins to be purely historical, and in that light its early history is now to be considered.

CHAPTER XLVII

THE EARLY GRAND LODGE WARRANTS

FROM what has been said in the immediately preceding chapter it appears that we may divide the narrative of the introduction of Freemasonry into the Colonies of North America into two distinct eras, which, in imitation of the archaeologists, we might almost call the pre-historic and the post-historic eras of American Speculative Freemasonry. The pre-historic era embraces that period of time which is included between the first immigration of settlers from Britain into the colonies and the granting of the first Deputation for a Provincial Grand Lodge. More strictly, it would be confined to the first thirty years of the 18th century.

Freemasonry was not, I think, in a condition, before the opening of the 18th century, to inspire its disciples with an enthusiasm which would lead to the propagation of the Order and the establishment of lodges in a new country.

Under the slow but persevering efforts of Speculative members of the Operative lodges, Freemasonry was gradually assuming a new character. The old Operative element was beginning to die off. It finally "gave up the ghost" about the year 1723, when the purely Speculative became not only the predominating but actually the sole element of the Institution.

It was while this transition was going on that many Freemasons, who were initiated under the old system before 1717, and under the new one after that date, emigrated into the American Colonies and carried with them their attachment for the Institution which they had acquired at home.

If any lodges were established before 1717, the act must have been a spontaneous one under the usage, which is described by Preston, by which a competent number of Masons were permitted to assemble for Masonic work without the sanction of a Warrant of Constitution, a thing which was unknown to the Craft until after the adoption of a special regulation in 1717.

After that year it is true that every regular lodge was required to be sanctioned and authorized by a Warrant from the Grand Lodge, and this regulation, which ought rather to be called a compromise between the four old Lodges, and the new Grand Lodge was generally obeyed in London, where we have no evidence that any lodges were formed after 1717 without the sanction of a Warrant of Constitution.

But such was not the case at that early period in other countries where the principles of English Speculative Freemasonry were carried by immigrants. We know that English lodges were formed in France before 1712 in the old, which had now become an irregular, manner.

The same thing occurred in the American Colonies before 1730.

Mention has been already made, in the preceding chapter, of an assembly of Masons in Philadelphia in 1716, and it has also been stated in that chapter, that a lodge without a Warrant was held in the same city in 1730 and probably for some years previously.

There is an excuse for this, if an excuse be needed, in the difficulty there was of obtaining a Warrant from England. Again the old regulation or custom was abrogated, only for those lodges within the "bills of mortality," that is to says in the city of London and its purlieus.

"It admits of little doubt," says Bro. Gould, "that in its inception the Grand Lodge of England was intended merely as a governing body for the Masons of the Metropolis."[72]

Hence we find in the Minutes of the Grand Lodge under the date of November 25, 1723, the declaration or agreement, "That no new lodge its or near London, without it be regularly constituted be countenanced by the Grand Lodge, or the Master or Wardens admitted to the Grand Lodge."

The earlier records of the Grand Lodge, contained in Anderson's second edition, show in other places very plain indications that the regulation which required a Warrant of Constitution was not intended to apply to lodges outside of London.

But the fact is, that even in England, the regulations were not at that period strictly enforced. "The general laws of Masonry, however," says Dr. Oliver, " were but loosely administered." It is not to be supposed

---

[72] "Four Old Lodges," p. 19.

that a more implicit obedience to them was paid in distant parts of the empire.

The Grand Lodge was too young and too weak to extend the influence of its newly created authority beyond the narrow limits of its domestic territory.

CHAPTER XLVIII

ORIGIN OF THE ROYAL ARCH

No event in the history of Speculative Freemasonry has had so important an influence upon its development, as a system of symbolism, as the invention of the Royal Arch degree and its introduction into the Masonic ritual.

It is evident that the limitation of the system to three degrees, terminating in the "Master's part," left the cycle of symbolism in as incomplete a condition as would be a novel with the last chapter unwritten.

The ritual, as it was devised and presented to the Craft in the beginning of the 18th century, when the Speculative element was wholly dissevered from the Operative, was an immature conception of its inventors, and was marked by the imperfections and deficiencies which are always attendant on immaturity.

Accepting the meagre ritual, principally intended to embody merely methods of recognition, Desaguliers and his collaborators had gradually extended it, first by the development of the one simple degree, which had been common to the whole body of the Craft, into two and finally into three degrees.

Here, unfortunately, they desisted from further labors in the construction of a ritual. The experiment had so far been successful. It had given renewed vitality to an institution which had long languished; it had excited the curiosity and gained the support of many who had hitherto felt no interest in the ruder system of the Operative lodges; and it had placed the society upon a much higher plane than that which it formerly occupied before the absolute disseverance of the two elements of which it was composed.

It is much to be regretted that the experiment of fabricating a ritual so prudently begun, and which was so successful in its results, had not been continued, and the Third degree been supplemented by a Fourth that should have given perfection to the symbolic scheme.

What was precisely the ritual of the Master's degree as fabricated by Desaguliers, Payne, Anderson, and their contemporaries, it is impossible for us to know. The knowledge of facts which has been only orally transmitted are often lost in the lapse of time; tradition is scarcely ever unchanged; and when there is no written record to guide our inquiries, we necessarily grope in the dark.

The Masonic system of symbolism as now constituted presents us with a triple series of antagonisms - that of ignorance and knowledge; that of darkness and light; and that of loss and recovery.

With the first and second of these antagonisms we have nothing here to do. It is the last only that interests us in the present connection.

The antagonism of loss and recovery, when it is symbolized by death and resurrection - by the ending of the present and the beginning of the future life, is perfectly represented in the Master's degree. But when it refers to the doctrine of Divine Truth symbolized by the Word, which being lost for a time is ultimately recovered, the Third degree, as now constructed, and as it probably always was, fails completely to carry out the symbolism.

Everyone who has devoted full attention to the study of the ritual of Speculative Freemasonry must admit that the Word constitutes the central point around which the whole system of Masonic symbolism revolves. Its possession is the consummation of all Masonic knowledge when lost, its recovery is the sole object of all symbolic, Masonic labor.

These are not mere truisms, having only a general bearing upon the subject of symbolism; they are important axioms, indispensably connected with the history of the origin of the Royal Arch degree, and with the primary cause of its invention.

Even in the time of pure, unadulterated Operative Freemasonry, the Word was an important secret of the institution. The German Stonemasons had, at a very early period, a word, sign, and grip, and in the 17th century, if not before, the Operative Masons of Scotland attached much importance to the secrets of the Mason Word.

Analogically we may infer that the English Operative Masons were also in possession of it, though no reference is made to it in the Old Constitutions or in the Legend of the Craft.

Whether this was or was not the same Word as that which afterward became the nucleus of the Royal Arch degree, it is impossible to determine. Most probably it was not. The Word given in the Catechism of the German Steinmetzen, which is to be found in Findel and that contained in the catechism of the Sloane MS., are different from each other and neither of them is the Word now used.

There may, however, have been another Word, communicated only to a select few, which for obvious reasons has not been referred to, in either of these records. But this is merely conjectural, and I confess is hardly probable.

The Word as we now have it is indicative of a more elevated character of religious symbolism, to which the purely Operative Freemasons never apparently attained.

On the other hand, it can not be denied that the Freemasons of the Middle Ages indulged to a great extent in a species of religious symbolism. Christian iconography abounds in their architectural decorations, among which we find the triangle in its various modifications.

The question is therefore by no means settled by the reticence of the old catechisms on the subject. Happily, its settlement is not a matter of vital importance in the discussion of the Origin of the Royal Arch degree. Its decision would only determine whether the fabricators of the high degrees of which the Royal Arch was the earliest were original inventors of the Word, or only the followers of the older Freemasons and the resuscitators of their ideas.

Leaving the settlement of this question in abeyance, let us pursue our historical investigations of the origin and growth of the Royal Arch degree.

It is the opinion of many eminent Masonic scholars that the original Third or Master's degree of Desaguiler's, which, with some modifications made from time to time by successive ritualists, continued to be recognized by the Constitutional Grand Lodge of England until the Union in 1813, contained the true Master's or Royal Arch Word.

Dr. Oliver has furnished, I think, a very convincing proof that the True Word was communicated in the original ritual of the Third degree, as practiced from 1723 onward. In his Origin of the English Royal Arch, he makes the following statement:

"I have now before me an old Master Mason's tracing-board or floor- cloth, which was published on the continent almost immediately after symbolical Masonry had been received in France as a branch from the Grand Lodge of England in 1725, which furnished the French

Masons with a written copy of the lectures then in use: and it contains the true Master's Word in a very prominent situation."[73]

It can not be denied that his deductions from this circumstance are very legitimate. He goes on to say:

"This forms an important link in the chain of presumptive evidence, that the Word, at that time. had not been dissevered from the Third degree and transferred to another. If this be true, as there is every reason to believe, the alteration must have been effected by some extraordinary innovation and change of landmarks. And I am persuaded, for reasons, which will be speedily givenw that the ancients are chargeable with originating these innovations for the division of the Third degree and the fabrication of the English Royal Arch appear, on their own showing to have been their work."

A future proof of the fact that the true Word was contained in the original Third degree may be found in Wilkenson's edition of the Book of Constitutions. That work was published at Dublin in 1769 and in front of the first page is a tracing-board, purporting to be the delineation of "A lodge fitted up for the reception of the most respectable Master." Among the emblems depicted are the hillock, the sprig of Acacia and the coffin surrounded by the heraldic guttes de larmes, or drops of tears, symbolic of grief, all of which refer to the Hlramic Legend of the Master's degree while, in a prominent place and in conspicuous letters, is the true Master's Word.

In another work Dr. Oliver says that the "Royal Arch Word was anciently the true Wordf of the Third degrees"[74] and he refers to a French writer of 1745 as stating that "the Master's Word was originally . . . but that it was changed after the death of Adoniram."

The writer here referred to is, I think, Guillemain de St. Victor, who, however, published the first edition of his Recueil Previezex de Ma Maconnerie Adonhiramite, not in 1745, but in 1781. Guillemain gives the Word in full, which is precisely the Royal Arch Word of the present day. It was engraved on the tomb of Hiram upon a triangular plate of gold, and it was, he says, l' ancien mot de maztre."[75]

Now, what Guillemain knew of the Third degree had for its basis the primitive ritual of the Constitutional Grand Lodge of England,

---

[73] "Origin of the Royal Arch," p. 20.
[74] "Discrepancies of Freemasonry," p. 75. In this posthumous work Dr. Oliver has evidently made the personages of his interesting dialogues merely the media for communicating his own opinions.
[75] "Recueil Preceiux de la Magonnerie Adonhiramite," p. 105, edition of 1787.

for this had passed over into France and been adopted on the Continent long before that Grand Lodge made the changes so much objected to by the seceding Masons of 1740, His authority may therefore be accepted as confirmatory of Oliver's statement that the Third degree originally contained the True Word.

But though it should be admitted that the Master's degree was known to the framers of the ritual of that degree, as it was fabricated soon after the organization of 1717, and was communicated in the last part of the degree, it will not follow that there was anything more than a mere communication of it, without comment or explanation.

Something in the teachings of the ritual must have been wanting; else why should there have been a secession of a part of the Craft, who sought professedly to supply a defect which they felt by supplementing a Fourth degree.

The loss and the recovery of the Word constitute the foundation on which the entire system of Masonic symbolism is built. Without these important points, Speculative Freemasonry as "a science of morality, veiled in allegory and illustrated by symbols" would be a total failure. As a moral and social institution inculcating the practice of virtue and cultivating the principle of brotherhood, it might remain. But it would in no respect differ from hundreds of other societies professing the same objects, which have sprung into existence, and recanting the vitality which a deep, religious symbolism has given to Freemasonry have all passed through only an ephemeral existence.

Hence, the invention about the middle of the 18th century of a Fourth degree which should supply the deficiency of the original "Master's part," gave an impetus to the institution, which history records in the successful progress of the seceders who had adopted the invention

The interpretation of the loss and the recovery of the Word, lie, as has already been said, at the very foundation of all Masonic symbolism.

Now, it is more than probable that the fabricators of the original Third degree were acquainted with and communicated to their initiates the history of the loss. We know that the Hiramic legend constituted an important part of the ritual, and the loss of the Word must have been included in the allegory which forms the substance of that legend.

But as the history of the recovery of the Word is not included in the legend, it is evident that the original Third degree could have made no reference to it, and the dual symbolism of a loss and a recovery could not have been perfect.

The degree, as originally intended, being founded on the Hiramic legend, gave, of course, a history of the way in which the Word was lost. But though afterward it was communicated, as it is said, to a select few, we do not learn from its ritual in what way it was restored to the graft. There was, therefore, an important defect in the symbolism of the system.

Now, this defect must have at length attracted the attention of some of the students of the ritual who were looking at Speculative Freemasonry as something more than a mere social organization, and who were desirous to lift it to a more elevated plane of intellectuality.

It was on the continent that the disposition to expand the ritual first displayed itself. It was this disposition which, in time, passed out of the limits of propriety and gave rise to the almost innumerable hauts grades, which have rather overclouded than purified the atmosphere of Masonic symbolism.

At first, however, the attempt at expansion was conducted with moderation, and was confined to only two points - to supplying the deficiency in the history and symbolism of the Word, and to inventing a new account of the origin of the institution.

With the latter of these expansions, the present subject has no connection. It is only to the former that we must direct our attention.

The first innovator on the original ritual of Desaguliers and his collaborators was the noted Chevalier Ramsay, and it is to him that we have to trace the first addition to that ritual which was to supplement the Third degree with another, which has since under great modifications been known to English-speaking Freemasons as the Royal Arch.

The Masonic labors of Ramsay entitle him to, at least, a brief sketch of his life and character.[76]

Andrew Michael Ramsay, commonly known as the Chevalier Ramsay, was born at Ayr, in Scotland, on June 9, 1668. Having completed his education at the University of Edinburgh, where he was distinguished for ability and diligence, he became, in 1709, the tutor of the two sons of the Earl of Wemyss.

Subsequently, he left his native country and retired to Holland.

There he became acquainted with Peter Poiret, a learned and philosophical disciple of the celebrated Quietist Antoinette Bourignon. Poiret was a prominent teacher of the mystic theology which then prevailed on the continent.

---

[76] See a biography of Ramsay in Mackey's "Encyclopedia of Freemasonry," from which the present sketch is condensed.

To his intimacy with this pious mystic, Ramsay was very probably indebted for that love of mystical speculation which he subsequently developed as the inventor of high degrees in Freemasonry, and as the author of a Masonic rite.

In 1710 Ramsay visited Fenelon, Archbishop of Cambray, became his guest and pupil, and six months afterward a proselyte to Romanism.[77]

Through the influence of the Archbishop he received the appointment of preceptor to the young Duke de Chateau-Thierry and the Prince de Turenne.

As a reward for his services in that capacity he was created a Knight of the Order of St. Lazarus, whence he derived the title of "Chevalier," by which he is always designated.

In 1724 Ramsay went to Rome and was appointed tutor to the two sons of the titular James III., who, as the son and heir of James II., the exiled King of England, still claimed the throne of his ancestors.

He is known in history generally by the more appropriate title of the is "Old Pretender."

Ramsay's close connection with the exiled family of Stuart, and with their adherents, the Jacobites, undoubtedly exerted much influence in the shaping of certain high degrees and in the modified interpretation of certain legends, so as to give a coloring to the preposterous theory that Speculative Freemasonry was invented or at least used as a political means of promoting the restoration of the House of Stuart to the English throne. Ramsay, himself, is not clear from the suspicion of having sown the germs of this theory. He was a firm believer in hereditary right, and, being an aristocrat at heart, he spurned the idea that Freemasonry could have had an Operative origin.

In the year 1728 he visited England and became an inmate of the family of the Duke of Argyle. While in England the University of Oxford conferred upon him the degree of Doctor of Laws, a tolerable evidence of his reputation as a man of letters.

On his return to France he took up his residence at Pointoise, a seat of the Prince of Turenne, and spent the remainder of his life as Intendant in the Prince's family, dying on May 6, 1743, in the seventy-fifth year of his life.

The literary career of Ramsay was marked by the production of only a few works, but each of these give evident proofs of his learning

---

[77] In his "Life of Fenelon" Ramsay gives the full details of the intellectual process and the arguments of the prelate through which his conversion was effected. "Life," pp. 189 - 247

and of his skill as a writer. His first work appears to have been The Life of Francois de Salignac de le Motte Fenelon, Archbishop, and Duke of Cambray. This was published at London in 1723, and gave rise to a severe criticism by "Britannicus" in several consecutive numbers of the London journals of that year.

In 1727 he published The Travels. This work, composed after the style of Fenelon's Telemaque, was enriched by a learned "Discourse on the Theology and Mythology of the Persians." The book was so favorably received as to be speedily translated into the French, the Dutch, the German, and the Danish languages. A much altered and improved edition was subsequently published by the author at Glasgow in Scotland. [78]

In the latter years of his life he wrote as a tribute of friendship a History of the Viscount Turenne. After his death his greatest work appeared, namely, The Philosophical Principles of Natural and Revealed Religion, Unfolded in a Geometrical Order. This work, published in two quarto volumes at Glasgow in 1748, stamps its author not only as a man of varied learning but as a profound metaphysician and an astute logician. Of all the adversaries of Spinoza, none has so adroitly and successfully attacked the errors of that incredulous philosopher as Ramsay.

His contributions of published works to the literature of Speculative Freemasonry are still fewer. They consist of only two productions, and the authorship of one of these is only conjectural.

In 1738 there was published at Dublin, Ireland, a work, reprinted at London in 1749, with the title of Relation apologetique et historique de la Societe des Francs-Macons, par J. G. D. M. E. M. Kloss, who styles it a comprehensive and fundamental apology for the Institution of Freemasonry, and attributes its authorship without doubt to Ramsay. By order of the Sacred Congregation it was burnt in the following year, at Rome, by the public executioner, for containing "impious propositions and principles," and "the faithful" were prohibited from reading it. This act of literary cremation was the first instance of the impotent persecution of the Order by the Roman Church after the publication of the celebrated Bull in eminenti of Pope Clement XII.

In 1740, when Ramsay was Grand Orator of the Grand Lodge of France, he pronounced a discourse before that body. It was first

---

[78] The copy in my possession bears the imprint of James Knox, Glasgow, but without a date. Kloss registers several London and Paris editions of the work varying from 1760 to 1829, but omits any mention of this Glasgow edition. See Kloss, " Bibliography," No 3936

published in 1741 in the Almanach des Cocus, under the erroneous title of Discours d'un Grand Maitre. Ramsay never attained to that official dignity.

This Discourse and the Apologetic Relation, conjecturally attributed to him, are the only published writings of Ramsay on Masonic subjects that have come down to us. It is not known indeed that he ever published any others.

But this Discourse is of great importance, inasmuch as in it he develops in explicit terms his theory of the origin of Freemasonry.

It is sufficient here to say that that theory repudiated the idea of its connection with an Operative art and traces its birth to Palestine and to the time of the Crusaders. He thus gave to Freemasonry not an architectural but a religious and military character which connected it with the Orders of Knighthood.

It is to the influence of this theory on the Masonic mind that we are to attribute the subsequent incorporation of Templarism into the system of Freemasonry, a thought that never suggested itself to the original founders of the Society.

But though Ramsay wrote but little on Freemasonry for the public eye, no one during the 18th century exerted a greater influence over continental Masonry, and that influence, as it will hereafter be seen, extended, in some degree, even into England.

He was an assiduous and enthusiastic ritualist, and sought to develop the Masonic system by the invention of new degrees.

To him we are indebted (though the value of the debt is questionable) for the invention of the system of Rites, wherein the science of Speculative Freemasonry is expanded by a superstructure of "high degrees," based upon the primitive three.

At that time the Grand Lodge of England recognized and practiced only the three degrees of Apprentice, Fellow-Craft, and Master Mason. The same system was pursued by the Grand Lodge of France.[79]

This simple system had no congruity with the theory of Ramsay. It made no reference to the Orders of Chivalry and bore no appearance of a relationship to anything but an Operative art.

Ramsay, therefore, found it necessary to construct a new system, which should bear the evidence not of an Operative, but of a Chivalric origin.

---

[79] La Grande Loge de France ne reconnaissait que les trois grades symboliques; ses constitutions ne s'etendaient pas au dela. Thory, "Fondation de la G. L. de France," p. 15.

If in carrying out these views he had rejected the primitive degrees, his new system would have had no pretensions to be a Masonic one.

He was unwilling to attempt such a revolution, which would, most probably, have been unsuccessful in its results.

Speculative Freemasonry had by that time become a popular Institution - it possessed wealth and influence, and men of rank and learning eagerly sought admission into the society. Ramsay, himself, was undoubtedly attached to it, though his aristocratic tendencies induced him to seek for it a more elevated sphere.

Besides, he must have seen that it furnished, even in what he deemed its imperfect state, a firm foundation on which to erect the edifice of his "high grades."

Ramsay, therefore, constructed a new system, which has since been called a Rite. His example was afterward imitated, but with less moderation as to the number of degrees, by ritualists who inundated Freemasonry with their new inventions. But of all the succeeding rites, though some of them extended to nearly a hundred degrees, only one of the original ideas of Ramsay, that, namely, of perfecting the Master's part, by the symbolism of a recovery of the Word, was sedulously preserved.

This first Masonic Rite, which has since been known by the title of "The Rite of Ramsay," consisted of six degrees, designated as follows:

1. Entered Apprentice.
2. Fellow-Craft.
3. Master Mason.
4. Ecossais or Scottish Master.
5. Novice.
6. Knight of the Temple or Templar.

Rhigellini adds a seventh degree, which he says was the Royal Arch; but I find no evidence elsewhere of this fact, and Rhigellini, I am sorry to say, is worse than useless as an historical authority.[80]

The fifth and sixth of these degrees embodied his ideas of the chivalric or Templar origin of the Institution. Their consideration would throw no light upon the investigation of the Royal Arch which we are now pursuing.

---

[80] Rhigellini, "La Masonnerie, etc.," tome ii., p. 125. It was a part of Ramsay's system to ascribe the invention of these degrees to Godfrey of Boulogne, in the days of the Crusades. It was Ramsay's legend with less foundation in truth than legends usually possess.

It is the Fourth only in which we are interested - the Ecossais - from which it is supposed that the suggestions were derived which gave origin to the invention of the Royal Arch degree in England and to the great Masonic schism which followed.

Ramsay went to England in 1728. How long he remained there is uncertain, but it was long enough to win the favor of the University of Oxford, and to obtain from that body one of its highest literary favors. He had also gained warm friends in that country, among whom may be named the Duke of Argyle, in whose family he resided, and Lord Landsdowne, to whom he dedicated his Cravens of Cyrus, and of whose "singular friendship" he boasts.

It is not, therefore, improbable that he possessed some influence with the Freemasons of England, among whom it is said he sought to introduce his new ritual.[81] But he failed in his effort to get it adopted by the Grand Lodge, which was then, as it still is and always has been, extremely conservative in its views.

But though unsuccessful with the Grand Lodge, his Royal Arch seems to have excited an interest in some of the Fraternity. His method of supplying the allegorical symbol of a recovery of the lost Word had awakened them to the fact that this symbolism, so necessary to perfect the circle of Masonic symbology, was wanting in the old system of three degrees as then practiced by the Grand Lodge.

For some few years no effort was made to incorporate the new system into the then accepted ritual. But the thought did not die. It continued to grow, and at last was given actual life when, about 1738 or perhaps a few years earlier,[82] certain of the brethren began to manipulate the Master's degree, and to add to the story of the loss of the Word the new legend of its recovery.

This tampering with the Third degree was met by the Grand Lodge first with grave censure, and then, as the participants in the scheme continued to be refractory, with their expulsion.

This led, as we have already seen, to the schism which divided the Masons of England into two parties, distinguished by the titles of the "Moderns" and the "Ancients."

The latter having organized a Grand Lodge, adopted a new ritual of four degrees, and called the last the Royal Arch.

---

[81] Ill voulut introducerie a Londres, en 1728, un nouveau Rite; mais il echoua dans ce projet. Thory, "Acta Latomorum," tome ii., p. 568.

[82] The Grand Lodge first officially noticed the "irregular makings" in 1738; but it does not follow that they had not been occurring for some time before attention was called to them.

It has been said that Ramsay invented the Royal Arch degree. He did no such thing. He did not even invent the name. But he did the symbolism which referred to the recovery of a Word that had been once lost and afterward recovered. And this constitutes the whole essential sum and substance of all Royal Arch Masonry, no matter under what name and in what Rite it is to be found.

We may suppose, and the supposition is a very tenable one, that he said to his disciples in England, " Your ritual gives you a recital of how the True Word of a Master was lost, but it does not tell you how it was afterwards restored to the Craft; and in this respect your system is perfect. The discovery of a lost Word constitutes a most important part of the symbolism of Speculative Freemasonry.

This symbolism and the Legend which refers to it, I offer you as necessary development and improvement of your system."

His disciples accepted the idea of the symbolism, but they rejected his Legend, and invented one of their own.

Neither the Legend of what has been called Dermott's Royal Arch, though he was not its author, nor Dunckerley's, nor that which has been in existence in England certainly since the Union of 1813, has any similitude to that of Ramsay's Ecossais degree.

So then, the correct historical statement would be that Ramsay suggested to the English Masonic mind the symbolism of a Recovered Word, for which Speculative Freemasonry was indebted to his inventive genius.

In this guarded sense of the expression it may be permitted to be said, that he introduced the doctrine of the Royal Arch into English Freemasonry. Without the suggestive influence of his ideas, Royal Arch Masonry would have been unknown to the Masonic system.

This theory, which is, I think, generally accepted as correct by Masonic scholars, has met with, so far as I know, only one opponent.

The late Bro. Charles W. Moore, the learned editor for many years of the freemasons' Monthly Magazine, published at Boston, Mass., in an article[83] "on the Origin of Royal Arch Chapters, at Home and Abroad," says, "it is not true that Ramsay had anything to do with the Royal Arch degree." His grounds for this unbelief are thus stated:

"Ramsay's system consisted of the three degrees of Ecossaizs, Novice, and Knight Templar only. If he ever invented a Royal Arch degree, which is very doubtful, no traces of it now remain."[84]

---

[83] "Moore's Magazine." vol. xii. April, 1853, p. 160.
[84] Ibid., p. 163, note.

Now the error of Bro. Moore consisted in his confounding the doctrine and symbolism of the Royal Arch degree with the specific name adopted in England. He could find no such title as Royal Arch among the degrees of Ramsay's Rite, and he rashly concluded that he had nothing to do with it.

It did not occur to him to look in Ramsay's system for the doctrine of the Royal Arch, under another name. Had he done so, he would have found it in the fourth degree, or Ecossais, of that system.

The word Ecossais, which may be correctly translated as Scottish Master or Scottish Mason, was invented and first used by the Chevalier Ramsay as the name of a grade in the Masonic ritual which he had constructed. In pure French the word signifies Scottish or Scotsman, and is said to have been adopted by Ramsay, because it was a part of his Legend, that though the degree, like the rest of Freemasonry, was originally fabricated by the Crusaders, it passed over from the Holy Land into Scotland, where at Kilwinning it found for a long period an abiding place, until it was disseminated over Europe.

From this as the original degree has sprung up numerous others having the same name and the same design.

That design is to detail the method in which the Lost Word was recovered, so that the true symbolism of the Word may be preserved.

This symbolism, which gave perfection to that of the hitherto incomplete Third degree, was so acceptable to the Fraternity everywhere, that in all the Rites subsequently established over the continent, the Ecossais of Ramsay was adopted with certain modifications

The extent to which this cultivation of Ecossaison, or the doctrine of the True Word, was carried by the ritualists who succeeded Ramsay may be shown from the fact that Ragon, in his almost exhaustive Nomenclature of the degrees, enumerates no less than eighty-three which bear the name of Ecossais.

In every legitimate Ecossais degree we meet with these two essential characteristics: first, there is a communication of the True Word which had been lost; and secondly there is a Legend which details the mode by which it was recovered and restored to the Craft.

In all these degrees the Word is substantially the same; in most of the Continental Rites the Legend of Ramsay, which accompanied it, has been preserved, with but little or no alteration.

The English Masons accepted the suggestions of Ramsay as to the necessity of expanding the Third degree or Master's partly They adopted the Word which indeed it is said had always existed in the original ritual of the Third degree; but they transferred its collocation from the Third to a Fourth degree; and they wholly rejected Ramsay's Legend, fabricating a new one for themselves, for which there is some reason for believing that they were partly indebted to a talmudic or rabbinical tradition. They also declined to adopt Ramsay's nomenclature, and having perhaps no liking for a name which, by implication at least, gave a Scottish origin to the Institution, they abandoned the title of Ecossais and took instead of it that of Royal Arch.

If the details of this narrative and the conclusions drawn from It are correct, then the theory has been established that the brethren who seceded about 1738 from the Constitutional Grand Lodge of England, with its three primitive degrees, and afterward organized a schismatic Grand Lodge of their own with an additional or Fourth degree, were indebted to Ramsay for the idea which led to the innovation.

Ramsay introduced the doctrine of the Royal Arch into English Masonry, but he did not succeed in introducing his degree.

Having thus settled the question of the origin of English Royal Arch Masonry, we are next to inquire at what time it was introduced into England and incorporated in the ritual of English Speculative Freemasonry.

There is no authority anywhere to be found which traces the existence of a Royal Arch degree in England anterior to the year 1738.

The earliest printed work which makes any reference to the degree is a book entitled A Serious and Impartial Enquiry into the Castle of the Present Decay of Free-masonry in the Kingdom of Ireland, by Fifield Dassigny, M.D., published in London in 1744.[85]

The references of the author of this work to the subject of Royal Arch Masonry, are, viewing the time when they were printed, of great interest, and may throw some light on a contested point of history. They are, therefore, here quoted in full, as follows:

"Now as the landmarks of the constitution of Free-Masonry are universally the same, throughout all kingdoms, and are so well fixt that they will not admit of removal, how comes it to pass that some have been led away with ridiculous innovations, an example of which I shall prove by a certain propagator of a false system some few years ago, who imposed upon several worthy men under a pretense of being Master of a

---

[85] The book is very scarce, there not being a copy in the British Museum. There is none to be found in any library in Ireland, and only one in America, which is in possession of Bro. Carson of Cincinnati, O. Bro. Hughan having obtained a copy, republished it in his "Memorials of the Union." The passage here quoted is from p.96 of his republication

Royal Arch, which he asserted he had brought with him from the city of York; and that the beauties of the Craft did principally consist in the knowledge of this valuable piece of Masonry. However, he carried on his scheme for several months, and many of the learned and wise were his followers, till at length his fallacious art was discovered by a Brother of probity and wisdom, who had some small time before attained that excellent part of Masonry in London and plainly proved that his doctrine was false; whereupon the Brethren justly dispised him and ordered him to be excluded from all benefits of the Craft, and altho' some of the fraternity had expressed an uneasiness at this matter being kept a secret from them (since they had already passed thro' the usual degrees of probation) I cannot help being of opinion that they have no right to any such benefits until they make a proper application, and are received with due formality, and as it is an organized body of men who have passed the chair, and given undeniable proofs of their skill in Architecture, it can not be treated with too much reverence, and more especially since the character of the present members of that particular lodge are untainted and their behaviour judicious and unexceptionable; so that there can not be the least hinge to hang a doubt on, but that they are most excellent Masons."

As Dassigny's book was published in 1744, the phrase "a few years ago" may be interpreted as applying to about the year 1741, or perhaps even 1740. With this explanation as to time, we may infer several facts from this passage.

In the first place, it appears that an adventurer coming to Dublin to propagate the Royal Arch thought it favorable to his interests to claim that he had brought the degree from the city of York. From this we may infer that it was a belief among the Freemasons of Ireland as well as elsewhere, that there was a Royal Arch organization then existing at York. This is not an absolutely essential inference, because he may have depended for its success on the prestige given to that city in the Masonic mind by the traditional belief that it was the cradle of Masonry.

But the inference gains some strength from what Dassigny says in a foot-note: "I am informed in that city (York) is held an assembly of Master Masons under the title of Royal Arch Masons, who as their qualifications and excellencies are superior to others, they receive a larger pay than working Masons."

Here we have the explicit statement of a Contemporary writer that such a belief was in existence. Whether it was founded in fact or in fiction is another question. Yet it is a proverbial dogma that there is no rumor without some foundation. "Flame," says Plautus, "is very close to smoke."[86]

However, Bro. Hughan, whose authority as a Masonic historian demands great respect, says it is doubtful whether an Assembly of Royal Arch Masons ever met in York so early as 1744, for there is no trace of such a degree until many years later in any of the Records preserved.[87]

But the absence of any records of a Royal Arch degree among the papers of the Grand Lodge of York, which have been preserved, is no sufficient evidence of the non-existence of that degree between 1740 and 1744. These wanted records may have been among those which have been lost or destroyed. Against this explainable deficiency of evidence by official records, which it is admitted are not complete, we have the testimony of a contemporary writer of repute and intelligence who says that there was in 1744 a rumor that the Royal Arch degree was conferred in York at that time.

The question therefore of this early existence of Royal Arch Masonry in York must still remain in abeyance; it is sub judice, nor can it ever be decided, until further testimony is produced.

But notwithstanding the high authority of Bro. Hughan, I am disposed to think that in 1744 and a few years before, the Royal Arch degree was conferred in the city of York, having of course been brought there from London, where it originated.

It does not follow that at that time there was any regular organization connected with the Grand Lodge (which, by the way, was at that time dormant, or of which we have no records) or with the lodge which was still in existence. The degree was about that time just beginning, even in London, to assume an official shape, and irregularities must have prevailed. Bro. Hughan tells us that Bro. William Cowling, an officer of the present York Lodge, is of opinion in reference to the later and undisputed organization of a Chapter in 1780, that "the Royal Arch Degree was kept distinct from the Craft at York, but that there was a very intimate connection between them."[88]

What is here said of the later organization may probably be applied to an earlier one. If so, it would be vain to look in the missing records of the York Grand Lodge from 1735 to 1760, if they are ever found, for any reference to Royal Arch Masonry.

Returning to the extract from Dr. Dassigny's Enquiry we infer, in the second place, that in the year 1744 there were Royal Arch Masons

---

[86] Flamma fiemo est proxima Plautus, "Curculio," i., 53.
[87] "Memorials of the Union,"p. 6.
[88] Hughan, "Memorials of the Union," p. 82.

in Dublin who appreciated the degree as a valuable addition to the Masonic system.

We infer, thirdly, that at that time there was an organized body of Past Masters there who regularly conferred the degree, restricting it, however, to those Masons who had passed the chair. As this was the regulation which existed in London, it is evident, if other proof were wanting, that the degree given in Ireland was originally derived from London and from the "Ancients."

After this digression for the purpose of demonstrating the time of the first appearance of the degree at the cities of York and Dublin, we may return to our investigation of the history of its origin in England.

We have seen that in 1728, soon after the Chevalier Ramsay had fabricated his system of high degrees, among which was one that, under the title of Ecossais or "Scottish Master" developed his doctrine of the Royal Arch or the recovery of the true Word, he came to England.

There he had personal intercourse with many Freemasons and communicated to them his views, and demonstrated to them the incompleteness of the established ritual, which, terminating in the Master's part, and the loss of the Word, made no provision for its recovery.

To the greater part of the English Freemasons his theory was either unintelligible as a doctrine or offensive as an innovation. Hence, the efforts he is said to have made for its adoption by tne Grand Lodge proved unsuccessful.

But, happily for the progress of Masonic light, there were some thinkers of more enlarged views. They saw the deficiency in the old ritual, and were ready to accept any modification that would improve it.

With this party, small at first but gradually increasing in numbers, the ideas of Ramsay became popular.

But while they adopted his doctrine concerning the recovery of the true Word as the basis of a new degree to be added to the ritual of three degrees, they refused in the end to adopt his legend.

It is not unlikely that the first English Freemasons who were engaged in 1738 in the "irregular makings" which were censured by the Grand Lodge may have used Ramsay's legend for a time.

This is mere guess-work. Still, it is very supposable that Ramsay taught his whole system to a few disciples who naturally would seek to propagate.

Dassigny, in his Enquiry, throws some gleams of light on this obscure subject in the following passage:

"I can not help informing the Brethren that there is lately arrived in this city a certain itinerant Mason whose judgment (as he declares) is so far illumined, and whose optics are so strong that they can bear the view of the most lurid rays of the sun at noon day, and altho' we have contented ourselves with three material steps to approach our Summum Bonum, the immortal GOD, yet he presumes to acquaint us that he can add three more, which, when properly placed, may advance us to the highest heavens."[89]

Now, it is at least a coincidence that Ramsay's newly invented Rite added just three degrees to the three of the original ritual. May not this "itinerant Mason" referred to by Dassigny have been a disciple of Ramsay, who was seeking to introduce his ritual into Dublin ?

But as I have said before, this is mere guess-work. It only gives a sort of probability to the hypothesis that Ramsay had succeeded in imbuing the minds of certain English Freemasons with the principles of his system, so that they were prepared to formulate out of it a degree, which, though differing in name and differing in legend, retained its doctrine.

And so out of this system of Ramsay the seceding Masons of England formulated a Fourth degree, which they called the "Royal Arch," and which, though owing its origin to Ramsay's Ecossais, resembled it only in the doctrine of a lost Word, recovered, which is the true and only doctrine of Royal Arch Masonry, under whatsoever name it may be known.

It may be considered as a well-settled fact in history that the Royal Arch degree was not known in England before the year 1738,[90] at which time it was practiced by certain brethren who afterward assumed the name of "Ancient Masons," and finally seceded from the Constitutional Grand Lodge.[91] The degree then conferred was suggested by and founded on the Ecossais degree of Chevalier Ramsay.

"If the Royal Arch degree," says Brother Hughan,[92] "in its separate and distinct form, existed prior to 1738, and indeed, was as old as the Third degree, how comes it that the regular Grand Lodge of England persistently refused to recognize it until 1813, but the body of Masons which seceded from this original and premier Grand Lodge,

---

[89] Dassigny's "Enquiry," in Hughan's republication in the "Memorials," p. 97.
[90] Hughan, "History of Freemasonry in York," p. 38.
[91] See Northouck's "Book of Constitutions." where, in a note to p. 239, a full but not altogether impartial account of the secession is given.
[92] In a Review of Higgins's "Anacalypsis," in the "Voice of Masonry," vol. xiii., p 887.

made much of the degree, and by it, we may truly say, succeeded in making their numerical position in a few years almost equal to the regular Grand Lodge itself ?"

The degree as practiced by the seceding Masons was, as Dr. Oliver[93] remarks, "imperfect in its construction," and its rude and unfinished state betrayed its recent origin.

Its form was, however, gradually improved. When the Grand Lodge of Ancients was organized in 1753, that body adopted it as one of its series of degrees, making it the Fourth in order of precedence.

At first, the degree was conferred in the lodges and as a supplement to the Third degree.

Dr. Oliver describes it as having at that early period "jumbled together, in a state of inextricable confusion, the events commemosrated in Ramsay's Royal Arch, the Knights of the Ninth Arch, of the Burning Bush, of the East or Sword, of the Red Cross, the Scotch Fellow-Craft, the Select Master, the Red Cross of Babylon, the Rose Croix," etc.[94]

I know not whence Oliver derived his authority for this statement.

But as none of the degrees which he mentions were then fabricated, it is impossible that he can be correct.

It is very probable that the Legend of Enoch which was embodied in Ramsay's Ecossais, and which was afterward adopted in the degree of Knights of the Ninth Arch, was at first used by the seceders in conferring their Fourth degree. But it was after ward changed for the very different Legend which is still taught in the English Royal Arch.

After a short time, when the degree had been nursed into a better shape by the Grand Lodge of Ancients, it was conferred into a body called a "chapter," but still constituting a part of a Warranted lodge.

The regulations "for the Instruction and Government of the Holy Royal Arch Chapter," adopted by the Atholl Grand Lodge, declare that severs regular and warranted lodge possesses the power of forming and holding meetings in each of these several degrees, the last of which from its pre-eminence is denominated among Masons a chapter." And this regulation continued in force until the Union of 1813.[95]

The earliest official minute of the Royal Arch degree among the "Ancients" bears the date of 1752.[96] At that time the "Ancients" were

---

[93] "Origin of the Royal Arch," p. 21.
[94] "Origin of the Royal Arch," p. 21.
[95] See the "Ahiman Rezon" published in 1807, p. 107.
[96] Hughan, "Memorials of the Union," p. 6.

organized in a General Assembly, which bore the name of a "Grand Committee."

The degree was then conferred in the lodges but only on those who had passed the chair. We have seen that this right of the lodges to confer the Royal Arch was always recognized by the Atholl Grand Lodge.

But a Grand Chapter was subsequently established, at what precise date is not accurately known.

On April 6, 1791, the "Ancients" published "Laws and Regulations for the Instruction and Government of the Holy Royal Arch Chapters, under the sanction of the Grand Lodge of England, according to the Old Constitutions." These Regulations were subsequently revised, amended, and approved "in a General Grand Chapter" held at the "Crown and Anchor Tavern," in the Strand, on April 1, 1807, and are contained in the Ahiman Rezon of that year.

The first of these Regulations that, "There shall be a General Grand Chapter of the Holy Royal Arch held half yearly at the 'Crown and Anchor,' Strand, on the first Wednesday in the months of April and October. That agreeably to established custom the officers of the Grand Lodge, for the time being, are considered as the Grand Chiefs, and are to preside at all Grand Chapters, according to seniority; they usually appoint the most expert R. A. companions to the other Offices; and none but Excellent Masons, being members of warranted lodges, in and near the Metropolis, shall be members thereof. Certified sojourners may be admitted as visitors only."[97]

It will be perceived that the organization of this Grand Chapter of the "Ancients," though not recognized as legal, prepared the model on which the subsequent Grand Chapter of England has been founded.

The government by three Chiefs has also been adopted in America, though they are no longer made identical, as they still are in England, with the three principal officers of the Grand Lodge.

Warrants were granted by the Grand Chapter for the formation of chapters, but only where the parties composing such chapter possessed a regular Warrant granted by the Grand Lodge.[98] Hence, every chapter under the system of the if "Ancients" was, though independent as to the degree, an appanage of a warranted lodge. An application for initiation to the Royal Arch degree was to be dlrected "to the presiding chiefs of the chapter of Excellent Royal Arch Masons, under sanction of lodge number_____."[99]

---

[97] "Ahiman Rezon," 1807, p. 108.
[98] "Laws and Regulations of the General Grand Chapter," No. iv.
[99] Ibid., No. vi.

This usage prevailed in America as long as lodges of "Ancient Masons" existed there. I have in the early part of my life personally known several old Royal Arch Masons who received the degree in lodges attached to chapters.

The chapters, though thus closely connected with the lodges, were so far under a separate jurisdiction as to be required to make returns of their exaltations and payment of fees to the Grand Chapter.[100]

Another regulation required that none should receive the Royal Arch degree but those who had "passed the chair."[101] The earliest custom was to confer it only on those who had been Masters of lodges. But this practice having been found inconvenient, as it too greatly restricted the number of candidates, the law was subsequently violated, and a fictitious degree of Past Master was instituted, brethren being permitted by a mere ceremony to "pass the chair" without having ever been elected Masters of lodges. Thus the distinction of actual and virtual Past Masters came in vogue, the degree or rank of Past Master being thus virtually conferred as a prerequisite to exaltation.

In 1813 the United Grand Lodge of England abolished this practice and it now admits Master Masons to be exalted. But the practice still prevails in the chapters of the United States, though efforts have at times been unsuccessfully made to abandon it.

The "Moderns" had seen with some envy, as we may suppose, the success which the "Ancients" were securing, and they very properly attributed it to the prestige given to the seceders by their fabrication of a Fourth degree.

It was therefore a very judicious movement on their part to avail themselves of a like prestige by the extension of their ritual and the adoption also of an additional degree.

Hence we find that some of the "Moderns" formed a chapter for conferring the Royal Arch degree on June 12, 1765. [102]It has been believed that Thomas Dunkerley was the founder of this chapter, but Bro. Gould denies this, because the minutes show that he did not become a member of it until January 8, 1766.

But I am unwilling to reject the almost universally accepted tradition that to him we owe the fabrication of the Royal Arch of the "Moderns" - a degree which is said to have differed in many points from that of the "Ancients."

---

[100] "Laws and Regulations of the General Grand Chapter," No. xii.
[101] Ibid., No. viii.
[102] Gould, "Atholl Lodges." p. 38.

Dunkerley, who was an illegitimate son of George the Second, and whose claims to that paternity received a sort of quiet recognition from the royal family, was a man of excellent character and of considerable talents. He was very popular with the Craft and was the author of a new system of lectures, or an improvement of the old, which had been sanctioned by the Grand Lodge.

In the course of his Masonic studies he appears to have been convinced of the policy, under existing circumstances, of supplementing the deficiencies of the original Third degree. We may indeed attribute to him a higher motive than that of policy, and believe that as a Masonic scholar he saw the necessity of completing the system by the fabrication of a Royal Arch degree.

It does not therefore follow that because Dunkerley's name does not appear as a member of the new chapter until six months after its formation, he may not have had an important part in its organization. If he was, as there can be no valid doubt, the original fabricator of the Royal Arch of the "Moderns," from whom, except from him, could the original members of the new chapter have received the degree which qualified them to enter upon its organization?

That he appeared later on the scene does not militate against his influence and his quiet work in its formation. There are no records extant to show what he was doing between the time when he invented the degree and that when it was first put into practice by the foundation of a chapter. The leading character in a drama does not always make his appearance in the first act, nor the hero of a novel in the first chapter.

It is more logical to suppose that the inventor of the Royal Arch of the "Moderns" was the founder of the chapter in 1765. But if Dunkerley was not the inventor, who was? History upon the best grounds assigns the invention to him, and to him also I am willing to ascribe the foundation of the chapter, though his name does not appear on its records until six months after its formation.

The chapter did not long continue to hold the position of a private body. In 1766, according to Bro. Hughan, [103]it assumed the rank of a Grand Chapter. This it must have done, just as the lodge at York in 1725 resolved itself into a Grand Lodge. There were no other chapters to unite with it, as the four Lodges did in 1717 to form a Grand Lodge. It simply changed its title and enlarged its functions.

Dr. Oliver places the date of the formation of the Grand Chapter at a later date, that of 1779.[104] This is, however, only an

---

[103] "Memorials of the Union." v. 8. note.
[104] "Origin of the Royal Arch," p. 38.

assumption, as he gives no proof of the correctness of his statement, and on a point of Masonic history dependent on the authority of old documents and the correctness of a deduction from them I am compelled to prefer the accuracy and the judgment of Bro. Hughan to those of even the venerable Oliver.

Notwithstanding that the Grand Chapter counted some of the most distinguished "Modern" Masons among its members, it was never officially recognized as a Masonic organization by the Grand Lodge.

In 1792 it was resolved that the Grand Lodge has nothing to do with the proceedings of the Society of Royal Arch Masons.[105]

Still, it met with marked success. In 1796 it had one hundred and four chapters under its obedience and to which it had granted warrants.

Unlike the Grand Chapter of the "Ancients," it was independent in its jurisdiction, being, as has been seen, wholly unconnected with the Grand Lodge. Its presiding officers were called the three Principals, and bore respectively as titles the initials of the names Zerubbabel, Haggai, and Joshua. Thus there was Principal Z., Principal H., and Principal J. This usage has been preserved in the present Grand Chapter of England. It had for its chief Principal Thomas Dunkerley as long as he lived, and for its first Patron, the Duke of Cumberland, who on his demise was succeeded by the Duke of Clarence.

In 1813, on the union of the two Grand Lodges of the "Ancients" and the "Moderns," the Royal Arch degree was recognized as a component part of Ancient Craft Masonry, and the Supreme Grand Chapter was established as one of the powers of English Freemasonry.

Of the two rituals then in use that invented by Dunkerley, which had been practiced by the "Moderns," was preferred but the regulation of the "Ancients," which closely united the Grand Lodge [106]and the Grand Chapter and vested the presiding officers of both bodies in the same persons, was adopted. Hence, the Duke of Sussex, who had been elected the Grand Master of the Grand Lodge, became, by virtue of his office, the chief Principal of the Grand Chapter.

---

[105] Hughan presents this fact in his "Memorials," p. 8. The Grand Chapter, he says, was purely a defensive organization to meet the wants of the regular brethren and to prevent their joining the "Ancients."

[106] Dunkerley's ritual was Christian in its character, and his principal symbol, the foundation stone, was made to allude to the Saviour. In 1834 this ritual was abolished by the Grand Chapter, and a new one, less sectarian in its interpretation of the symbols, was adopted, which still continues in England and in English chapters.

Lyon says that the Royal Arch degree was introduced into Scotland about the middle of the last century, through the medium of military lodges whose members had received it in Ireland.[107] The statement that the degree was first worked in Scotland by the " Ancient Lodge of Stirling" in 1743 in connection with the Knight Templar and other high degrees, is said by Bro. Lyon to be without authentic evidence. But the writer of the introduction to the General Regulations for the Government of the Order of Royal Arch Masons of Scotland asserts that the Minute Mook of the Chapter from 1743 is still extant.[108]

About 1800 several Templar Encampments were founded in Scotland by charters granted by a body assuming that prerogative in Ireland.

These charters authorized the conferring of the Royal Arch degree.

There were other chapters which at that time practiced the degree without a charter.[109] The establishment of a Grand Encampment in 1811 by a charter granted by the Duke of Kent, the head of Templarism in England, put a stop to the practice of Royal Arch Masonry in Encampments, and that branch of the institution was for some time in a very irregular position, though there were many working chapters.

But on August 28, 1817, the Supreme Grand Royal Arch Chapter of Scotland was established by the representatives of thirty-four chapters at a General convocation of the Order held at Edinburgh.[110]

The Grand Lodge of Scotland, persistently wedded to the idea that Speculative Freemasonry consists of only three degrees, has always refused to recognize the Royal Arch as a part of the system. At first it prohibited its members from receiving the degree, but as that extreme of opposition has long since ceased, the antagonism now reaches only a quiet, official non-recognition.

The introduction of Royal Arch Masonry into the continent of America, and especially into the United States, will occupy our attention in the following chapter.

---

[107] "History of the Lodge of Edinburgh," p. 291.
[108] "General Regulations of the Grand Chapter of Scotland," Introduction, p. vii.
[109] Ibid.
[110] Lyon's "History of the Lodge of Edinburgh," p. 290.
P. 1263

CHAPTER XLIX

THE INTRODUCTION OF ROYAL ARCH MASONRY INTO AMERICA

THE Royal Arch degree was introduced into the North American Colonies not very long after its invention or adoption in England.

The Grand Lodge of Ancients granted its first Warrant for a lodge in the colonies in the year 1758.[111] In the same year, as will be seen hereafter, a chapter connected with an Atholl lodge was established. This alone would prove, if such proof were necessary, that the Royal Arch Masonry of Pennsylvania, where it first appeared on this continent, was derived from the "Grand Lodge of England, according to the Old Institutions," and that the degree which was then worked was what is commonly known as Dermott's Royal Arch.

Of course, the degree must have been conferred in a chapter working under a Master's Warrant, as at that time no Grand Chapter had been organized.

The Grand Lodge of Ancients had always granted this privilege to its lodges, and it was maintained up to the early years of the present century by several of the American lodges. Thus as late as January, 1803, Orange Lodge of Ancient York Masons, an Atholl lodge in Charleston, S.C., granted the privilege of its Warrant for the use of the Royal Arch Chapter of South Carolina."[112]

The first Royal Arch Chapter in America of which we can find an account, was held in Philadelphia in the year 1758. The author of

---

[111] It is so stated in Gould's "Register of the Atholl Lodges," p. 16, and the fact is confirmed by the recent researches of the Grand Lodge of Pennsylvania.

[112] "Historical Sketch of Orange Lodge." See Mackey's "History of Freemasonry in South Carolina," p. 471.

the Historical View prefixed to Pennsylvania Ahiman Rezon, says that it was held "anterior" to that year. This is manifestly an error, as the date of the Warrant of the first lodge of the "Ancients" in that city, and indeed in the country, was June 7, 1758, and it is evident that no chapter could have preceded the lodge in date of birth, as the former derived its authority from the latter, and worked under its Warrant.

The author of the Historical View, which has just been referred to, stated that it worked under the Master's Warrant of Lodge numbers and that it was recognized by and had communion with a military Chapter working under a Warrant number 351 granted by the Grand Lodge of England, meaning, as the context clearly shows, the Atholl Grand Lodge or the Grand Lodge of the Ancients.[113]

There can be no doubt of the truth of the statement that a chapter of Royal Arch Masons was established in Philadelphia about the year 1758 and that it worked under the Master's Warrant of Lodge number 3. Bro. Clifford MacCalla, who is the very best authority on the early history of Freemasonry in Pennsylvania, says that the minutes of this Chapter, which he designates as Jerusalem Chapter number 3, are in existence as far back as 1767, and that they mention prior minutes.[114]

But it is not easy to reconcile the statement that it held communion with a military lodge, numbered 351, granted by the Atholl Grand Lodge, with the facts of history.

Up to the year 1756 the Atholl Grand Lodge had granted only two military Warrants, numbers 41 and 52, one in 1755 and the other in 1756. In fact, at the end of the year 1757 the numbers on the roll of that Grand Lodge as accurately arranged by Bro. Gould amounted to only 68.[115]

There was a military Warrant numbered 351, but it was not granted until October, 1810.[116]

Indeed, number 351 is too high for the year 1758 roll of either of the Grand Lodges of England, or of those of Ireland or Scotland.

Even in England, the oldest of the four bodies, the numbers had not at that early period gone far into the two hundreds.

What then was this military Lodge, numbered as 351, at a time when no such numbers could have been reached by the existing registrations, and what was this Lodge number 3 on the Pennsylvania

---

[113] "Ahiman Rezon of Pennsylvania," edition of 1825, p. 79.
[114] "Philadelphia, the Mother City of Freemasonry in America," p.99.
[115] Gould's "Atholl Lodges," p. 16.
[116] Ibid., p. 102. By a typographical error the number is printed 361 instead of 351 as it should evidently have been.

roll which held communion with it, and both of which were thus engaged in the propagation of the Royal Arch degree in America ?

Bro. MacCalla, referring to the military lodges in Pennsylvania, during and before the war of the Revolution, says that "Lodge number 18 was in the 17th Regiment British army." Nowin the first official list of the Atholl lodges given in the Ahiman Rezon for 1807, we find if "18, 17th Regiment of foot," as the third of the military lodges. No date is given for its Warrant, but from its position in the list we may presume that it was one of the oldest lodges Gould says it was originally warranted as number 237, and he gives the original 18 as having been constituted as a civil lodge at London in 1753. This lodge becoming extinct, the number seeme by a system of registration peculiar to the Atholl Masons to have been taken up by the military lodge instead of its original number, 237.

Again this military Lodge number 18 makes its appearance in another official quarter.

C. Downes, Past Master of Lodge number 141, on the registry of Ireland, published at Dublin in 1804, Lists of lodges "according to the 'Old Constitutions' of the kingdom of Great Britain, and also of America, the East and the West Indias, &c." Downes was the printer to the Grand Lodge of Ireland and with its permission had edited the Irish Ahiman Reman. His Lists are therefore possessed of some official authority.

In his List of military lodges he also gives Lodge number 18, in the 17th Regiment, as third lodge in order of sequence as having been warranted by the Atholl Grand Lodge of England.

But he also gives a list of the lodges which had been warranted up to the year 1804, amounting to 65. How many of these had been discontinued, and what was the date of any of their warrants we can not learn from the List, which gives only the numbers and places and times of meeting.[117]

The 8th Pennsylvania lodge in Downes's List is marked as number 18, British 17th Regiment of Foot." The coincidence here apparent would indicate that this was the same lodge as that marked in Downes's, Harper's, and Gould's list of military lodges warranted by the Atholl Grand Lodge of England. By what process it changed its

---

[117] In an article on "Military Lodges," published by Bro. Gould in the "Freemasons' Chronicle," and copied into the "Keystone" (July 31, 1880), he finds after much research, much difficulty in "disentangling the history of Lodge number 18." The only explanation at all satisfactory, and that nose altogether so, is the one given in the text.

obedience from its Mother Grand Lodge to the Grand Lodge of Pennsylvania, Downes does not inform us.

We have an authentic record that in 1767 there had been and was a military lodge in an Irish regiment stationed at Philadelphia.

The records of Lodge number 3, which have been copied in the Early History and Constitution of the Grand Lodge of Pennsylvania,[118] contained the following item:

"Dec. 9, 1767. The majority of (the) Body was of opinion that it would not be proper to admit Bro. Hoodless a member of this or to enter, pass, or raise any person belonging to the army, in this lodge, as there is a lawfull warranted Body of good and able Masons in the Royal Irish regiment."[119]

So much for the military lodge which is said to have introduced Royal Arch Masonry into the American Colonies, and through whose instrumentality the degree was first conferred in Lodge number 3.

Our next inquiry must be directed to the character and position of this lodge, which, without rhetorical exaggeration, may be well called the Mother of Royal Arch Masonry in America.

The Lists of the Atholl lodges show that the Grand Lodge of the Ancients granted a Warrant for a lodge at Philadelphia in the year 1758. On the Pennsylvania roll this lodge was known as number 2, but in Gould's List it is marked as "No. 69, Philadelphia, 7 June 1758." On June 13, 1761, the Grand Lodge of Ancients granted a Warrant for another lodge, which Gould records as is 89, number 1 Philadelphia." This Warrant was, however, lost. and another one was issued on June 20, 1764.

It is from the date of this Warrant that the organization of the Provincial Grand Lodge of Pennsylvania is reckoned.

Why the lodge warranted in 1758 should be designated as number 2, while that warranted three years afterward should be designated as number 1, can be accounted for in only one way. There was most probably a deputation accompanying the Warrant for number 2, which deputation must have organized a Provincial Grand Lodge which took the number 1. The Ahiman Rezon of Pennsylvanza, for 1825, referring to Lodge number 2, says that "the patents to Provincial Grand Masters were usually in force for one year, at the expiration of which, if a Grand Lodge was formed, it elected its Grand Master,

---

[118] Compiled and published by authority of the Grand Lodge, 1777.

[119] "Early History," etc.,p. 11. The "Royal Irish Regiment" afterward became the 8th on the Muster roll of the British army. See Debrett's "British Imperial Calendar for 1819," p. 137

Wardens, Secretary and Treasurer. . . If no Grand Lodge was constituted upon a patent, it expired, and another patent was issued as occasion required."[120]

The writer then concludes that "it is probable that no Grand Lodge had been organized upon the first patent issued for Pennsylvania since a second was issued on June 20, 1764, by the Grand Lodge of England to William Ball, Esqr., and others authorizing them to form and hold a Grand Lodge for the then province." [121]

This conjecture is very plausible. The deputation which accompanied the Warrant for number 69 in Philadelphia may have been intended for a Provincial body, which was not, however, completely organized, but which nevertheless took the number 1, while the lodge which on the registry of the Atholl Grand Lodge of England bore the number 69 was changed on the Pennsylvania roll to number 2. The Provincial deputation which had been appointed in 1758 not having completely fulfilled its functions by the permanent establishment of a Provincial Grand Lodge, another Warrant for that purpose was issued in 1761, and that having been lost on the way, a second was issued in 1764, and the Provincial Grand Lodge was formed. In fact this must have been merely a continuation of the first lodge or deputation, and the Lodge number 69, which had been originally transmuted into number 2, retained that number, and, excepting the Provincial Grand Lodge, we find no number 1 on the registry of Pennsylvania.

But though this deputation of 1758 did not formally and permanently organize a Provincial Grand Lodge, or if it did, has left no record of the transaction, it performed the functions of one by warranting another lodge, which received the number 3.

Of this fact we have the following evidence. When the Grand Lodge of Ancients granted its warrant for a lodge in 1758, no further notice of Pennsylvania was taken by it until it granted the Warrant numbered 89 on its register in 1761, which being lost was replaced by another of the same tenor issued in 1764, and which Gould calls number 1, at Philadelphia.

Between 1758 and 1764 it granted no more Warrants for the establishment of lodges in Pennsylvania, nor did it ever afterward do so. With the exception of the Warrant issued at first in 1761 and renewed or rather replaced in 1764, Freemasonry in Pennsylvania appears, from the year 1758, to have been controlled solely by some authority within

---

[120] "Ahiman Rezon of Pennsylvania," for 1825, p. 67.
[121] Ibid., p. 68.

the Province, and from that authority Lodge number 3 must have received its Warrant.

The first act of the Provincial Deputation, or Provincial Grand Lodge, or whatever may have been the character and designation of the authority existing in Philadelphia in the year 1758 was to grant a Warrant for the establishment of another lodge as number 3.

There is no record extant of this Warrant but the author of the Early History of the Grand Lodge of Pennsylvania says that in Lodge number 3 of Philadelphia by tradition dates its warrant about the same time as number 2."[122]

This Lodge number 3 is the one which in 1758, with the concurrence and under the instruction of the military lodge in the 17th Royal Irish Regiment, introduced the Royal Arch degree into Pennsylvania and worked it, as all "Ancient" lodges at that time did, under the authority of its Master's Warrant.

The absence of the records of early Freemasonry in Pennsylvania, which were lost or destroyed during the revolution, forces us to trust, more than is desirable in writing history, to conclusions mainly based on conjectures; but the conjectures are reasonable, sustained by the strongest evidence and entirely consistent with facts derived from the very few authentic documents that remain.

We are told in the Pennsylvania Ahiman Rezon that other Chapters were afterward established "upon like principles." That is, they were established under the shadow of Master's Warrants.

The writer of the Historical View of Masonry, contained in the 1825 edition of the Pennsylvania Ahiman Rezon, tells the story of the further progress of Royal Arch Masonry in that State in the following words:

"In November, 1795, an irregular attempt was made, at the instance of one Molan, to introduce innovations in the Arch degree and to form an independent Grand Royal Arch Chapter, under the Warrants of numbers 19, 52, and 67, held in the city of Philadelphia, and a lodge constituted by authority of the Grand Lodge of Maryland, and another holding under the Grand Lodge of Georgia. Chapter number 3 instituted an enquiry into these proceedings, which they declared, after investigation, to be contrary to the established uniformity of the Craft. The Grand Lodge, upon complaint made, unhesitatingly suspended the Warrants of numbers 19, 52, and 67, and having received the report of the committee raised for that purpose, resolved that Molan

---

[122] "Early History and Constitution of the Grand Lodge of Pennsylvania." p. 35

ought not to be received as a mason by the lodges or brethren under its jurisdiction. The offending lodges, by the mild and firm course of the Grand Lodges were convinced of their errors, and were received into favora having their Warrants restored to them.

"Throughout this controversy, the Grand Lodge acknowledged the right of all regular warranted lodges, so far as they have ability and number, to make masons in the higher degrees, but lest differences might exist, or innovations be attempted in such higher degrees, which for want of some proper place to appeal, might create schism among the brethren, they resolved that a Grand Royal Arch Chapter should be opened, under the immediate sanction of the Grand Lodge of Pennsylvania; and that all past and present officers of the Grand Lodge, having duly obtained the degree of Royal Arch, and all past and existing officers of Chapters of Royal Arch masons, duly and regularly convened under the sanction of a warrant from the Grand Lodge of Pennsylvania, to be considered as members of the Grand Rowral Arch Chapter; and that all members of the regular Chapters shall be admitted to their meetings, but without the right to vote or speak therein, unless requested."[123]

It has, from this record, been maintained that this was the first Grand Chapter established in America, and that Webb was mistaken in giving the priority to that organized at Hartford in 1798.

But the truth is that the Grand Chapter established at Philadelphia in 1795 was not a Grand Chapter in the sense attached to such a body by those who organized at Hartford the Grand Chapter of the Northern States.

The Grand Chapter of Pennsylvania was merely an instrument of the Grand Lodge. That body alone could grant permission to hold a Chapter, and no Chapter could be held unless with the sanccion of the Warrant of a lodge, and it was expresslydeclared that the Grand Chapter was to be opened "under the immediate sanction of the Grand Lodge."

Now all these prmcipies oil dependence were repudiated by Welbb and his associates. They expressly declared in the very outset of their labors of organization - no matter whether the statement was historically accurate or not - that no Grand Lodge could "claim or exercise authority over any convention or Chapter of Royal Arch masons." In the first constitution which they formed they placed Chapters exclusively under the control of Grand Chapters, and by implication abolished all authority of Grand Lodges over them and at

---

[123] "Ahiman Rezon of Pennsylvania," edition of 1825, p. 79.

the same time denied the right of any Chapter to work under the Warrant of a Master's lodge.

This system has ever since prevailed in the United States. It was subsequently adopted by the Grand Chapter of Pennsylvania itself.

The Grand Chapter established at Philadelphia in 1795 was only an organization for the more convenient administration of Royal Arch Masonry in the bosom and under the superintendence of the Grand Lodge.

The Grand Chapter established in 1798 at Hartford was, as has been shown, of a very different construction, and based on very different principles of Masonic law.

To the Grand Chapter formed at Hartford in 1798 must therefore in all fairness Ibe given the precedency of date as being the first independent Grand Chapter established in the United States - indeed we may say it was the first in the world, as the Grand Chapters previously established in England were like that of Pennsylvania, dependent instruments of the Grand Lodge.

The credit, however, must be given to Philadelphia of having introduced Royal Arch Masonry into the British Colonies. We have no record of the establishment of a Chapter in any other of the Provinces before the year 1758, at which time, as we have seen, the degree was conferred in a Chapter attached to Lodge number 3 .

But during the succeeding years of the 18th century the degree, under various modifications, was introduced into other States, principally by Atholl, or as they were pleased most incorrectly to style themselves, "Ancient York Masons."

The original system inaugurated by the "Ancients" was strictly followed, and as Thomas Smith Webb, the founder of the American system, has said, during all that period "a competent number of companions, possessed of sufficient abilities, under the sanction of a Master's Warrant, proceeded to exercise the rights and privileges of Royal Arch Chapters, whenever they thought it expedient and proper, although in most cases the approbation of a neighboring Chapter was deemed useful if not proper."[124]

The degree practiced was that of the Grand Lodge of Ancients from whom it was derived. Virginia was, however, an exception. Whether the English Royal Arch was worked in the early period of Freemasonry in that State is not known. Dr. Dove, the author of the

---

[124] "Freemason's Monitor," p. 155.

Virginia Text Book of Royal Arch Masonry, our best authority on the subject, does not inform us.

Joseph Myers was one of the deputies of M. M. Hayes, who had, under the authority of Stephen Morin, been engaged in the dissemination of the twenty-five degrees of the Rite of Perfection, which was afterward developed into the Ancient and Accepted Rite of thirty-three degrees.

Soon after 1783 Myers removed to Richmond, Va., where, says Bro.Dove, he imparted the degrees of the Rite Ecossats to many Master Masons.[125]

Among these degrees was the Arch of Enoch, which was really Ramsay's Royal Arch. This degree, Dove says, was taught in Virginia until the year 1820, when it was abandoned and Webb's degree, which was the modification of the English system, and which is novn universally practiced in the United States, was adopted.

During the latter part of the 18th century several Chapters were organized in Virginia, each of which worked under the authority of Master's Warrant. Such were the Chapters at Norfolk, Richmond, Staunton, and Dumfries. In the year 1808 the first three united in the organization of a "Supreme Grand Royal Arch Chapter," which immediately assumed jurisdiction over the degree in the State.

The Royal Arch degree was introduced into New York not long after its introduction into Pennsylvania, and most probably by some of the English military lodges, many of which were at that time in the Province.[126]

Independent Royal Arch Lodge was warranted in December, 1760. Bro. John G. Barker, the author of the Early History of Masonry in New York, says "that the history of this lodge, prior to the year 1784, is involved in obscurity, as is also the derivation of its name."[127]

But it is evident that the peculiarity of the name refers to the fact of its having been engaged in working the Royal Arch degree.

I do not therefore hesitate to place, conjecturally, the introduction of that degree into the Province at a time contemporaneous with the organization of the lodge.

---

[125] "Virginia Text Book," p. 91.
[126] Of the nine lodges engaged in 1782 in the organization of the Provincial Grand Lodge of New York, six were military lodges, attached to different regiments in the British Army.
[127] "Early History and Transactions of the Grand Lodge of the State of New York," published by Kane Lodge, 1876, p. 17.

From New York, Royal Arch Masonry extended into other Northern Provinces, and independent Chapters were established which eventually gave birth to the General Grand Chapter.

Chapters were successively formed in different parts of the Province, each acting under the authority of a Master's Warrant.

One of the most important of these was Washington Chapter in the City of New York, which, as it will hereafter appear, granted Warrants for the establishment of other Chapters.

In 1798 a Deputy Grand Chapter was formed under the newly adopted constitution of the Grand Royal Arch Chapter of the Northern States, and when in 1799 that body changed its title to that of the General Grand Chapter," the Deputy Grand Chapter of New York assumed rank and name as a " Grand Chapter."

In the Province of Massachusetts, Royal Arch Masonry was introduced about the year 1769, probably a year or two later.

In that year the Grand Lodge of Scotland granted a Warrant for a lodge under the title of "St. Andrew's Lodge number 82." In the same year, if we may credit the statement of Bro. C. W. Moore,[128] "the degree was conferred in Boston in a "Royal Arch Lodge," which he "thinks" was attached to St. Andrew's Lodge Subsequent researches have removed all uncertainty on that point.

There is no positive information as to the original source whence the ritual of the degree as it was practiced by the St. Andrew's Chapter was derived. Its introduction has been attributed to Moses Michael Hayes, who is said to have introduced it from France, under the authority of a patent dated December 6, 1778. This statement Bro. Moore declares to be not true,[129] and his close official connection for a long series of years with the Masonry of Massachusetts, certainly makes him a competent judge.

But besides Hayes was one of the Inspectors appointed by Stephen Morin for the propagation of the Rite of Perfection which subsequently became the Ancient and Accepted Rite, and if the degree had been instituted by him, it would have assumed, which it did not, the form of Ramsay's Royal Arch, or the thirteenth degree of that Rite, as it did in Virginia, where Royal Arch Masonry was introduced by Myers, who was one of the collaborators of Hayes.

But according to Moore, the degrees conferred by the St. Andrew's Chapter corresponded in number and name with the degrees which were then conferred in Scotland, and hence he asserts with great

---

[128] "Freemasons' Monthly Magazine," vol. xii., p. 165.
[129] "Freemasons' Monthly Magazine," vol. xii., p. 165.

plausibility that the system was brought over from Scotland, perhaps at the same time that the Warrant for St. Andrew's Lodge was issued.

The degree had no rapid growth in Massachusetts. In 1798 there were but two Chapters in the State. St. Andrew's at Boston, and King Cyrus's at Newburyport. These two united to form a Deputy Grand Chapter, and in 1799 became the Grand Chapter of Massachusetts, under the new Constitution of the General Grand Chapter.

The history of the introduction of Royal Arch Masonry into Rhode Island presents some interesting facts in reference to the degrees which were at that time conferred preparatory to the Royal Arch.[130]

In the year 1793 a number of the members of St. John's Lodge number 1, in the city of Providence, met to consult upon the proper steps to be taken for the establishment of a Royal Arch Chapter, after consulting with those brethren who were already in possession of the degree.

An agent was accordingly sent to New York, who, on October 5, 1793, returned with a Dispensation issued by Washington Chapter in the city of New York.

Though called in the official records a Dispensation, the words of the instrument show that it was really a Warrant of Constitution.

Its date is September 3, 1793.

The brethren proceeded under this Warrant to organize Providence Chapter number 2. This was done on November 23, 1793, with the assistance of certain Royal Arch Masons who had been invited from Newport, and who were members of a Chapter.

As we learn from the records of this Chapter, the essential officers were, a High Priest, King, Scribe, Royal Arch Captain, and Zerubbabel, the latter officer evidently being the one now known as Principal Sojourner. The fact that an inferior office was attributed to Zerubbabel instead of the more exalted station of King, as is now the case, shows that the ritual used in New York and in Rhode Island was different from the present one.

Such a position for the "Prince of the Captivity" is more conformable to the ritual of the Sixteenth degree or Prince of Jerusalem, in the Rite of Perfection which afterward became the Scottish Rite, but altogether incompatible with the functions ascribed to him in the Royal Arch of the present day.

---

[130] The facts stated in this narrative are derived from the Records of St. John's Lodge, extracts from which were published in "The Warden," a Masonic magazine, printed at Providence, No. IV., September, 1879, p. 23 et seq.

This circumstance would indicate that there is some foundation for the hypothesis that in its early introduction into the American Colonies, Royal Arch Masonry was to a considerable extent affected by the rituals of the Hautes Grades or High Degrees, which were brought over from France in 1761 by Stephen Morin as the Agent of the "Deputies General of the Royal Art," for the purpose of "multiplying the sublime degrees of High Perfection."[131]

Morin appointed his Deputies, who spread over the West India islands and the continent of North America, and there isvery strong evidence that they or some of them exercised an influence in the organization of Royal Arch Masonry in several parts of the country.

Charters for Mark Lodges were originally issued by Grand Councils of the Prince of Jerusalem. The Select degree was one of the honorary degrees conferred by the Inspectors - we have seen that Myers, one of Morin's Inspectors, organized the Royal Arch Masonry of Virginia according to the ritual of the Thirteenth degree - Moses Michael Hayes, who was also an Inspector of the new Rite, was at one time Grand Master of the Grand Lodge of Massachusetts, and as he was a very zealous Mason and a very energetic officer, it can scarcely be doubted that he exercised an influential connection with St. Andrew's Chapter, the first Chapter established in that State - and finally we have a significant fact stated in the records of the organization of the chapter at Providence, which shows the intimate relation which existed at that time between the Royal Arch Masons who founded the Chapter and certain possessors of the High Degrees imported into this country by the deputies and agents of Stephen Morin.

When the Dispensation or Warrant had been issued by Washington Chapter for the holding of a Chapter at Providence, the brethren to whom it had been granted, feeling perhaps incompetents from their want of skill and experience to undertake unaided the task of organization, invited the assistance of the Royal Arch Masons who resided at Newport to give their assistance in the ceremony. The invitation having been accepted, the lodge met on Tuesday evening, October 29th. But "unavoidable necessity having prevented the attendance of the brethren from Newport, the brethren who had met, agreed to postpone any further meeting until they should arrive." Nearly a month passed before any further steps were taken toward the organization, and it was not until November 23d that the Newport Royal

---

[131] The language of the Patent issued to Morin.

Arch Masons having then made their appearance, the organization was completed.

The evidence of the connection of these Newport brethren with the "High Degrees" is to be found in the following extract from the record of the proceedings:

"Our worthy and respectable Brethren from Newport, viz.: R. W. Moses Seixas, 45th Degree or Deputy Inspector General of Masonry in and thro'out the State, and Master of St. John's Lodge number 1, in Newport, the W. Peleg Clark 28th Degree or Knight of the Sun, and Senior Warden of the Grand Lodge in this State, and the Hon. Thomas W. Moore 28th Degree or Knight of the Sun and Consul of his Britannic Majesty in this State, having this Day cheerfully attended at the Council chamber in this Town, agreeably to invitation, for the express Purpose of assisting in the Formation of a Royal Arch Chapter, the Brethren of the Royal Arch here, with the brethren aforesaid and our worthy Brother, Samuel Stearns, 7th Degree, R. A. (who also attended by Invitation), proceeded agreeably to the Directions in that case provided to open and consecrate a Royal Arch Chapter, by the name of 'Providence Chapter of Royal Arch Masons' under the Dispensation from the M. W. Washington Chapter of R A. Masons of New York, etc."[132]

The figure "45 " is evidently either an error of the pen in the manuscript record or of the press in the printed copy in The Warden. It should be " 43." In David Vinton's Short Historical Account of Masonry appended to his Masonic Minstrel, which was published at Dedham, in Massachusetts, in the year 1816, will be found a list of the degrees said to be conferred in Charleston, New York, and Newport. The number is 43, and the last, or 43d, is Sovereign Grand Inspector-General. The number is made up by adding to the thirty-three degrees of the Scottish Rite ten others, embracing the degrees of the American Rite and several Orders of Knighthood. In this enumeration the Knight of the Sun is made the 38th, and therefore I suppose that the number "28" prefixed to that degree in the extract above quoted is also an error. This enumeration of 43 degrees was never accepted nor used by the legitimate bodies of the Scottish Rite, but only by some spurious associations which then existed. Newport was the locality of one of these associations, and Moses Seixas was its chief. This does not, however, affect the truth of the statement that the possessors of the "High Degrees," whether legally or illegally

---

[132] Proceedings of Providence Chapter, published in " The Warden," No. iv., p. 24.

obtained, sought, in the infancy of Royal Arch Masonry in this country, to take a part in its institution and in giving complexion to its ritual.

There is another record in these minutes of the proceedings of Providence Chapter which is of far greater importance, as it shows, officially, the number, names, and sequence of the degrees which in the year 1793 and for some time before were considered asessentially preliminary to the reception of the Royal Arch.

At the meeting on October 5, 1793, when the Dispensation was received from New York, we find the following proceedings recorded:

"Our M.W. having suggested that in order to confer the R A. Degree it would be necessary that the Brethren who were Candidates for the same should previously be initiated in Three Degrees which were between that of Master Mason and the R A., and to accomplish the business as soon as possible, proposed the immediate opening of a lodge for that purpose, which was done accordingly.

"Present,

M. W. DANIEL STILLWELL, M.
W. JONA. DONNISON, S. W.
W. JACOB SMITH, J. W.
BR. WILLIAM MAGEE.

"And the Brethren whose names here follow after due preparation were regularly initiated in the degrees of Master lWark, Past Master, and Most Excellent Master."

This record conclusively proves that Thomas Smith Webb was not the inventor of the Mark and Most Excellent degrees, an opinion that has been entertained by several Masonic writers Webb was not initiated into the symbolic degrees until about the year 1792; certainly not before, for having been born in October, 1771, he was not qualified by age to receive those degrees at an earlier period.

The Royal Arch degree he of course obtained at a still later date, and it is certain that in October, 1793, he could not have been competent by skill or experience to invent a ritual, nor could he have had influence enough to establish it.

All that can justly be ascribed to him is that in 1798, and in the subsequent years in which he was engaged in teaching a ritual, he modified the degrees of the Chapter, as well as those of the lodge, so as to give them that permanent form which they have ever since retained.

But though it appears very satisfactorily from this record that about the year 1793 the system of degrees given in a Royal Arch Chapter was well settled in the Northern States, at least in New York and in New England, yet in other parts of the United States and in Canada there remained for a long time, even to the early years of the 19th century, a great diversity in the names and number of the preparatory degrees.

In Philadelphia, where Royal Arch Masonry made its first appearance, having been derived from England through a military lodge, warranted by the Ancient Masons, the system pursued by the Atholl Grand Lodge appears to have adopted, and the Royal Arch immediately followed the Master's degree. Such was the case in Royal Arch Lodge number 3, whose minutes, as far back as 1767, have been preserved.[133]

This lodge was so styled because it conferred the Royal Arch degree as well as the three symbolic degrees. In its minutes, so far as they have been published, we shall find no allusion to any preparatory steps. Indeed, the only reference to the degree in the earlier minutes is on December 3, 1767, when the important admission is made that the initiation into the symbolic degrees of a candidate who had been Entered, Passed, and Raised by three Royal Arch Masons acting without a Warrant was lawful.[134] There is no evidence elsewhere, either in England or America, that this prerogative was ever claimed or admitted for the possessors of the Royal Arch degree.

It was, however, from the earliest period made the qualification of the Royal Arch degree that the candidate should have passed the chair either by election or by a dispensation from the Grand Master.

We learn from the minutes of Jerusalem Chapter number 3 that in 1783 the Royal Arch as given in Pennsylvania differed so much from that conferred in Scotland that Bro. George Read, coming from the latter country, where he had been made a Royal Arch Mason, "not being able to make himself known in some of the most interesting points, he was (in consequence of his certificate) granted the privilege of a second initiation." Bro. Charles E. Meyer, when quoting this extract from the Minutes, in his History of Royal Arch Masonry and of Jerusalem Chapter number 3, as a proof that the rituals of Scotland and Pennsylvania were not alike, says: "It would be interesting to know what these points were that Bro. Read did not possess."

---

[133] "See Early History and Constitutions of the Grand Lodge of Pennsylvania," Part 1., p. 11.

[134] "It appearing by good authority that Bro. John Hoodless has been duly and lawfully entered, passed and raised at Fort Pitt in the year 1759 by our brethren, John Maine, James Woodward and Richard Sully, all Royal Arch Masons." Minutes of Royal Arch Lodge, No. 3.

I think it very probable that there was a difference in the rituals of the two countries at that time, as there is at the present day.

But the proof of it from this record is not positive, since the question may very naturally arise, whether the difficulty in this case arose from the difference of ritual or from the ignorance or forgetfulness of the candidate, who had possibly not retained in full the lesson which he had been taught.

In May, 1795, we have the first record of the adoption of the Mark as a preparatory degree, though Bro. Myers thinks it was doubtless previously conferred as a side degree.

The first record of the Most Excellent Master's degree in the minutes of Jerusalem Chapters is on November 5, 1796, and from that time the three preparatory degrees have been conferred in Pennsylvania as they are in the other States.

In Virginia, the Royal Arch was introduced as we have already seen by Myers, and was not the degree practiced either by the Ancient Masons of England or by the Chapters of this country. It was the Thirteenth degree or Royal Arch of Solomon, contained in the series of degrees of the Rite of Perfection. Dislocated from its proper place in the original Rite to which it belonged, it was made to follow the Third degree, without the interpolation of any preparatory step.

Subsequently the Virginia Chapters introduced preliminary degrees, derived from other sources. In the minutes of the Grand Chapter, as late as 1808, we find references to the degrees of "Most Excellent Master," and of "Arch and Royal Arch Excellent and Super-Excellent Masons."[135]

In Connecticut all the Chapters except one had derived their Warrants from Washington Chapter of New York, and necessarily adopted the system of degrees which was practiced by it and by the Chapters which it established. These degrees, as we have already seen in the instance of Providence Chapter in Rhode Island, were the Master Mark, Past and Most Excellent Master as preliminary to the Royal Arch.[136]

But in Vanden Broeck Chapter, at Colchester, which was warranted in 1796 by the Grand Chapter of New York, the names and

---

[135] Dove, " Royal Arch Text Book," p. 132.
[136] There was not, however, absolute uniformity. According to Wheeler ("Records of Capitular Masonry in Connecticut," p. 21), the minutes of Solomon Chapter No. 5 at Derby contain no notice of the Past Master's degree until January, 1796, and the Mark and Most Excellent Master are not mentioned until a later period.

sequence of the preparatory degrees was as follows: Mark Master, Excellent Master, and Super-Excellent Master. In 1800 it conformed to the system which has been established by the General Grand Chapter.

Excellent Master was exchanged for Past Master, and Super-Excellent for Most Excellent.[137] It is probable that the change was rather in the nomenclature than in the ritual.

We have already seen that the names and ranks of the officers of Chapters in the 18th century differed from those now used. For instance, Zerubbabel, who now occupies one of the prominent places in our modern ritual, was formerly placed at the bottom of the list.

The by-laws of Hiram Chapter, at Newtown, which were adopted March 3, 1792, give the following succinct account of the duties of these officers, and throw considerable light upon the ritualistic history of the time:

"It shall be the duty of the High Priest to preside at every meeting, to direct the business and to give occasionally a lecture; of the King to preside in the absence of the High Priest, and to assist him in his duty; of the Scribe, to preside in the absence of both, to cause the Secretary to enter in a fair and regular manner the proceedings of the Chapter in a book provided for that purpose, to summons the members for attendance at every regular and special meeting and also to administer the obligation; of Zerubbabel, to superintend the arrangements of the Chapter; of the Royal Arch Captain, to keep watch at the Sanctuary; of the three Grand Masters, to watch the vails; of the Treasurer, to receive the monies, to keep an account thereof and to pay none but on the warrant of the High Priest, and to render an account at the meeting previous to the annual election; of the Secretary, to keep the minutes under the direction of the Scribe, to receive the fees for admission, and to pay the same to the Treasurer; of the Clothier, to provide and to take care of the clothing; of the Architect, to provide and take care of the furniture."[138]

The Royal Arch was probably introduced into many of the Southern States, as it had been into the Northern, either by possessors of the degree coming direct from England, or by military lodges in the British army, and which held their Warrants from the Grand Lodge of the Ancients.

Chapters were, however, not organized as independent bodies, but the degree was, until some time after the beginning of the 19th century, conferred both in South Carolina and Georgia, and, I think,

---

[137] "Records of Capitular Masonry in Connecticut," p. 24.
[138] By-laws of Hiram Chapter, Article VIII. See Wheeler's "Early Records." D. 10.

also in North Carolina,[139] in Chapters dependent on and deriving their authority from Master's Warrants.

Many years ago, while investigating the history of Royal Arch Masonry in South Carolina, I was led to make the following statements, the correctness of which I have since had no reason to doubt.[140]

I have in years past made the acquaintance of several Royal Arch Masons in the upper part of South Carolina, who had received their degrees in Master's lodges. The long period which had elapsed since their withdrawal from the active pursuits of Freemasonry, and the imperfection of memory attendant on their extreme age, prevented them from furnishing me with all the particular information in reference to the ritual which I desired, but I learned enough from my frequent conversations with these Patriarchs of the Order (all of whom must long since have succeeded to their heritage in the Celestial Lodge) to enable me to state, positively, that in the upper counties of the State, at as late a period as the year 1813, the Royal Arch degree was conferred in Master's lodges. The same condition of things existed in the neighboring State of Georgia.

The manuscript Minutes of Royal Arch Chapter number 1, under the sanction of Forsyth's Lodge number 14," are now, or were, some years ago, on the Archives of the Grand Chapter of Georgia. For an examination of these interesting records I was indebted to the kindness of the Grand Secretary, Comp. B. B. Russell.

The Chapter met in the City of Augusta, and the Minutes, to which I shall have occasion again to refer, are restricted to the year 1796.

These records state that the chapter at Savannah, having announced its intention to apply to the Grand Lodge of Georgia for a dispensation or warrant, a letter was written to the brethren at Savannah by the chapter at Augusta on May 27, 1796, in which the following declaration appears:

"If there is any rule or by-law that requires a Royal Arch Chapter to apply for a special dispensation or Warrant, it is unknown to us. We conceive that the Warrant given to Forsyth's Lodge was sufficient

---

[139] The first warrant for an independent chapter in North Carolina was granted in 1808 by the Grand Chapter of Virginia to "sundry Royal Arch Masons" in Bertie County. But the petition was recommended by the Lodge at Windsor, and by the Master of the Lodge at Winston. The Royal Arch Masons who signed the petition had, it is to be supposed, previously received the degree in these Lodges. Dove, "Royal Arch Text Book," p. 122.

[140] Mackey's "History of Freemasonry in South Carolina," 1861, p.471.

for the members thereof to confer any degree in Masonry agreeable to the ancient usages and customs."[141]

The same usage was pursued at the same time in South Carolina, where, as has been previously stated, Orange Lodge number 14 in 1796 adopted a resolution to "sanction the opening of a Royal Arch Chapter under its jurisdiction, and again in January, 1803, resolved "that the privilege of the Warrant of this lodge be granted for the use of the Royal Arch Chapter of Charleston." [142]

That this usage was not confined to the Atholl lodges is seen from the fact that while Orange Lodge in South Carolina was a lodge of "Ancient Masons," all the lodges in Georgia were "Moderns," the Atholl Grand Lodge of England never having extended its jurisdiction over that State nor organized any lodges in it.

The first Chapters in these States, under the constitution of the General Grand Chapter, were established in 1805 at Beaufort in South Carolina and at Savannah in Georgia.

The Grand Chapter of the former State was formed in 1812; that of the latter in 1816.

But reverting to the subject of the early ritual of Royal Arch Masonry and to the differences which prevailed toward the end of the 18th century in the names and character of the degrees, we shall meet with some interesting information in these Minutes of the Royal Arch Chapter at Augusta.

The business of electing candidates for the Royal Arch having been accomplished in an informal meeting of Royal Arch Masons. a Master Mason lodge was opened, when, the qualification for exaltation being to "pass the chair," they were made what are now called "Virtual Past Masters."

We find this in the records of the first meeting of the Chapter of which the following is an exact transcript made by me from the original manuscript.

"At a meeting of the subscribers, Royal Arch Masons at Forsyth's Lodge room the 29th February, 1796.

"Read a petition from Brothers Joseph Hutchinson, William Dearmond, and John McGowan, Master Masons of Forsyth's Lodge, praying to become Royal Arch companions; and the same being agreed to, a Master's lodge was then opened.

---

[141] "MS. Minutes of Forsyth's Royal Arch Chapter."
[142] "Historical Sketch" appended to By-laws of Orange Lodge, p. 4

"Present: Thomas Bray, Master; Thomas Davis, S.W.; D.B. Butler, J.W.; Joseph Hutchinson, Tyler; William Dearmond, John McGowan.

"Brothers Hutchinson, Dearmond, and McGowan were regularly passed the chair and obtained the degree of Past Master, and returned thanks for the same. The lodge was closed.

"A Royal Arch Chapter was then opened in ancient form.

"Present: Thomas Bray, H. P.; Thomas Davis, C.S.; D.B. Butler, K.

"Bro. Hutchinson (attending) received the preparatory degree; also Brothers Past Masters Dearmond and McGowan. They were then in rotation raised to the super-excellent degree of Royal Arch Masons, and returned thanks for the same."

Subsequent minutes are of the same character, except that the election of the candidates took place in a Master's lodge and not as in the first in an informal meeting of Royal Arch Masons. But, of course, we are to suppose that all the Master Masons present were not only Past Masters but also Royal Arch Masons.

But what were the preparatory degrees? That question is answered by the Minutes of November 29, 1796 these degrees are for the first time given. The record is as follows:

"At an extra meeting of Forsyth's Lodge, convened by the order of the W. M. and held at the court-house on Tuesday 29 November, 1796.

"Present: Thomas Bray, Master; Thomas Davis, S.W.; William Dearmond, J. W. pro tem.

"A Master's Mark lodge was opened for the purpose of conferring the degrees of Fellow-Craft Mark and Master Mark on Brothers John McGowan, Lawrence Trotti, and John B. Wilkinson, when they, attending, received the same and returned thanks to the lodge; which was then closed. A Past Master's lodge was then opened.

"Present: Thomas Bray, M.; Thomas Davis, S.W.; William Dearmond, J.

W. pro tem., John McGowan.

"The lodge was opened for the purpose of conferring the degree of Past Master on Brothers Lawrence Trotti and John B. Wilkinson, when, they attending, were regularly passed the chair and obtained the degree of Past Master, and gave thanks for the same. The lodge was then closed in ancient form. The Royal Arch Chapter was then opened.

"Present: Thomas Bray, H. P.; Thomas Davis, C. S.; John McGowan, K.; William Dearmond, R. A. C.

"The minutes of the last Chapter were read. The M. E. H. P. informed the companions present that the Chapter was called for the purpose of conferring the Super-excellent degree on Brothers Lawrence Trotti and John B. Wilkinson, who were then attending.

Bro. Trotti was then duly prepared and received the preparatory degree of R. M. and R. A., also Brother Wilkinson. They were then raised to the super-excellent degree of Royal Arch Mason, and returned thanks. The Chapter was then closed by order of the M. E. H. P."

These records supply us with several interesting and important facts relating to the ritual and the organization of Royal Arch Masonry in America about the close of the 18th century.

The Chapter degrees were then, as has been already shown from other sources, conferred under the sanction of the Warrant of a Master's lodge, but the body in which the Royal Arch degree was given was called a Chapter.

Nine Royal Arch Masons were not then deemed necessary to the opening of a Chapter or the conferring of the degree.

The only officers mentioned are a High-Priest, Chief Scribe, King, Royal Arch Captain, Treasurer and Secretary, and the Scribe appears to have taken precedence of the King. The officer called "Zerubbabel" in the Northern Chapters, is not mentioned in the Southern. In the latter it is probable that the same officer was called the "Royal Arch." The Royal Arch Captain could not have supplied his place, for both officers are recorded in the Minutes of the Providence Chapter in Rhode Island. The absence of an officer called "Zerubbabel" in the Southern Chapters, while it is found in all Northern ones, would evidently indicate some difference in the rituals of the two sections of the country. It is also significant on this point, that in the records of the Chapters at Augusta, no mention is made of the three Grand Masters of the Vails. They are included in the list of officers of all the Chapters in Connecticut which derived their Warrants and, we may suppose, their rituals from the Washington Chapter in New York.

It was always deemed an indispensable qualification for the reception of the Royal Arch degree that the candidate should be a Past Master. This practice, established in England at the origin of the degree, was followed by all the Chapters in America. As the restriction of the degree to those only who had presided for twelve months over a Symbolic lodge and thus become "Actual Past Masters" would have circumscribed the number of candidates within a very narrow and inconvenient limit, the ceremony of passing the chair was invented, by which the candidate became a "Virtual Past Master." This usage, which was the real origin of what is now called the Past Master's degree, was adopted by all the American Chapters, and thus the earliest records of the Augusta Chapter show that each person before being raised to the degree of Royal Arch was made to "pass the chair."

At first, as is shown by the minutes of February 29, 1796, the ceremony was performed in a Master's lodge. The same usage was observed at several subsequent meetings, but on December 26, 1796, for the first time it is recorded that the Master's lodge was closed and a Past Master's was opened for the purpose of conferring what had then become, not a mere qualification, but a preparatory degree.

Other preparatory degrees are mentioned in the earliest Minutes, but their names are not given until a later period. From the later minutes we learn what these degrees were. They are recorded in the November minutes as having the following names and being given in the following order:

Past Master, Fellow-Craft Mark, Master Mark, R.M., and R.A. These last two degrees are never recorded otherwise than by their initials, but we have every reason to believe, from other authorities, that they were Royal Master and Royal Ark, or Royal Ark Master.

Samuel Cole, writing in 1826, says of these two degrees that "they are considered as merely preparatory and are usually conferred immediately before the solemn ceremony of exaltation." Cole's work received the sanction of the Grand Lodge of Maryland, and it is hence evident that these two degrees were at one time conferred in the Chapters of the State. They were not known to or practiced in the chapters of the Northern States.

It will be noticed also, as a further evidence of the want of uniformity in the rituals of the 18th century, that the Minutes of the Chapter at Augusta make no reference to the Most Excellent Master's degree, which from an early period was always conferred as a preparatory step to the Royal Arch in the Northern States.

Passing over from the United States to Canada, we shall find the Royal Arch ritual at the close of the 18th century in another but still confused condition.

In the year 1856 the members of Ancient Frontenac Chapter, attached to the St. John's Lodge number 491, English Register, situated at Kingston in Canada, published a history of the Chapter from its organization. From this little but interesting work may be gleaned a very satisfactory statement of the character and condition of Royal Arch Masonry at the end of the 18th and the beginning of the 19th century.

Ancient Frontenac Chapter, which is or was the old Chapter in Canada West, was established at Freemasons' Tavern, in the town of Kingston, on June 7, 1797, under the sanction of a Warrant which had been granted to Lodge number 6 on November 20, 1795, by R. W.William Jarvis, at that time Provincial Grand Master of Canada, under the Atholl Grand Lodge of England.

Master's lodges in Canada, as in the neighboring United States, assumed the right to hold Chapters for conferring the Royal Arch degree. It was a right always sanctioned by the usages of the "Ancients" and tolerated by the "Moderns," nor ever denied until after the organization of the General Grand Chapter at Hartford. As late as February, 1806, at a convocation held in Kingston a charge was preferred against a member of Frontenac Chapter of "unmasonic conduct in striving to separate the Holy Royal Arch Chapter from the body of number 6."

Until the year 1809, the three principal officers of the Chapter were designated as "1, High-Priest; 2, Solomon, King of Israel; and 3, Hiram, King of Tyre." Judging by this, we must conclude that the ritual used in Frontenac Chapter differed very materially from all the various systems which prevailed at the time in other parts of America.

The earliest records of the Chapter do not show any recognition of preparatory degrees. The "Most Excellent" was first conferred on April 17, 1807, and the "Mark" on July 20, 1818. These degrees were not, however, even then obligatory, but appear to have been taken or not, at the action of the candidate; and as there was an attendant expense, few of the brethren availed themselves of the opportunity of receiving them. The Past Master's was, however, a prerequisite qualification toward exaltation, and, as elsewhere, it was always conferred in the Master's lodge to which the Chapter was attached.

Up to the end of the last century, many candidates were exalted when only seven Royal Arch Masons were present, the mystical number nine not being then required to constitute a quorum for conferring the degree.

Capitular Masonry seems to have been separated in Canada from Lodge Masonry in 1806, for on January 18th in that year a decision was received from the Provincial Grand Master for holding a Chapter at Kingston, which, says the pamphlet from which I have been quoting, was "the first step towards this Chapter working under a warrant separate from that of the Craft lodge."

On February 10, 1818, the Grand Royal Arch Chapter of Upper Canada was established, and on March 25th of the following year Frontenac Chapter number 1 received its Charter as one of its constituents.

The extracts given in the preceding pages, from the records of Chapters working at the close of the last and the beginning of the present century, have been sufficient to show that there prevailed at that time, in the different parts of the American Continent, a very confusing variety in the ritual of the Royal Arch and in the number of preparatory degrees, which clearly demonstrates that the conflicting systems must have been derived from different sources.

What these sources were it is impossible to precisely say, at least in every instance, in consequence of the unavoidable scantiness of the records. The general drift of history leads us to believe that among these sources were the Grand Lodge of Ancients, in England, and at a later period the Grand Lodge of Moderns, both of whom disseminated the degree through their military lodges, the Grand Lodge of Scotland, or rather the Royal Arch Masons of that kingdom, who practiced the degree without the recognition of their Grand Lodge, and as in Virginia and the Southern States the possessors of the "Sublime degrees," as they were called, which had been introduced into this country from France by Stephen Morin and his emissaries or deputies.

The result of borrowing rituals from so many different sources inevitably led to a deplorable diversity in the ceremonies, which led the Royal Arch Masons in some of the Northern States to attempt the laying of a firm foundation on which a uniform system might be established, and the constitution of a superintending authority which should maintain that uniformity, and give to Capitular Masonry a symmetry and shapeliness which should secure to it a permanence and success such as had been previously given to Craft Masonry by the ritualistic labors of Desaguliers and his associates in the second and third decades of the 18th century.

This work of reformation and of purification, in which the dross was rejected and the pure ore only retained, was finally accomplished by the institution of the General Grand Chapter of the United States, which was one of the most important events in the Masonic history of the United States.

To this event we must therefore next direct our attention. But the extent and interest of the subject demand a separate chapter for its consideration.

CHAPTER L

THE GENERAL GRAND CHAPTER OF THE UNITED STATES

As the system of Royal Arch Masonry which is practiced in the United States of America is really indebted to the organization of the General Grand Chapter for its existence and popularity, no history of that body could be complete without some account of the Masonic life of Thomas Smith Webb, who was the founder of both the system and the General Grand Chapter.

I shall therefore precede the history of the origin of the General Grand Chapter by a brief sketch of the Masonic services of that distinguished ritualist.[143]

Thomas Smith Webb was the son of English parents who had emigrated to this country a few years before his birth, and settled at Boston, in the State of Massachusetts, where he was born, on October 13, 1771.

Having received an elementary education in the public schools, he was bound as an apprentice to the art of printing, or perhaps of bookbinding. There is some uncertainty about this question, but the testimony preponderates in favor of the former. It is, however, not material as, in after life, he did not pursue either calling.

Having soon after removed to Keene, in New Hampshire, he there married, and about the year 1792 was initiated in the primary degrees of Freemasonry.

Subsequently he removed to Albany in New York. It is probable that he there received the higher degrees, as we find him, while residing there, engaged in the establishment of a Chapter of Royal Arch Masons

---

[143] In "Mackey's Encyclopedia of Freemasonry" will be found a copious memoir of Webb, from which, as the creation of my own pen, I have not hesitated to borrow the materials and indeed much of the language of the present sketch.

and a Commandery of Templars. We may also suppose that while living in Albany he became acquainted with the Ineffable degrees of which Albany was an early seat.

It was about this time that Webb commenced his career as a Masonic ritualist and teacher. In 1797 he published the first edition of his Freemasons' Monitor, or Illustrations of Masonry.[144] In the Preface to this work he acknowledges his indebtedness to Preston for the observations on the first three degrees. But he states in his Preface that he has made an arrangement of the lectures which differs from that of Preston, because the latter's distribution of the sections is not "agreeable to the present mode of working."[145] If other proof were wanting this would be enough to show that the "Prestonian work," as it has been called, differed from that then practiced in the United States, and ought to be an answer to those who at a later period have attempted to claim an identity between the ritual and lectures of Webb and those of Preston.

About 1801 he removed to Providence, R. I., and commenced the manufacture of wall-paper on an extensive scale. But he did not abandon his labors in the field of Speculative Masonry. By invitation he became a member of St. John's Lodge number 2, of Providence. He passed through the various grades of office and was elected in 1813 Grand Master of the Grand Lodge of Rhode Island.

His labors in the constitution of a Grand, and afterward a General Grand Chapter, will be hereafter referred to.

While continuing his interest in the manufacture in which he was engaged he did not neglect his Masonic labors, but in 1816 visited the Western part of the United States and appeared to have been actively employed in the organization of Chapters and Encampments.

He died at Cleveland, O., where he was on a visit on July 6, 1819, and was buried with Masonic honors. The body was subsequently disinterred and carried to Providence, where it was reinterred by the Grand Lodge of Rhode Island.

---

[144] This edition is very rare. The title-page, in a copy now lying before me, is as follows: "The Freemasons Monitor; or Illustrations of Masonry: in two Parts. By a Royal Arch Mason, K. T. - K, of M. - &c., &c. Printed at Albany, for Spencer and Webb, Market street, 1797," p. 284.

[145] "The observations upon the first three degrees are principally taken from Preston's 'Illustrations of Masonry,' with some necessary alterations. Mr. Preston's distribution of the first lecture into six, the second into four, and the third into twelve sections, not being agreeable to the present mode of working, they are arranged in this work according to the general practice First edition. Preface.

As to Webb's Masonic character and services, I see no reason to say otherwise than what I have already said on a former occasion.

His influence over the Freemasons of this country is to be ascribed almost wholly to his personal communication with them and to his oral teachings. He has made no mark in Masonic literature of any importance. His labors and his reputation as an author are confined to a single work, and that one of but little pretension. It is, indeed, only a meager syllabus of his Lectures. He seems, though the author of a Masonic system now universally practiced in the United States, to have been but very inadequately imbued with the true philosophical spirit of symbolism. He was an able workman of the ritual which he had invented, and an effective teachers and to this he owed his popularity. The deficiencies of his system are to be regretted, but Webb undoubtedly deserves commendation for his devotion and perseverance in the establishment or a system of ritualism which has been productive of such abundant fruit.

The Freemasons of America have generally attributed to him the invention of the preliminary degrees of the Chapter. But of this fact we have no satisfactory evidence, while there is much to the contrary. It has been seen in a preceding chapter that the Mark and Past degrees, as well as the Most Excellent, though probably under a different name, had been conferred in Chapters before Webb had been exalted in Albany to the Royal Arch.

But what Webb really did, was to change the rituals of these degrees and to give to them the form which is now universally adopted in the Chapters of this country.

For instance, the Mark Master's and the Most Excellent Master's songs, which now constitute essential parts of the working of those degrees, and are indispensably connected with their most important ceremonies, were composed by him and first published in his FreeMason's Monitor. They could therefore have been introduced into the work only after his composition of them.

In short, Webb can be deemed the founder of what is now called the "American Rite" only in so far that he modified the degrees which had previously existed, and gave to them not only a new and improved form, but established them in a legitimate sequence which has ever since been recognized by the constituted authorities.

Previous to his teaching, there was no regularity in the management of the preliminary degrees. In some Chapters they were conferred as preparatory to the Royal Arch; in others they were omitted, and the Royal Arch immediately followed the Third degree. For the permanent regularity now existing, we are certainly indebted to Thomas Smith Webb.

With this brief sketch of the Masonic life of this popular ritualist, we are now prepared to direct our attention to that portion of his labors which were especially given to the establishment of Royal Arch Masonry on a plan peculiar to this country.

The supplement of the Master's degree, which had been introduced by the Seceders into the English system, about the middle of the last century, was not long after imported into this country. This importation has been generally attributed to the military lodges which worked under the regime of the Atholl Grand Lodge, and which had received, at the time of their constitution, the instructions and the privileges of the Royal Arch.

It has been seen that the first American Chapter was instituted at Philadelphia in 1758, and that the degree had been received from an English military lodge, at that time stationed in that city.

At a somewhat later period in the century the Royal Arch degree was conferred in many lodges in the United States, under a Master's Warrant. This custom continued for several years to be observed in the Southern States, where distinct Chapters were unknown until the 19th century.

But in the Northern States, the control of the Royal Arch was assumed by independent Chapters at an earlier period.

From the records of the General Grand Chapter it appears that St. Andrew's Chapter was instituted at Boston, in 1769; King Cyrus Chapter at Newburyport, Mass., in 1790; Providence Chapter at Providence, R. I., in 1793; Solomon Chapter at Derby, Conn., in 1794; Franklin Chapter at Norwich, another of the same name at New Haven, Conn., and Hudson Chapter at Hudson, N. Y., in 1796.[146]

Temple Chapter at Albany, N. Y., is mentioned in the Proceedings of a convention held in 1797, and was probably instituted at an earlier period.

On October 24, 1797, a convention of Royal Arch Masons was held in Boston, for the purpose of forming a Grand Chapter.

At this convention delegates from three Chapters were present:

St. Andrew's, of Boston; Temple, of Albany, and King Cyrus, of Newburyport.

This convention, probably in consequence of the small number of Chapters represented, did no more than issue a circular addressed to

---

[146] "Compendium of Proceedings of the General Grand Chapter from 1797 to 1856," p. 8.

the various Chapters in the Northern States, recommending a future meeting to be held at Hartford.

In this circular the delegates at Boston enunciated the principle which has since been universally accepted as the law of Royal Arch Masonry in the United States; namely, that "no Grand Lodge of Master Masons can claim or exercise authority over any convention or Chapter of Royal Arch Masons, nor can any Chapter, although of standing immemorial, exercise the authority of a Grand Chapter."[147]

On January 24, 1798, a convention of delegates from seven Chapters assembled at Hartford, in the State of Connecticut.

At this convention the following Chapters were represented: St. Andrew's, of Boston; King Cyrus, of Newburyport; Providence, of Providence; Solomon, of Derby; Franklin, of Norwich; Franklin, of New Haven; and Hudson, of Hudson.

The States represented were, therefore, Massachusetts, Rhode Island, Connecticut, and New York.

It was then unanimously resolved that the delegates should establish a Grand Chapter for the States of New Hampshire, Massachusetts, Rhode Island, Connecticut, Vermont, and New York, to be denominated " The Grand Royal Arch Chapter of the Northern States of America."[148]

On the next day, delegates from Temple and from Horeb Chapter, both of New York, presented their credentials. These nine Chapters then proceeded to the organization of a Grand Chapter.

On January 26, 1798, a constitution was adopted and immediately afterward the officers were elected.

The preamble to this constitution ordains and establishes the body as "The Grand Royal Arch Chapter for the Northern States of America," a title under which jurisdiction was assumed over the States of New Hampshire, Massachusetts, Rhode Island, Connecticut, Vermont, and New York.

In each of these States there was to be under the jurisdiction of the Grand Chapter a Deputy Grand Chapter, over which a Deputy Grand High-Priest was to preside, assisted by a Deputy Grand King and a Deputy Grand Scribe.

The Grand Chapter was to be composed of its officers elected for the time, of the Past Grand High-Priests, Kings, and Scribes, and of the first three officers of the Deputy Grand Chapters.

---

[147] "Compendium of Proceedings," p. 6.
[148] Ibid., p. 9

The Deputy Grand Chapters were to be composed of the elected officers, of the Past Deputy Grand High-Priests, Kings, and Scribes, and of the High-Priests, Kings, and Scribes of the subordinate Chapters.

The Grand Chapter was to meet biennially and the Deputy Grand Chapters annually, and the first meeting of the former body was to be held at Middletown, Conn., on the following September.

In this Constitution the nomenclature and precedency of the Capitular degrees, which had hitherto been somewhat unsettled, was finally determined, so that the names and order of sequence should remain forever thereafter as they were then established.

This arrangement has ever since remained unchanged and makes the Mark Master, Past Master, and Most Excellent Master essentially preliminary degrees, to be followed by the Royal Arch degree as the consummation of the system.

This constitution gave to the Grand Chapter an exclusive power to hear and determine all controversies between Chapters within its jurisdiction, and an appellate jurisdiction over all the proceedings of the Deputy Grand Chapters.

As far as regards the States of Massachusetts, Rhode Island, Connecticut, and New York, which States were represented in the convention, the Constitution was definitely adopted. But the Chapters in Vermont and New Hampshire, not having sent delegates, a committee was appointed to solicit their concurrence in the organization.

The convention then proceeded to the first election on the newly adopted constitution, which resulted in the following choice of officers:

Ephraim Kirby, of Connecticut, Grand High-Priest; Benjamin Hurd, Jr., of Massachusetts, Grand King; Thomas Smith Webb, of New York, Grand Scribe; William Woart, of Massachusetts, Grand Secretary; Rev. Abraham Lynsen Clarke, of Rhode Island, Grand Chaplain; Stephen Titus Hosmer, of Connecticut, Grand Treasurer, and Gurdon Lathrop, of Connecticut, Grand Marshal.

It will be seen that the meeting here described was only that of a convention to take the preliminary steps for the organization of a Grand Chapter. The first meeting of the "Grand Chapter of the Northern States," after that organization, was holden on October 19, 1798, at the city of Middletown in Connecticut. The object of the meeting, as expressed in the Proceedings, was "for the choice of officers." Although these had already been elected, at the meeting of the convention in January preceding, that election was not by the Grand

Chapter, which was at that time inchoate, and could hardly have been considered as regular. It was therefore legalized by the subsequent action on October 1, 1798, which was in fact the first meeting of the Grand Chapter.

"Agreeably to the Constitution," says the compendium, "the Grand Chapter proceeded to the choice of officers, when on sorting and counting the votes the old officers were all declared reselected."[149]

No other business was transacted, and the Grand Chapter adjourned to hold its second meeting on the second Wednesday of January, 1799, at Providence, in the State of Rhode Island.

The Grand Chapter accordingly convened at Providence on January 9, 1799, when the representatives of the Deputy Grand Chapters of Massachusetts, Rhode Island, and New York were present.

At this Convocation some important changes in the regulations were made, and the constitution was revised.

The title of the Grand Chapter was altered to that of the "General Grand Chapter of Royal Arch Masons for the six Northern States of America," and its meetings were changed from a biennial to a septennial period. The Deputy Grand Chapters were in future to be styled "State Grand Chapters." The powers of the General Grand Chapter were much abridged. The section giving it appellate jurisdiction over the State Grand Chapters was omitted from the new Constitution, and has never again been re-asserted. Its powers were confined to a control of the ritual and to the establishment of Chapters in States where there were no Grand Chapters. It continued, however, to maintain the prerogative of defining the powers and functions of State Grand Chapters. This prerogative has never been denied, and the law of Royal Arch Masonry, as it now exists and has ever since the close of the last century existed in this country, is dependent on the Constitution of the General Grand Chapter.

Thus, the internal regulations of the State Grand Chapters and their subordinates are all directed by this Constitution. It prescribed the method of granting charters, the number of petitioners, the fee to be paid, the titles of the officers, the time of election, the price of the degrees, and the rule for receiving candidates, with several other points, all of which have always been implicitly obeyed.

In a word, the Constitution of the General Grand Chapter has been received as, in some sort, the common law of Royal Arch Masonry in this country. This law, derived from and formulated by that body, has

---

[149] "Compendium of Proceedings," p. 18.

universally been accepted, and it is admitted that it cannot be repealed or rescinded in any of its parts by any inferior body.

If the General Grand Chapter had accomplished no other good result by its organization, this alone would furnish a sufficient defense of its institution, and an answer to those discontented spirits who from time to time have sought for its dissolution.

The third convocation was holden at Middletown, Conn., on January 9, 1806. Representatives from only four States were present. The Constitution was again revised, and some important changes were made. Hitherto the General Chapter had claimed jurisdiction over only the six Northern States. But it now sought to extend its territorial limits over the whole country and assumed the more pretentious title of "The General Grand Chapter of Royal Arch Masons for the United States of America." This title it has ever since retained.

An oath of allegiance was also for the first time prepared, and every officer of a lodge or Chapter under the jurisdiction of the General Body was required, on assuming office, to swear that he would support and maintain the General Grand Royal Arch Constitution.

The exclusive right of issuing charters to subordinate Chapters, in States where there were Grand Chapters, was conferred by this constitution on those bodies, while the General Grand Chapter reserved to itself the right of issuing warrants for Chapters which were to be established in States where no Grand Chapters existed.

The next septennial convocation of the General Grand Chapter should have taken place in 1813. But at that time the United States were engaged in a war with Great Britain, and the situation of the country incidental to such a cause was such as to prevent the General Grand Chapter from convening.

A special session was called in 1816 at the city of New York. But no business of any especial importance was transacted, except the admission of the Grand Chapter of Maryland and the District of Columbia, under a provision which permitted it to confer the degrees of Royal and Select Master as preliminary to the Royal Arch. This permission has always been refused to other Grand Chapters, as being in positive contradiction of the terms of the constitution, which recognizes only three preparatory degrees in the Chapter. In the subsequent history of the General Grand Chapter this too liberal action has been found to be productive of some trouble.

Indeed, in the very inception of this proceeding there was an evident irregularity. The Grand Chapter of Maryland proposed to enter the Union of the Grand Chapters and to support the Constitution of the General Grand Chapter, but "requests that it shall not be forced to alter its mode of working."

This was reported to the General Grand Chapter by the Committee of conference, which recommended the admission of the Grand Chapter of Maryland, "under a consideration of all the circumstances," which of course must have referred to its request to continue its peculiar mode of working. The terms of the report were agreed to by the Maryland delegates, and accepted by the General Grand Chapter, which immediately afterward resolved that the Grand Chapter of Maryland and the District of Columbia be admitted under its jurisdiction, "subject to the Constitution and Regulations of the said General Grand Chapter."

It is very difficult to discover the real meaning and result of this action. The acceptance of the report permitted the Maryland body to confer its two additional preliminary degrees. The adoption of the subsequent resolution prohibited it from so doing, because the Constitution to which it was made subject as a condition of admission, recognized only three preliminary degrees, and excluded the two conferred in Maryland.

The Maryland companions selected the explanation which was most agreeable to their own views. They entered the Union of Grand Chapters, and continued, for a time, to confer the Royal and Select Master's degrees as preliminary to exaltation to the Royal Arch.

Subsequently they dropped the Council Degrees and confined themselves to the usual four degrees.

In 1829 the General Grand Chapter recommended that these degrees, which have always been under the control of independent organizations, known as Grand Councils, should be conferred in Royal Arch Chapters, but in 1853 it retraced its steps and declared that the Mark, Past, and Most Excellent Master were the only captular degrees, thus returning to the original arrangement of Webb.

In 1870 another attempt was made by several of the Grand Chapters to get the two degrees of Royal and Select Master incorporated as preparatory steps in the Capitular system, but it did not succeed, and most probably never will.

According to adjournment another session of the General Grand Chapter was holden in the city of New York on September 9, 1819. No business of great importance was transacted and it was ordered that the next convocation should be held at the city of Washington in February, 1823. No such meeting was held.

The sixth session of the General Grand Chapter was holden at the city of New York on September 14, 1826, which was the regular septennial convocation. The Grand Chapters were largely represented, delegates from no less than fifteen of them being present.

The Constitution was again revised, and among other amendments the word "triennial" was substituted for "septennial," so that the Convocations were thenceforth to be holden every three years. This regulation has ever since been continued.

Probably the most important event that occurred at this meeting was an attempt made to dissolve the General Grand Chapter. This was the first effort at a suicidal policy which has since been several times repeated, but always without success.

The attack was made by the Grand Chapter of Kentucky, which presented a memorial, copies of which had previously been transmitted to the different Grand Chapters with the hope that they would unite in the action.

In this memorial the Grand Chapter of Kentucky set forth at great length its reasons for desiring a dissolution of the organization.

They are the same arguments which have since been advanced at different times.

The objections urged against the General Grand Chapter were its nationality, the danger of its usurping the functions and destroying the sovereignty of the State Grand Chapters, the existence in it of life members, whose voice and numbers might become more potential than the votes of the elected delegates who would soon be in a minority, and, finally, the great expense of supporting such an organization.

But the arguments, plausible as they might have appeared, had no weight with the Grand Chapters, nearly all of which expressed their opposition to any such movement. When the question was submitted to the convocation, only two votes, those of the delegates from Kentucky, were found in its favor. Every other officer and member voted against a dissolution.

It is "passing strange" that an institution whose utility has been proved by ample experience, should ever have met with opposition to its existence. We have already seen that to it we are indebted for that common and universal law, which has done so much good in the establishment of an organized system.

When we remember the discordant condition of Royal Arch Masonry at the close of the last century, when the number of the degrees, their names and the order of their sequence, which varied in every State and sometimes even in adjacent Chapters, when there was no positive and generally recognized principles of Masonic law, and no authority to which to appeal for the settlement of controversies in ritual or in custom, and when we view the uniformity which now prevails in all parts of the country, which is undoubtedly owing to the weight and influence of the General Grand Chapter as a well- organized head, it can not be denied that all American Royal Arch Masons owe a debt of gratitude to the founders of that institution which thus wisely brought order out of chaos.

It is not worth while to extend this history beyond the period at which we have arrived. From the year 1826 the General Grand Chapter, now placed on a stable foundation, has continued to meet triennially at different cities of the United States. There has been but one interruption to this continuity. In 1862 a civil war then dividing the country into two hostile sections so that there was a military impossibility for the convocation to be held at the appointed place, which was Memphis in Tennessee, the General Grand High Priest, Albert G. Mackey, suspended the meeting until the restoration of peace, and by his proclamation the session was held at Columbus, O., in 1865. The session lasted but one day, when it adjourned to meet in the same place and on the next day in a new triennial session.

Its jurisdiction now extends over the whole of the United States, embracing all the Grand Chapters except those of Pennsylvania and Virginia, which have never entered into the confederation, and Texas, which withdrew during the war, 1861 - 65, and has never reunited.

The following list of all the Presiding officers of the body since its organization will be of interest as an historical document. It will be seen to embrace the names of some who have been distinguished in Freemasonry or in political life:

1798, EPHRAIM KIRBY, of Connecticut.
1799, EPHRAIM KIRBY.
1806, BENJAMIN HURD, of Massachusetts
1816, DEWITT CLINTON, of New York.
1819, DEWITT CLINTON.
1826, DEWITT CLINTON.
1829, EDWARD LIVINGSTON, of Louisiana
1832, EDWARD LIVINGSTON.
1835, Rev. PAUL DEAN, of Massachusetts
1838, Rev. PAUL DEAN.
1841, Rev. PAUL DEAN.
1844, Rev. PAUL DEAN.

1847, ROBERT P. DUNLAP, of Maine.
1850, ROBERT P. DUNLAP
1853, ROBERT P. DUNLAP.
1856, CHARLES GILMAN, of Maryland.
1859, ALBERT G. MACKEY, of South Carolina.
1865, JOHN L. LEWIS, of New York.
1868, JAMES M. AUSTIN, of New York
1871, JOSIAH H. DRUMMOND, of Maine
1874, ELBERT H. ENGLISH, of Arkansas.
1877, JOHN FRIZZELL, of Tennessee.
1880, ROBERT F. BOWER of Iowa.
1883, ALFRED F. CHAPMAN, of Massachusetts.
1886, NOBLE D. LARNER, of District of Columbia.
1889, DAVID F. DAY, of New York.
1891, JOSEPH P. HORNOR, of Louisiana.
1894, GEORGE L. MCCAHAN, of Maryland.
1897, REUBEN C. LEMMON, of Ohio.
1900, JAMES W. TAYLOR, of Georgia.
1903, ARTHUR G. POLLARD, of Massachusetts.
1906, JOSEPH E. DYAS, of Illinois.
1909, NATHAN KINGSLEY, of Minnesota.

REPRINT
In Deo Fiducia Nostra.
Or of Washington, June 24th, 1881.

THE GRAND COMMANDER OF THE SUPREME COUNCIL FOR THE SOUTHERN JURISDICTION OF THE UNITED STATES:

To the Free-Masons of the Ancient and Accepted Scottish Rite throughout this Jurisdiction

DEAR BRETHREN: Sickness and old age have brought the ending of his days to the Dean of the Supreme Council, its Secretary-General, Brother ALBERT GALLATIN MACKEY, Born at Charleston, in South Carolina, on the 12th of March, 1807, made a Mason there, it is said, in the year 1831, he became a member of the Supreme Council and Secretary General in 1844, and continued to be both until his death, at Fortress Monroe, in Virginia, on the 20th of June, 1881.

The Masonic Text-books written by him for the Symbolic Lodge, the Chapter of Royal Arch, and the Council of Royal and Select

Masters, his Treatises on Masonic Jurisprudence, on Parliamentary Law as applied in Masonry, and on Symbolism, his Lexicon and Encyclopaedia of Free-Masonry, and the Masonic Periodicals at different times edited by him, have made his name as an Author widely and well known in this and in other countries. He stood, indeed, at the head, facile princeps, of all the Masonic writers of the world. A ripe scholar and an accomplished writer as well as an educated physician, he would have won even a larger fame in other and wider fields of literature.

Bro. Mackey was Grand Secretary of the Grand Lodge of South Carolina for many years, a Commander of Templars, Grand High Priest of the Grand Chapter of Royal Arch Masons of the State, and General Grand High Priest of the General Grand Chapter of the United States. In the Sessions of 1856 and 1859 of that Body, he was especially prominent in debate. In our Supreme Council, in 1870, he was elected Lieutenant Grand Commander, and declined, preferring to continue to be Grand Secretary. The Symbolic Masonry, above all, is his debtor, because most of his works were written for the use of the Masons of the Blue Degrees; and he intended to render it further service, if he had lived, by exploding some of the fictions that have been imposed upon Masons for history and truth.

Bro. Mackey had lived all his life among gentlemen, and had the manners and habits of a gentleman. Tall, erect, of spare but vigorous frame, his somewhat harsh but striking features were replete with intelligence and amiability; he conversed well, and was liked as a genial and companionable man, of a cheerful, tolerant and kindly nature, who if he had quarrels with individuals, had none with the world. Idolized by his wife and children, he loved them devotedly, and suffered intensely when, one after another, his two intelligent and amiable daughters died. He had many friends, and made enemies, as men of strong will and positive convictions will always surely do. He plotted no harm against any one, and sought no revenge, even when he did not forgive, not being of a forgiving race, for he was a McGregor, having kinship with Rob Roy.

Masonry will not soon lose as great a man, and she may well put dust upon her head and wear sackcloth in her Lodges, where, in Masonry, his heart always was.

Of course, as he grew old, he had his crosses and troubles, and fortune was not kind to him. Adversity may be profitable; but the world goes too hardly with too many of us; and Sallust truly says:

'In luctu argue miseries mortem arumnarum requtem, non cruciatum, esse:'

'In grief and sorrows, death is a rest from troubles, and not a misfortune.

A great man hath fallen in Israel; and, in the words of Pushmataha the Chahta Chief, it is like the falling of a huge oak in the woods The fall will be heard afar off, and the sound be re-echoed from many and far-off lands.

Upon the reading of this letter in the Bodies of our Obedience, the altars and working-tools will be draped in black, and the Brethren will wear the proper badge of mourning during the space of sixty days. And may our Father Which is in Heaven have you always in His holy keeping!

Albert Pike 33d, Grand Commander.

REPRINT
Supreme Council, 33d, A\ A\ S\ Rite,
For the Northern Masonic Jurisdiction of the U.S.
ORIENT, BOSTON, MASS
Office of the the M\ P\ Sov\ G١\ Commander,
Milwaukee, Wis., July 10th, 1881.

The M\ P\ Sovereign Grand Commander, to all Free Masons of the Ancient Accepted Scottish Rite of the obedience of the said Supreme Council.

Sorrow !   Sorrow !   Sorrow !

BRETHREN:

With profound sorrow I announce to you the decease of our Illustrious Brother ALBERT GALLATIN MACKEY of the A.'.A.'.Scottish Rite of the Southern Masonic Jurisdiction of the U. S. He died at Fortress Monroe, Virginia, on the 20th of June, 1881. Bro.'. MACKEY was born at Charleston, South Carolina, on the 12th of March, 1807. and had long since passed the allotted span of three score years and ten.

For a full half century he had been an active, zealous Mason, always laboring where his work was most needed, to elevate and dignify Masonry and enlarge the sphere of its usefulness. During his long and active Masonic career he honored many exalted official stations, the duties of all of which he discharged with signal fidelity. He was for many years Grand Secretary of the Grand Lodge of South Carolina, "a Commander of Templars, Grand High Priest of the Grand Chapter of

Royal Arch Masons of the State and General Grand High Priest of the General Grand Chapter of the United States."

In the Ancient Accepted Rite he was the Dean of the Supreme Council of the Southern Masonic Jurisdiction, and at the time of his decease and for many years prior thereto, the Grand Secretary General of our sister Supreme Council. A ripe scholar and an accomplished writer, his taste naturally led him to enter the literary field of the craft, in which his labors were of immeasurable value to the Great Brotherhood he loved so well. The various works he prepared and published, and without which no masonic library is complete, have rendered his name a household word among the fraternity everywhere, and constitute a fitting monument of his love for masonry and his patient and intelligent labor in its behalf. After a long and useful life he has been called to rest, his departure leaving a void to be filled - when ? by whom ? Others may indeed extend and enlarge the work he commenced, but it was he who laid the foundation, and first reared the superstructure. In addition to the various text books prepared by him for the use of Lodges and Chapters, and his other works of a more general character, the Fraternity are more indebted to him than to any other one man for its present admirable system of masonic jurisprudence. When such a man falls, it is meet that his brethren, who alone can appreciate his entire worth, should deplore his loss.

While we tender our sincere sympathy to our Brethren of the Southern Jurisdiction, who were more immediately connected with our deceased Brother, we also feel the loss we have all sustained, and mingle our tears with theirs.

Let these letters be read in all the Bodies of our obedience at the first meeting thereof held after its receipt, and let the altars and working tools be draped with the usual badge of mourning for the space of sixty days.

Given at the Grand Orient, the day and year aforesaid.

REPRINT
ROYAL ORDER OF SCOTLAND IN CRUCE STAT SECURUS
AMOR
Washington, 24 June, 1881, A. O. 568.

The Brethren of the Provincial Grand Lodge of the United States will already have learned that their Brother, the Senior Provincial Grand Wardens SIR ALBERT GALLATIN MACKEY, closed his eyes upon this world, and his life here ended, at seven of the clock on the morning of the 20th day of this month of June. Worn and wasted by age and disease, he fell into unconsciousness a little while before he died, and his life passed painlessly away, as when one falls asleep.

He was Forn at Charleston, in South Carolina, on the 12th of March, 1807, and so was an old man. Made a Mason in 1831, he had laboured in Masonry during half a century, and the works of his brain, published for the use of Masonic Bodies and for the instruction of the Brethren, are known to all reading Masons at home, and to many abroad By them he will be long remembered. He was a man of mark, who toiled in the Masonic field assiduously, an accomplished writer and impressive speaker, and one who made many friends, a genial and companionable man, whose death a host of Masons will regret.

I invite the Brethren of the Provincial Grand Lodge to wear with me the badge of mourning of the Order, on account of the death of this Veteran Brother and Knight, during the space of thirty days from the receipt of this letter.

Morte detur aliquando otium Quiesque fessis.

ALBERT PIKE PROV'L GRAND MASTER.
THE HISTORY OF THE INTRODUCTION AND PROGRESS
OF FREEMASONRY IN THE UNITED STATES
THE HISTORY OF THE SYMBOLS OF FREEMASONRY
AND THE
HISTORY OF THE A.'. A.'. SCOTTISH RITE
BY
WILLIAM R. SINGLETON, 33D
PART THREE
THE HISTORY OF THE INTRODUCTION
AND PROGRESS OF FREEMASONRY
IN THE UNITED STATES

SALUTATORY

THE death of Dr. Albert Gallatin Mackey, June 21, 1881, prevented the completion of his great work on the "History of Freemasonry." The preceding chapters, ending on page 1302, were all written by him, and, as he had contemplated continuing his labors until the whole history of the Masonic Orders and Degrees should have been completed, his publishers have complimented the present writer by selecting him to do, imperfectly as it will appear, what so able a writer as Dr. Mackey would have done, had his life been spared a little longer. Dr. Mackey's long and useful career as a Masonic savant and writer had endeared him to all Masonic students over the wide world of Masonry. Wherever the English language is spoken may be found the Masonic works of our distinguished brother. In the conclusion of the admirable "Historical Sketch of the Order of Knights Templar," by Theodore S. Gourdin, of Charleston, S. C., 1855, he says: "The history of our Order remains yet to be writs ten. It can not be attempted by an American, alone and unaided. in fact, it can not be written at all in this country; for we have not the materials. But this great work can and ought to be undertaken by the Templars of the United States. . . . Let them select a Brother, who, from his great learning and his thorough knowledge of the principal modern languages, as well as the dead, is fully qualified for the work. I know but two brethren in the United States who are qualified to execute the work proposed: Bro. Albert G. Mackey, of Charleston, S. C.; and Bro. William S. Rockwell, of Milledgeville, Ga."

We thus see that, at as early a date as 1855, Bro. Mackey shared, with that other eminent and distinguished Brother, Rockwell, the highest reputation for scholarship among all the Masons of the United States. He then continues: "Then would a history be written worthy of our illustrious Order, and of the distinguished body which governs it in this country ! The author of such a work would earn, for himself, an immortal reputation, and each individual brother who contributed his mite would enjoy the delightful consciousness that the Masonic world was, in a measure, indebted to him for a work which would prove the great desideratum of the age."

The rapid and continued increase of the membership of the Templar Order has kept pace with the growth of the population of the United States, and the progress in all branches of human knowledge, in science, and arts, as we shall demonstrate when we give a history of the Order and show in each particular State, what is the present membership, and the great field for usefulness laid open and the prospect before us, for the great battles which are yet to come, between truth and error, light and darkness, ignorance and enlightenment, crime and obedience to lawful authority, fanaticism, bigotry, and persecution against toleration, liberality and freedom of thought.

The Templars, in the Crusades, for two hundred years fought with material armor against the Infidels and Turks of Syria, but our modern Templars are engaged against more powerful and insidious foes, scattered everywhere in our midst. The Templars of the Crusades were carried from the West to the East, to fight for the Christianity as then known and practiced, a system of ignorance, the great parent of superstition, bigotry, fanaticism, intolerance, and persecution; these are the elements which finally culminated in the Middle Ages, in the Inquisition; and by which the Templar Order, for so many centuries the instrument of the Church of Christ in oppressing mankind, was totally destroyed, and the leaders burned at the stake by Clement V. and Philip the Fair, after they had no further use for them.

"God works in a mysterious way His purpose to fulfill!"

The Templars, now only such in name, may be the instruments of God, in turn, in the next century, to deliver His true children from the fangs of the monster who for so many ages has kept mankind, so far as they could be, within his power, in total ignorance of the TRUTH as it was, and is yet, in Christ the Lord, for whose sake and in whose name the original Templars fought, bled, and died upon so many hard-fought battle-fields of Syria. Let this thought be in the mind of every Knight Templar of the present day and in the future, whose eyes may see these words, written in the year 1899: That this great country, beginning with a few emigrants from several European nations, bringing with them to Virginia, first, at Jamestown, the descendants of the pride and chivalry of Old England; then the Puritans in New England - while these differed greatly in their method of interpreting the Scriptures, they were yet agreed in the great principles therein inculcated, viz.: EQUALITY, FRATERNITY, AND LIBERTY.

These, the descendants of the Reformation, have grown from the original Thirteen Colonies, despised and looked down upon by the great monarchies of Europe and Asia, with scorn and sometimes with contempt. Now these scornful peoples begin to appreciate what is before them in the future.

We therefore say to the Commanderies, Preceptories, and Encampments, and also to each private member of the Knightly Order of the Temple, remember your vows of obedience to the Grand Master of all Temples. The sword which you wield is not a weapon of carnal warfare, but a symbol, whose significance you have learned, and should ever put in practice in the defence of Truth, not as explained by the Mother Church of the Middle Ages, for the purpose of propagating error, but the truth as so well understood by every Templar, and in whose cause he should be prepared to make every sacrifice, and perform his pilgrimage even to the loss of life while engaged therein, and remember that you shall reap your reward if ye faint not.

"Magna est Veritas, et prevalebit."
WILLIAM R. SINGLETON

CHAPTER LI

GENERAL HISTORY OF CHRISTIAN KNIGHTHOOD

In our examination of various authors who have written on Templarism, we have found it very difficult, if at all possible, to determine, categorically, when the American Rite of the " Commandery " was really formulated. We learn from ancient as well as recent writers that the Knights of the Red Cross of Rome and Constantine, Knights of the Holy Sepulcher, Knights of St. John the Evangelist, and Knights of the Grand Cross were of a much earlier date than the Knights of the Templar Order. The Knights of the Red Cross of Rome and Constantine was the first Order of Christian Knights. The Knights of the Red Cross, which is the first degree conferred in the Commandery of Knight Templars in the United States, has no connection whatever with the Templar Order of the Crusades, nor the events in the history of the other Knightly Order of the Red Cross of Rome and Constantine first above mentioned.

The real history of the present American degree of the Red Cross is, that it is composed of the 15th and 16th degrees of the A.'.A.'. S.'. R.'.; and the incidents commemorated therein are located at the time of the captivity of the Jews, after the destruction of King Solomon's Temple, and the return of the Jews to Palestine by direction of Cyrus, and after him by Darius the Persian monarch.

The original symbol of the red cross, which is a Christian symbol, has no place in the Ritual of the Commandery degree of Red Cross, which relates to the Jews in captivity and the Persian Court of that date. The first red cross of Constantine, with its motto, "In hoc sings vinces," was adopted by Constantine the Great as the "Labarum" from the following circumstance, according to tradition: The night before the battle between himself and Augustus Maxentius the sign of the cross appeared to him in the heavens, with the inscription "In hoc signo vinces." This battle has been called "of Saga Rostra," which was an ancient station on the "Flaminian Way," eight miles north of Rome, which meant "red stones."

Having been successful in defeating his opponent, Constantine, on December 25, A.D. 312, instituted a new order of knights, of the "Red Cross of Rome and Constantine." The red cross became a badge, and was worn on the right arm of each knight or on his shield, this insignia thereafter being the highest honor of knighthood.

The Order of the Knights of the Holy Sepulcher, some writers say, "was instituted by Constantine, at the prayer of his mother Helena, for the avowed purpose of protecting the Holy Sepulcher, and defending it from the enemies of the Christian faith. Only Knights of the Red Cross, by royal decree, were eligible for the Order." It is also said that Constantine " instituted the Order of Knight of the Grand Cross, which he conferred (in 326) on several of his generals and ministers, as a special mark of merit and distinction."

The same writers say: "After the death of Constantine (337) the popes of Rome claimed, and exercised, sovereign authority over the Order throughout Christendom, delegating to the Papal Nuncios and Cardinal Princes, at the various Catholic Courts, the right to nominate candidates fos the Order of Knights of the Red Cross of Rome and Constantine. Samuel Cole, in the Freemason's Library, gives a list of the various Masonic degrees and says:

"In a later publication, 1816, we find the following list of Masonic degrees, which the author states are conferred on the Sublime Grand Lodges in Charleston, S.C., in the city of New York and in Newport, R. I.: No. 9 is Knight of the Red Cross; No. 10, Knight of Malta; No. 11, Knight of the Holy Sepulcher; No. 12, Knight of the Christian Mark; No. 13, Knight Templar. The degrees enumerated amount to forty-three. Besides these degrees there were ten others which were in the possession of most of the Inspectors given in different parts of the world, and which they generally communicate, free of expense, to those brethren who are high enough to understand them - such as Select Masons of 27, and the Royal Arch, as given under the Constitution of Dublin; six degrees of Maconnerie d' Adoption , Compagnon Ecossais, le Maitre Ecossais, et le Grand Master Ecossais, etc., making, with the regular number of forty-three, in the aggregate fifty-three degrees.[150]

---

[150] "Freemason's Library " and General Ahiman Rezon. Baltimore, Md., 1826.

"It will be well here to notice that the Select Masons of 27, which the Grand Chapter of Virginia alone retains in her curriculum and confers prior to the Royal Arch, was designed, by the Consistories of the Ancient and Accepted Rite of the last century, and by the Supreme Council of the A.'. A.'. A.'. S.'. Rite of 1802, to follow the Royal Arch. A great many of our distinguished Masons think that the Select of 27 should precede the Royal Arch, as, by its chronology, it does; but they forget that the same chronological circumstances occur in the present arrangement of the Mark degree, which not only follows the Fellow-Craft but also the Master's degree, while chronologically the events of the first section were prior to the completion of the Temple."

Cole thus refers to the Knight of the Red Cross: " After having, as we had supposed, satisfactorily shown that the Order of Knights Hospitalers of the Order of St. John of Jerusalem, who were afterwards called Knights of Rhodes, and now Knights Templars and Knights of Malta, is indisputably the oldest order of knighthood in the world, we are suddenly transported into the distant regions of Persia, and instructed to believe that the Order of the Cross was instituted 520 years before the birth of Christ, namely during the reign of Darius." [151] This was written prior to 1826, and he continues: "This Order has not, until late years, been practiced in America. I have, indeed, conversed with well-informed knights, who received the degree in Ireland; perhaps it may have originated there - be that as it may, it has found its way into our books, and is practiced, though very imperfectly, in some of our encampments, usually preceding the degrees of Knights Templars and Knights of Malta. A reference to the foregoing list will show us that the author has given us two other degrees, which are intended to precede the two last mentioned, namely, Knights of the Holy Sepulcher and Knights of the Christian Mark. Nor shall we have cause to wonder, if, in the process of time, an attempt should be made to precede the important Degree of Knights Templars, etc., with that of Knight of the Golden Spur, Knight of the White Elephant, or of the Golden Fleece."

Cole does not seem to have been aware that the 15th and 16th degrees of the A.'. A.'. S.'. R.'. were the materials for the so- called Red Cross, which has no connection historically with the Templarism of Christianity.

The Caleph Muez destroyed the church of the Holy Sepulcher, which was rebuilt by the Red Cross Knights and Knights of the Holy Sepulcher, in 969. In 1093 Philip I., King of France, revived the Order

---

[151] Samuel Cole: "Freemason's Library," p. 321, 1826. Note. - Cole refers of course, to the Red Cross of Rome and Constantine. - EDITOR.

of Knights of the Holy Sepulcher, and nominated his son, the Dauphin of France, as Grand Marshal. After the return of the Crusaders from the Holy Land, the Knights of the two Orders were called the first and second grades of the " Knight of the Red Cross of Rome and Constantine."

From A.D. 337 to 1094 the Popes exercised sovereign authority over the Orders. In 1099 there was held a Grand Conclave of the Orders of the "Knights of the Red Cross and Knights of the Holy Sepulcher."

Addison says: "The Holy Sepulcher presented itself to the eyes of the pilgrims, surrounded by a magnificence which redoubled their veneration.

"An obscure cavern had become a marble temple paved with precious stones and decorated with splendid colonnades. To the east of the Holy Sepulcher appeared the Church of the Resurrection, in which they could admire the riches of Asia, mingled with the arts of Greece and Rome. Constantine celebrated the twenty first year of his reign, A.D. 333, by the inauguration of this church, whose corner-stone had been planted under the auspices of his sainted mother, and thousands of Christians came, on occasion of this solemnity, to listen to the panegyric of Christ from the lips of the learned and holy Bishop Eusebius. St. Jerome, who, toward the end of the 4th century, had retired to Bethlehem for literary labors and religious solitude, informs us, in one of his letters, that pilgrims arrive in crowds in Judea, and that around the holy tomb the praises of the Son of God were to be heard uttered in many languages. From this period pilgrimages to the Holy Land were so numerous that several doctors and fathers of the Church thought it their duty to point out the abuses and dangers of the practice.

They told Christians that long voyages might turn them aside from the path of salvation; that their God was not confined to one city, that Jesus Christ was everywhere where faith and good works were to be found. But such was the blind zeal which then drew Christians toward Jerusaiem that the voices of the holy doctors severe scarcely heard. The councils of enlightened piety were not able to abate the ardor of the pilgrims, who believed they should be wanting in faith and zeal if they did not adore Jesus Christ in the very places where, according to the expression of St. Jerome, ' the light of the Gospel first shone from the top of the Holy Cross.'

"As soon as the people of the West became converted to Christianity, they turned their eyes to the East. From the depths of France, from the forests of Germany from all the countries of Europe, new Christians were to be seen hastening to visit the cradle of the faith they had embraced. An itinerary for the use of pilgrims served them as a guide from the banks of the Rhone and the Dordogne to the shoresof the Jordan, and conducted them on their return from Jerusalem to the principal cities of Italy. When the world was ravaged by the Goths, the Huns, and the Vandals, pilgrimages to the Holy Land were not at all interrupted. Pious travelers were protected by the hospitable virtues of the barbarians, who began to respect the Cross of Christ, and sometimes even followed the pilgrims to Jerusalem. In these times of trouble and desolation a poor pilgrim who bore his scrip and staff often passed through fields of carnage and traveled without fear amidst armies which threatened the empires of the East and the West.

"Illustrious families of Rome came to seek an asylum at Jerusalem and by the tomb of Christ. Christians then found, on the banks of the Jordan, that peace which seemed banished from the rest of the world. This peace, which lasted several centuries, was not troubled before the reign of Heraclius, A.D. 610 - 641. Under this reign the armies of Chosroes, King of Persia, invaded Syria, Palestine, and Egypt. The Holy City fell into the hands of the worshipers of fire.

The conquerors bore away into captivity vast numbers of Christians and profaned the churches of Jesus Christ. All the faithful deplored the misfortunes of Jerusalem, and shed tears when they learned that the King of Persia had carried off, among the spoil of the vanquished, the Cross of the Saviour, which bad been preserved in the Churches of the Resurrection."[152]

At the Council of Clermont in Auvergne, November, 1095, Pope Urban addressed himself to all the nations represented at the council, and particularly to the French, who formed the majority:

" Nation beloved by God," said he, " it is in your courage that the Christian Church has placed its hope. It is because I am well acquainted with your piety and your bravery that I have crossed the Alps and am come to preach the word of God in these countries. You have not forgotten that the land which you inhabit has been invaded by the Saracens, and but for the exploits of Charles Martel (A.D. 732) and Charlemagne (A.D. 768-800), France would have received the laws of Mohammed. Recall without ceasing, to your minds, the dangers and glory of your fathers. Led by heroes, whose names shall never die, they delivered your country, they saved the West from shameful slavery. More noble triumphs await you under the guidance of the God of armies. You will deliver Europe and Asia; you will save the city of Jesus Christ - that

---

[152] "Addison," p. 66

Jerusalem which was chosen by the Lord, and from whence the law is to come to us."

As Urban proceeded, the sentiments by which he was animated penetrated to the very souls of his auditors. When he spoke of the captivity and misfortunes of Jerusalem, the whole assembly was dissolved in tears; when he described the tyranny and the perfidy of the Infidels, the warriors who listened to him clutched their swords and swore in their hearts to avenge the cause of the Christians.

"When Jesus Christ summons you to his defense, let no base affections detain you in your homes. See nothing but the shame and the evils of the Christians; listen to nothing but the groans of Jerusalem, and remember well what the Lord has said to you: He who loves his father or his mother more than Me is not worthy of Me; whoever will abandon his house, or his father, or his mother, or his wife, or his children, or his inheritance, for the sake of My name, shall be recompensed a hundred-fold, and possess life eternal."

At these words the auditors of Urban displayed an enthusiasm that human eloquence had rarely before inspired. The assembly arose in one mass as one man and answered him with the unanimous cry, " Dieu le veut ! Dieu le veut ! "It is the will of God ! It is the will of God!" "Yes, without doubt, it is the will of God," continued the eloquent Urban; "you to-day see the accomplishment of the word of our Saviour, who promised to be in the midst of the faithful when assembled in His name. It is He who has dictated to you the words that I have heard. Let them be your war-cry, and let them announce everywhere the presence of the God of armies." On finishing these words, the Pontiff exhibited to tne assembled Christians the sign of their redemption. " It is Christ himself," said he to them, "who issues from His tomb, and presents to you His Cross. It will be the sign raised among the nations, which is to gather together again the dispersed Children of Israel. Wear it upon your shoulders and upon your breasts. Let it shine upon your arms and upon your standards. It will be to you the surety of victory or the palm of martyrdom. It will unceasingly remind you that Christ died for you, and that it is your duty to die for him."

When Urban had ceased to speak, loud acclamations burst from the multitude. Pity, indignation, despair at the same time agitated the tumultuous assembly of the faithful. Some shed tears over Jerusalem and the fate of the Christians. Others swore to exterminate the race of the Mussulmans. But all at once, at a signal from the Sovereign Pontiff, the most profound silence prevailed. Cardinal Gregory, afterward St. Innocent II., pronouncing, in a Bud voice, a form of General

Confession, the assembly all fell upon their knees, beat their breasts, and received absolution for their sins.[153]

Joseph Francois Michaud, in his History of the Crusades, states: "To the feudal Princes, assembled in the Holy Land in A.D. 1099, belongs the glory and honor of reviving the Order of the ' Knights of the Holy Sepulcher.' The Order was conferred on the Knights of the Red Cross for rare personal valor and courage. Every recruit receiving the Order of 'Knight of the Holy Sepulcher,' or that of 'Knight of St. John,' was required to wear a Red Cross on his arm or shield."

In 1100 the Crusaders of every country carried the banner of the Order of Knights of the Red Cross of Rome and Constantine.

A Grand Conclave of that Order assembled in Rome, May, 1119.

Emperor Michael Angelo Comnenus was chosen Sovereign Grand Master.

The Sovereign Grand Council issued an edict limiting the active membership of Knights of the Grand Cross to fifty Sir Knights in each kingdom or independent country, and that a Grand Cross Knight shall have precedence, in all assemblies of Sir Knights of the Red Cross, immediately after the Sovereign Grand Master.

Pope Innocent III. urged the Knights of the Red Cross, Knights of the Holy Sepulcher, and Knights of St. John to overthrow the Infidels in Constantinople in 1193. Richard of England in 1195 was proclaimed Sovereign Grand Master of the Knights of Rome and Constantine, and Senior Knight of the Grand Cross, by the Duke of Burgundy, for valorous services in front of Jerusalem. After the return of the Crusaders (1200), to about 1654, the history of the Order of Knights of Rome and Constantine is somewhat uncertain. No General Assembly was held. The Kings of Spain and France and the Emperor of Germany asserting sovereignty by Divine authority in their respective countries. In 1270 the Knights of the Red Cross of Rome and Constantine, under the leadership of the monarch of France, a Knight of the Grand Cross of the Order, drove the Mohammedans out of Carthage. In 1460 the germs of a new civilization had been scattered over Europe by this Order. They opened up the East to the nations of Europe and brought Asia and Europe in closer relations. In 1550 Father Boniface, a Prior of the Order, was appointed Warden of the Holy Sepulcher, by Pope Julius III. The Orders of Red Cross, Holy Sepulcher, and St. John were resuscitated in England, the first conclave being instituted by the

---

[153] McCoy's " Addison," pp. 87, 88.

German embassador to the Court of St. James, February, 1688. The Abbe Guistiniani, a Venetian priest of great learning, while visiting England, May, 1692, conferred these three Orders, of Red Cross, Holy Sepulcher, and of St. John, on several of the attaches of the English Court. The Abbe was the first writer to gather, prepare, and preserve the traditions and rituals of the Order as now existing. Sir Bernard Burke says: "Duke Francis I., of Parma, of the house of Farnese, was installed (September, 1699) Grand Master of the Knights of the Red Cross of Rome and Constantine with much pomp."

Baron Hunde states: "The great and rapid progress of Freemasonry on the European Continent is largely due to the efforts of the Knights of the Red Cross of Rome and Constantine." He also credits the Knights of the Red Cross as being the true Templars and as the only Order of Christian Knighthood that has had a regular succession since it was instituted in 312. After the Royal Arch degree was introduced into English Freemasonry prior to 1760. Many companies of the Royal Arch, in England, petitioned the local conclaves to modify the ancient landmarks of the Order, in age interest and welfare of Royal Arch Masonry, by changing the qualifications of membership in the Knights of the Red Cross of Rome and Constantine and the Appendant Orders, from a Master Mason to Royal Arch Mason.

From time immemorial a Master Mason, if a believer in the Christian religion, has been the qualification necessary for membership. In January, 1760, the Grand Masters of the English and Scottish Knights of the Red Cross of Rome and Constantine assembled in London, and adopted as a requirement for Knighthood in the Order that the applicant be a Royal Arch Mason and a believer in the Christian religion.

At Charleston, S.C., November 12, 1783, in St. Andrew's F. & A. M. Lodge, the Order of Knight of the Red Cross of Rome and Constantine was conferred on a class of eight, a dispensation having been obtained in England by a retired British officer, then residing in Charleston. This is the second authentic account of the conferring of the Order in America.

The history of the Order of the Red Cross of Rome and Constantine and also of Masonry being both silent as to the first connection of these two, there is some authority in the statement of the Grand Secretary of the Grand Lodge of Masons of England, that (in 1788) all the Grand Officers of the Grand Lodge of England and Scotland received the Order of Knight of the Red Cross of Rome and Constantine on their election, and before being installed as a Grand

Officer. The retiring Grand Master, if he served two or more terms, receiving the Order of Knight of the Grand Cross on retiring from the Grand East. Masonry and Knights of the Red Cross evidently became closely allied early in the 17th century. All of the above extracts, referring to the Knights of the Red Cross of Rome and Constantine, Knights of the Holy Sepulcher, and Knights of St.John, have been taken, with some slight alterations of language, from a small pamphlet, issued by C.L. Stowell, K.T. 33d, Sovereign Grand Master of the Knights "of the Red Cross of Rome and Constantine," and Thos. Leahy, K. T. 32d, Grand Registrar General - which pamphlet is an addition to the literature on the subject of the Knightly "Appendant Orders," and shows the chronological sequence of those degrees from their origin and present connection with freemasonry through the degree of Knights of Malta - which at present is conferred after the degree of Knight Templar.[154]

Peter Heylinl in his Cosmography of the World (1660), says:

"The Chief Orders of Knighthood in this Kingdom (Jerusalem), after the recovery from the power of the Turks, were:

"1. Of the Sepulcher, said to be instituted originally (A.D. 314) by Queen Helena, the Mother of Constantine the Great, by whom the Temple of the Sepulcher was indeed first built; but more truly by Philip, King of France. Anna 1099, at such time as that Temple was regained from the Turks. The Arms, the same with that of the Kings (the Arms of the Christian Kings in Hierusalem was Luna, a cross Crosset, crossed, Sol, which was commonly called the Hierusalem Cross), representing the five wounds of our Saviour CHRIST. At the first, conferred on none but Gentlemen of blood and fortunes, now (A.D. 1660) salable to any that will buy it of the Pater-Guardian who with a Convent of Franciscans doth reside near that Temple.

"2. Of Saint John of Hierusalem, begun by one Gerrard, Anno 1114, and confirmed by Cope Paschalis the second. Their Badge or Cognizance is a White Cross of eight points. Their duty to defend the Holy Land, relieve Pilgrims, and succor Christian Princes against the Infidels. They were to be of Noble Parentage and Extraction; and grew in time to such infinite riches, especially after the suppression of the Templars (most of whose lands were after given to the Order), that they had at one time in the several parts of Christendom no fewer than 20,000 Mannors; and of such reputation in all Christian Kingdoms, that in England the Lord Prior of this Order was accounted the prime Baron in the Realm. But now (1660) their Revenue is not a little diminished,

---

[154] See Mackey in chapters xxviii. - xxix., ante.

by the withdrawing of the Kings of England, and other Protestant Princes, from the Church of Rome; who on that change seized on all the Lands of that Order in their several Countries, and either kept them to themselves, or disposed them to others, as they pleased.

"Their first Great Master was that Gerrard by whom they were founded; the last that had his residence in the Holy Land was one John D. Villers, in whose time, being driven out of Palestine, they removed unto Cyprus, and in the time of Fulk de Villaret, Anno 1309, to the Isle of Rhodes. Outed of which by Solomon the Magnificent, Anno 1522, they removed from one place to another, till at last by the magnificence of Charles V., Anna 1530, Whey were settled in Malta; and there we shall speak further of them.

"3. Of the Templars, instituted by Hugh of Pagennes, Anno 1113, and confirmed by Pope Euggenius. Their ensign was a red cross, in token that they should shed their blood to defend Christ's Temple. They were buried cross-legged, and wore on their backs the figure of a Cross; for which they were by the common people called Cross-backs, and by corruption crook-backs. Edmund, Earl of Lancaster, second son to Henry the Third, being of this Order, was vulgarly called Edmund Crook-back; which gave Henry the Fourth a foolish occasion to feign that this Edmund (from whom he was descended) was indeed the eldest son of King Henry the Third, but for his crookedness and deformity, his younger brother was preferred to the Crown before him. These knights had in all Provinces of Europe their subordinate Governors, in which they possessed no less than 16000 Lordships; the greatness of which revenue was not the least cause of dissolving the Order. For Philip the Fair, King of France, had a plot to invest one of his sons with the Title of King of Hierusalem, and hoped to procure of the Pope the revenue of this Order to be laid unto that Kingdome, for support of the Title: which he thought he might the better do, because Clement the V., then Pope, for the love he bore to France, had transferred his seat from Rome to Avignon. But herein his hopes deceived him; for this Order being dissolved, the lands thereunto belonging were given to the Knights Hospitallers or of St. John. The crimes objected against this Order were - first, their revolt from their professed obedience unto the Patriarch of Jerusalem, who was their Visitor.

Secondly, their unspeakable pride; and, Thirdly, their sins against Nature. The House of our Law-Students in London called the Temple was the chief house of the Knights of this Order in England; and was, by the Knights of St. John, whose principle Mansion was in Smithfield, sold unto the Students of the Laws, for the yearly rent of

10l., about the Middle of the reign of Edward III. These three Orders M. Selden (and deservedly) put not in his Title of honour, in that they were prohibited to kiss a woman; honorary Knighthood and the love of Ladies going together, like Virtue and Reward."

Hugo de Paganis, after arriving in Palestine, as a Crusader and pilgrim, finding that the Moslem inhabitants infested the approaches to Jerusalem and other sacred places, and persecuted such pilgrims as were not in sufficient numbers to protect themselves, gathered with him eight other companions, viz.: Godefroi de St. Aldemar, Roral, Gundemar, Godefroi Bisol, de Montdidier, Archibald de St. Aman, Andrew de Montbar, and the Count of Provence, and bound themselves to the Patriarch of Jerusalem, in A.D. 1118, "to guard the approaches to the Holy City, so that pilgrims to the sacred places might have easy access; to live as regular Canons of the Church, under the Benedictine rule; and to fight for the King of Heaven and the Bride of Christ, in chastity, obedience, and self-denial. In 1119 Hugo de Paganis became the first Master. The palace of the Latin Kings of Jerusalem, which had been a Mosque on Mount Moriah - which Mount constitutes now the Haram Es Sheriff - and then was known as "Solomon's Temple," was assigned to them as their quarter[155] This Mosque, after many vicissitudes from the time of its first erection, is at the present day called the "Mosque of Omar," because at one time in its history he was supposed to have been its builder, but it has been well determined by good authority that he was not; but when he conquered Jerusalem, between A.D. 640 and 644, he put it in thorough repair.[156]

---

[155] In consequence of the services to the Christians performed by the "Poor Fellow Soldiers," Baldwin II., King of Jerusalem, gave them for a habitation, for hitherto they seem to have had no fixed place of abode, " the palace or royal house to the South of the Temple of the Lord, vulgarly called the Temple of Solomon " (Addison). There seems to be confusion in this locality, by different writers, owing to the ignorance concerning the various buildings on this site. - EDITOR.

[156] Mosque of Omar or Kubbet es Sakra (Dome of the Rock). This building, which is on the Platform or Original Site of Solomon's Temple, is an Octagon of 66 feet to each side, having four porticoes and a range of pointed windows incrusted with beautifully colored Persian tiles. Within are two concentric ranges of columns and square pillars - the interior range supporting the drum of the magnificent dome, which is nearly too feet in height and over 60 feet in diameter. Within the central range is a rock 60 x 50 feet rising seven feet above the pavement - tradition saying that it was upon this rock Abraham was about to sacrifice his son Isaac.

Underneath this rock is a cave - a chamber 14 x 16 feet, in which the Mohammedans now worship. The walls and the drum are covered with beautiful Byzantine Mosaics of different dates, and the windows are filled with splendid sixteenth century colored glass.

It is supposed that this Mosque was originally a very early Byzantine church. It was no doubt greatly improved by Omar, when the Mohammedans occupied Jerusalem. Some writers say, by Abd-el- Malek Ibn Marwan, before the time of Omar.

From this palace, or "Solomon's Temple," these Knights took the name of "Templars," and were also called "poor fellow soldiers of Christ and the Temple of Solomon." They had every one of them seen hard service under the leadership of Godefroi de Bouillon, and were well qualified to render efficient service in aid of pilgrims and all others requiring their assistance.

Their fame and valuable services soon spread over all Europe, and many of the sons of noble houses were induced to enter into this body, so distinguished by its acts of benevolence and charity. The Order was brought prominently to the especial notice of St.Bernard, Abbot of Clairvaux, by whom a pastoral was issued praising the valor and extolling the merits of the Templars. At the Council of Troyes, in 1128, statutes were formulated for the new Order.

Seventy-two rules of discipline were adopted, which met the concurrence of Pope Honorius II. and the Patriarch of Jerusalem. So rapid was the growth of this Order that they had been established in every kingdom of Latin Christendom. Domains in Normandy were granted to them by Henry I. of France. In 1129 they were established in Castile, in 1131 in Rochelle, in Languedoc in 1136, in Rome in 1138, in Brittany in 1141. The White Mantle was chosen to be worn to distinguish them from the Hospitalers, who wore a robe of black. The Red Cross was added in 1146 by Pope Eugenius III., to be placed on the breast as a symbol that the Order was expected to invite martyrdom.

Hugo de Paganis, the first Master of the Templars, visited England, and many English knights followed him to Palestine as Members of the Order. Among these was Fulk, Count of Anjou, who afterward was King of Jerusalem, in II3I. Hugo de Paganis died in 1136.

Robert de Craou, a nephew of Anselm, Archbishop of Canter bury, succeeded Paganis as Grand Master of the Order.

The Second Crusade was excited by the troubles and dangers to which the Christians of Syria were exposed from the conquering arms of the Turks, who defeated the Franks at Antioch, and had taken Edessa, and threatened the destruction of all the Christian kingdoms of Syria. In this crusade Everard de Baris, the third Master of the Templars, was greatly renowned for his deeds of valor. This crusade, as before stated, was incited by St. Bernard, Abbot of Clairvaux in Champagne, who was distinguished for his learning and devotion. Under Louis VII., King of France, and Conrad III., Emperor of Germany, two immense armies marched for the Holy Land - this was in 1147. Manuel Comnenus, the Greek Emperor, through whose country the armies marched, by his treacherous conduct, caused great and a long series of disasters. A fruitless attempt was made to take Damascus, and the expedition was finally abandoned; only a small remnant of this vast host returned to Europe. Saladin, the Sultan of Egypt, in 1187 caused a Third Crusade to be started. Frederick Barbarossa, Emperor of Gem many; Philip Augustus, King of France; and Richard I. of England, were the Leaders of this crusade. In 1189 the Emperor of Germany set out first, but unfortunately died of a fever caused by imprudently bathing in the Orontes River, the modern Nahr-el-Asi, the chief river in Northern Syria; it flows past Antioch, and empties into the Mediterranean Sea. His army was then joined to the forces of the other two monarchs at Acre. Nearly two years were passed by these armies in the siege of Acre before it was surrendered, although Saladin made every effort to relieve the defenders. Nine battles were fought, and over 100,000 Christians perished during the siege. Unfortunately, from the peculiar temperaments of Philip of France and Richard of England, they could not agree; and Philip returned to Europe. Richard led his army to Ascalon and defeated Saladin; but was finally driven from Jerusalem. Richard performed prodigies of valor during this crusade, by which the admiration of the Saracens was excited, and from which he derived his name of "Coeur de Lion." He made a treaty with Saladin, by which the pilgrims were protected from injury and oppression; he then returned to Europe, in 1192. Saladin died in 1193; the unity of his empire was destroyed. The Sultans of Damascus, Egypt, and Aleppo became hostile to each other, and the Christians of Syria were not molested for many years. Pope Innocent III., in 1203, promoted the Fourth Crusade. At Venice an extensive armament was fitted out. The expedition, however, was diverted from its true mission against the Mohammedans, and, led by Baldwin, Count of Flanders, proceeded against Constantinople. In 1204 the Crusaders took this city, and then founded there the Latin dynasty of emperors who continued to fill the throne for fifty-six years.

Frederick II., Emperor of Germany, in 1228 led the Fifth Crusade, and it was ended by a treaty which he made with the Sultan of Egypt, according to which Palestine was ceded to Frederick, and free toleration granted to the two faiths of Christianity and Mohammedanism. By this arrangement the Christians lived in Jerusalem in peace and prosperity, until the Mongols, in the middle of the 13th century, disturbed this harmony.

Louis IX. (St. Louis) of France, in consequence of the capture and pillage of Jerusalem by the barbarous Mongols, in 1249, undertook the Sixth Crusade. After he had taken Damietta he was completely defeated by the Sultan of Egypt and taken prisoner; but was, in 1250, ransomed by his subjects. In alliance with Prince Edward (afterward Edward I.), son of Henry III. of England, St. Louis undertook the Seventh and last Crusade, in 1269, because of the capture of Antioch by the Mame-luke[157] Sultan of Egypt. Louis went to Africa, expecting to receive the King of Tunis as a convert to Christianity; he, however, found him to be a determined enemy. A pestilence having seized upon the French camp, they perished by thousands upon the burning sands. St. Louis died in his tent; and his son, after making a treaty with the King of Tunis, returned to France. Prince Edward, who at the age of fifteen had been married (August 5, 1254) to Eleanora of Castile (infants donna), not ten years of age, sister of King Alphonso, surnamed the "Astronomer," proceeded to Palestine, accompanied by his wife, who, leaving her three infants in England at Windsor, met her lord at Bordeaux, and from thence they sailed to Ptolomais, and in that campaign he won a great battle and stormed Nazareth. Embarking at Cyprus he won another victory, June, 1271, at Cahow.

The Saracens became greatly alarmed, and an attempt was made against Edward by the prince of the Assassins, called the "Old Man of the Mountains." He employed a fanatic, who, pretending to be a Christian convert, was admitted to the presence of Edward, aimed a dagger at his side, but stabbed him in the arm. Although wounded as he was, he overcame and killed the assassin before his attendants reached him. Being fearful that the weapon had been poisoned, for the wound turned black, when the Master of the Temple and the doctors recommended incision, the Princess Eleanora, agonized at what her lord had to suffer, cried and lamented, until his brother Edmund said: "My sister, it is better you should cry than all England weep." Edward, holding out his arm, bade his surgeons "cut away and spare not, he would bear it," and told his favorite knight, John de Vesci, to "carry the Princess away from a sight not fit for her to witness." Sir John carried her away to her ladies, she shrieking and struggling all the time. The surgical

---

[157] Mame-luke, meaning in Arabic slave.

operation was effectual, and, owing to Edward's virtue of temperance and Eleanora's tender care of him, he was convalescent in fifteen days.[158]

The forces of Edward, having been greatly reduced by sickness and want, prepared to leave the Holy Land, where his wife had given birth to a daughter, celebrated under the name of "Joanna of Acre," in which city she was born, and who afterward married Gilbert de Clare, the first nobleman of England. On their arrival in Sicily sad news met them - that their heir, Prince John, had died suddenly, and his brother Henry also. A messenger arrived on the third day, announcing that Edward's royal sire, Henry III., had expired, and Edward was now King of England. He had borne the loss of his sons with firmness, but was thrown into agonies upon the news of his father's death. When surprise was expressed at this he replied, "Eleanora may bring me more sons, but the loss of a father can never be replaced."

This closed the era of the Crusades. Antioch had fallen by the hands of the Sultan of Egypt, and the inhabitants were slaughtered or carried into slavery in 1268. All the other towns in Syria, successively, were reduced and fell into the hands of the Mohammedans excepting Acre, which for some time was the seat of the Christians. It was captured by the Sultan in 1291, and 60,000 of its inhabitants were massacred or sent into slavery. Soon afterward all the churches and fortifications of the Latin Christians throughout Syria were destroyed.

We might with some profit here pause, and reflect upon the wonderful effect that resulted from these vast and religious wars, between the Western Christian nations and the hordes of ignorant and benighted Mohammedan believers of the East, which successively followed from the First Crusade in 1096 No less than 275,000 men, mostly the dregs of the population of the various nations of Europe, were commanded by a religious fanatic, Peter the Hermit.

The first detachment, under Walter the Penniless, was destroyed by the Bulgarians, a few only succeeding in reaching Constantinople, where those led by Peter himself joined with them. After many difficulties a part of these succeeded in reaching Asia Minor, opposite Constantinople, where, upon the plains of Nice, they were defeated with great slaughter by the Turkish Sultan. A third and fourth expedition met with similar misfortune. However, the real Crusaders very soon thereafter arrived at Constantinople, who consisted of six armies of veteran soldiers, who were commanded by the most skillful and experienced commanders of that age: Godfrey of Bouillon; Duke of

---

[158] Agnes Strickland, "Queens of England," 1871, p. 97.

Lorrain; Hugh the Great, brother of Philip I., King of France; Robert, son of William the Conqueror of England; Count Robert of Flanders; Bo'he-Mond, Count of Tarentum, with his cousin, the noble and illustrious Tancred; and Count Raymond of Toulouse; amounting to nearly 600,000 men.

This force, under these noble leaders, defeated Sultan Sol'i-man, and took possession of his capital, Nice, in 1097, and afterward marched on to Syria, and besieged and took Antioch, in 1098, after seven months' siege; during which time Peter the Hermit, with multitudes of others, deserted the Crusaders. The Persian Sultan, having sent an immense army of Mohammedans to aid the others, they were also defeated and routed. The Crusaders then marched to Jerusalem, and found their numbers reduced to 40,000. This city surrendered to the Crusaders in 1099, after a short siege; and Godfrey de Bouillon was unanimously chosen King. Soon thereafter he met the Sultan of Egypt, with an immense army, at Ascalon, and there defeated him.

The Kingdom of Jerusalem, in a short time, was extended, until it embraced the whole of Palestine; nearly all or the best parts of Asia Minor were restored to the Eastern Empire; Bohemond was made Prince of Antioch. At this time the two Orders of Knights Hospitalers of St. John and Knights Templars above referred to were founded, " and for nearly fifty years the three Latin principalities or Kingdoms of the East - viz.: Edessa, Antioch, and Jerusalem - maintained themselves against the Mohammedans, and increased in power and wealth."

Then a Turkish Emir, who, having been made Governor of Aleppo, had defeated the Franks at Antioch, had taken Edessa, and threatened the destruction of all the Christian Kingdoms in Syria.

The influence of these crusades, extending from 1090 to 1291, a period of two hundred years, was very evident upon the European nations who had so repeatedly furnished their contingents to supply the armies who fought so hard and through so many difficulties in that unfavorable climate of Syria. In reading the accounts of these various crusades we are constantly reminded that in nearly every successful battle the conduct of the brave and gallant Knights Templars insured a complete victory.

The great reputation which they gained caused a constant increase of their numbers from the very best elements of the higher classes in Europe - and a constant increase of lands and monasteries and other estates. The political and social improvement of the nations of Europe followed. They tended to break up the feudal system, and the great barons were compelled to sell their extensive estates, in order to get the means of paying for the equipments of their armies; and their estates were divided up among the people generally. Popular freedom was given to towns and cities, with political privileges, in return for contributions of money to pay for troops and equipments. Commerce was encouraged by the demand for so many ships to transport such immense amounts of supplies and men - and every branch of trade was greatly stimulated and increased to furnish arms, equipments, and food supplies. Knowledge was diffused among the people, who formerly were almost as ignorant of the outer world as their domestic animals. Where was in those two centuries a wonderful advance in science, art, and literature.

The Greek and Saracenic civilization was soon imbibed by those who visited the East, and on their return to Europe, their own countries soon felt the influence in every branch of human knowledge.

Among those who returned, and thus impressed at home the great improvement in manners and customs, none were more influential than the Knights of the several Orders. Their influence was greater by far than any others who were fortunate to return; and consequently, according to human nature everywhere, these Orders became distasteful to all classes by their arrogant and tyrannical conduct, both to high and low; until the King of France, Philip the Fair, and Pope Clement V., for their own selfish purposes, and to gain the wealth of these Orders, determined to suppress them, which resulted in, first, their imprisonment for several years, until the plot was ripe; then by their execution, after the minds of the people had become sufficiently reconciled to their suppression.

During A.D. 1118, some writers say 1188, according to a Swedish Legend, "the Rose Croix came from the East into Europe, to propagate the doctrine of Jesus. Three of them founded in Europe the Order of Masons of the East [some writers say that our Knight of the Red Cross may probably have been derived from this degree], to serve as a preparatory seminary for those pupils whom they intended to instruct in the sublime sciences."[159]

To Ormesius, a priest of Alexandria in Egypt, is attributed the origin of the Order of Rose Croix. He with six others embraced Christianity at the solicitation of St. Mark the Evangelist, A.D.46.[160]

This tradition may be reconciled with the tradition of the formation of the Order of the Temple in Paris, which declares that the "Order of the East gave birth to the Order of the Temple; that, in Ancient Egypt, we find the cradle of the Order of the East." Also, "the

---

[159] "La Maconnerie," tome ii., p. 431.
[160] Ibid., tome ii., p. 431. "Acta. Lat.," tome i., p. 336.

Swedish brethren," as Reghellini observes, "have always enjoyed in the Order a very brilliant reputation for their learning; the proof of which is that all nations have adopted, in the Master's degree, the distress stgn as it was established in the catechism of their symbolic degrees." [161]This, however, can not be reconciled with that, which gives the origin of the Rose Croix, by the admission of the Order of St. John of Jerusalem of 27,000 Scottish Masons, who had given their aid to the Christian Princes during the wars of the First Crusade, as given by Oliver[162] and several others.[163] Addison says[164]: "That the first authentic notice of an intention on the part of the Hospitalers to occupy themselves with military matters occurs in the bull of Pope Innocent the Second, A.D. 1130." It is very probable that the latter Order was not of a military character at this time.

The Order of the Templars, by the exertions of Baldwin, King of Jerusalem, was greatly extended throughout Europe. The church, through the Pope and clergy, was enlisted in their favor. A code or set of rules was given them, afterward confirmed by a Papal Bull.

Large grants of land, and also money, were made to the Templars, after the visit of Hugode Payens, to Normandy, England, and Scotland, as before mentioned (A.D. 1128). According to Reghellini, "Eighty-one Masons, under the conduct of Garimont, Patriarch of Jerusalem, crossed into Europe, in 1150" (date probably erroneous).

"They went to the Bishop of Upsala, in Eastern Sweden, who received them very favorably, and by this means the Bishop was initiated into the mysteries brought from the Copts; afterward they intrusted to him the sacred depot of these doctrines, rites, and mysteries.

The Bishop of Upsala took care to conceal them in the subterranean vault of the tower of the four crowns, which at that time was the treasure-house of the King of Sweden. Nine of these Masons, among whom was Hugo de Payens, established in Europe the Order of the Templars, who subsequently received the depot, which had been given to the Bishop of Upsala, which held the doctrines, dogmas, and mysteries of the Coptic Priests. Reghellini adds: "It was by this action that the Templars became the conservators and guardians of the mysteries, rites, and ceremonies brought from the East by the Masonsand the Levites of the true light."[165] Hugo of the Temple, as he is

---

[161] "La Maconnerie," tome ii., p. 430.
[162] "Historical Landmarks," vol. ii., p. 135, note 40.
[163] "Dalcho's Oration," Appendix, note A, p. 66, Lexicon.
[164] "Addison," p. 55.
[165] "La Maconnerie," tome i., p. 437.

sometimes called, before he left England, appointed a Prior to govern[166] the Order in England.

The enthusiasm which prevailed in favor of the Templars was so great over Europe at this time that the King of Navarre bequeathed his kingdom to the Order. Most of the Barons of Navarre and Aragon ratified the act; notwithstanding which, the claims of the Templars were afterward successfully resisted. After Hugo had laid the foundations of the Order, he returned to Jerusalem and was greeted with great distinction (A.D. 1129), and a grand Council of War was called; soon after which he died.

Hugo de Payens was succeeded by Robert de Craou, surnamed the Burgundian, son-in-law of Anselm, Archbishop of Canterbury in 1136, who became a Templar after the death of his wife. The Templars were defeated in several battles by Zenghis and Naureddin, and lost several towns, the principal one being Edessa In consequence of these defeats application was made to the Pope for assistance by the clergy of the Eastern Churches, and he commissioned St. Bernard to preach the Second Crusade. In 1146 Everard des Barres, or de Barri, succeeded; Lord Robert convened a general chapter at Paris, where the Second Crusade was arranged. The Red Cross was permitted to be worn by the Templars by Eugenius III. In 1148 the red cross banner was first unfurled in battle, it is supposed, at Damascus.

It was a white standard, having in the center the blood-red cross, the symbol of martyrdom. Reghellini supposes the origin of this symbol to be of the highest antiquity. The Second Crusade having been a failure, the Master returned with King Louis to Paris. The Templars could only collect one hundred and twenty knights and one thousand serving brethren to recover the province of Antioch, which had been invaded by the enemy. The Master abdicated, and spent the rest of his life in the Monastery of Clairvaux.

He was succeeded by a nobleman of illustrious family of Burgundy, in France, Bernard de Tremelay, a valiant and experienced soldier, who was chosen Master in 1151. The Infidels were defeated near Jerusalem (1152) in a night attack, and driven to the Jordan, five thousand being left dead on the plain near the ford. Against this victory a disastrous defeat was encountered by the Templars, who in 1153 attempted to take the city of Ascalon. "They penetrated, at dawn of day, through a breach in the wall, reached the center of the town, were

---

[166] "Addison," p. 27.

surrounded by the Infidels, and 'slain to a man.' Their bodies were exposed in triumph from the walls."

Bertrand de Blanquefort, of a noble family of Guienne, a pious and God-fearing man, succeeded to the Mastership in 1154. The enemy captured him, with Otho, the Marshal, and eighty-five others in an ambuscade near Tiberias in 1156. Shortly thereafter, thirty Knights Templars put to flight, slaughtered, and captured two hundred Infidels. At the instance of Manuel Comnenus. Emperor of Constantinople, the Master was liberated (1158). in 1167 "Phlilp of Naplous became Master; he was the first Master who had been born in Palestine. He had been lord of the fortresses of Krak and Montreal in Arabia Petrsea; having assumed the habit and taken the vows of the Order of the Temple, after the death of his wife." Philip resigned his office in 1170, and Odo de St. Amand, of undoubted courage and resolution, succeeded as Master of the Temples according to William, Archbishop of Tyre, "having the fear neither of God or man before his eyes." In 1168, because the Master of the Temple refused to invade Egypt, in violation of certain treaties, Gilbert d'Assalit, the Guardian of the Hospitalers, the friend and confident of Almaric, King of Jerusalem, armed the Hospitalers as a great Military Society, in imitation of the Templars.

Egypt having been unjustifiably invaded by the Christian Knights, without the Templars, Saladin crossed the desert with 40,000 horse and foot, and after ravaging the borders of Palestine, advanced to and laid siege to Gaza, but was forced to retire again into Egypt by the Templars.

After this the Templars and Hospitalers became the guardians of the true cross - the former marched on the right, and the latter on the left of the sacred emblem.

The Templars conquered the Assassins in 1172, and their chief, "the Old Man of the Mountains," was forced to sue for peace. Near Ascalon, in a battle (November 1, 1177), "the Infidels were defeated. Odo with eighty Knights broke through the famous guard of Mamelooks, slew their commander, and forced Saladin to fly, almost naked, on a fleet dromedary." At the battle of Jacob's Ford, "where there was much hard fighting, the Master of the Hospital, covered with wounds, having fled, and the Count of Tripoli also, the Templars were all killed or taken prisoners and the Master Odo de St. Amand fell into the hands of the enemy. The fortress was burned down, and all the Templars taken in the place were sawn in two except the most distinguished."

During the difficulties between Philip, King of France, and Boniface VIII., the Templars coincided with the Pope. The King had issued coin below the proper standard, which caused a rebellion, and as the rents of the Templars were very great, they were thought by the King to be the instigators of the disaffection. The King determined to be revenged, and was not long in finding someone suited to his purpose. The evidence of the party who, to obtain the royal pardon, gave his testimony, was merely "hearsay," but two apostates from the Order, who were expelled and condemned to imprisonment for their crimes, corroborated this testimony. This information was treasured up by the King, to be made use of at the right time. Clement, an unprincipled man, in order to gain the summit of his ambition, had pledged himself on the holy sacrament to comply with a condition of which he was then ignorant. He became the instrument of the vindictive and wily monarch This Order, which had been for one hundred and seventy years the admiration of all Christendom, its members having shed freely their blood, and given thousands of lives to defend Christianity, and lavished their treasures in defense of the Cross against the Infidels, were declared to be heretics and apostates; they were accused of the blackest crimes, all of which were impossible. All the Templars in French dominions were simultaneously arrested and cast into prison.

Tortures of every kind were unsparingly applied. Some, to escape these horrible pains, confessed these crimes and absurdities imputed to them, in hopes of obtaining pardon. Most of these, after being restored to liberty, renounced their confessions and solemnly declared that the excessive torments to which they had been put alone induced them to confess that which they knew to be false.

They were then treated as relapsed heretics and cast into the flames. Neither age nor rank could escape of those who persisted in denying the guilt of the Order. Some languished in loathsome dungeons for years and perished from neglect disease, and starvation. Others, more robust, were in time restored to liberty, to wander about the world with mutilated limbs, to gain a living as best they could.

It would seem that these events, so well known to the nations of Europe, would have taught them all along the ages, from the Crusades to the 19th century, the humanitarian principles inculcated in their religion. Unfortunately, cruelty of every kind was so deep set In the very nature of all the Latin races, that where the religious sentiment was prevalent it was utterly impossible for the Roman Church ever to forgive any individual, high or low, who dared to controvert in the least manner any dogmatic utterance which might be promulgated from the Church authorities. Total obedience, the most abject and servile, was exacted from every individual. The history of every nation upon the continent of Europe, and where the Pope of Rome had authority elsewhere, shows that cruelties of the worst description were visited upon all who would not conform to the exactions of the Church of Rome. Such were the influences of that "curse of the world" which followed upon the suppression of the Templars by that "Curse of France" - as Philip the Fair was styled by Dante - that cruelties for differences in religious matters have been continued to the present day where any particular church is sustained by secular authority. The conduct of Spain in her treatment of her West and East Indian colonies in political matters is but the continuation of the old religious persecutions of the "Inquisition," " which caused countless millions to mourn." The persecutions of the Spanish governors in Cuba, Porto Rico, and Philippines, are the latest phases of the Spanish "Inquisition" and the "French Bastile" - The Devil's Island being but an outgrowth of that famous fortress destroyed in Paris during the Revolution.

Let us now complete the history of the Templars of the Crusades.

One recent author says: "The last scene of this dreadful tragedy was yet to be enacted. The four most noble victims were reserved for the last. James de Molay, the Grand Master; Guy, the Grand Preceptor; Hugo de Paralt or Peraldes, the Visitor General. and Theodore Bazile de Merioncourt, who had returned from the East (1307), when summoned by the Pope, and who had languished In prison for five years and a half, were (March 11, 1313) led out to a scaffold which had been erected in front of Notre Dames publicly to avow confessions which the Grand Master had declared were forged.

The confessions were read, their assent was required. Two were silent, and were condemned to be incarcerated for life. "But the Grand Master raising his arms, bound with chains, toward heaven, and advancing toward the edge of the scaffold, declared, in a loud voice, that to say that which was untrue was a crime, both in the sight of God and man. 'I do,' said he, 'confess my guilt, which consists in having to my shame and dishonor suffered myself, through the pain of torture and the fear of death, to give utterance to falsehoods, imputing scandalous sins and iniquities to an illustrious Order, which hath nobly served the cause of Christianity. I disdain to seek a wretched and disgraceful exist ence by engrafting a naked lie upon the original falsehood.' He was here interrupted by the Probo and his officers, and Guy, the Grand

Preceptor, having commenced with strong asseverations of his innocence, they were both hurried back to prison."[167]

King Philip was then informed of the occurrence, and in his blind fury ordered them to be immediately executed. This took place at four o'clock the same day, Addison says at dusk. There is no apparent discrepancy in this, as in March it often occurs that it is dusky soon after 4 P.M. They were conducted to the "Isle de la Cite," a funeral pile having been erected, and not yet completed, near where now stands the equestrian statue of Henry IV.

While the work of completion was going on, the Grand Master solemnly declared the innocence of his brethren, and then prayed as follows: "Permit us, O God! to remember the torments which Jesus Christ suffered to ransom us, and to imitate the example which he set us in enduring, without a murmur, the persecutions and tortures which injustice and blindness prepared for him. Pardon, O my God! the false accusations which have caused the total destruction of the Order of which Providence appointed me the head. And if thou wilt deign to hear the supplication which we now offer thee, grant that the deceived world may, at some future day, better know those who have endeavored to live for thee. We hope to receive, from thy goodness and mercy, the reward for the torments and death which we are about to suffer - to enjoy thy divine preset ence in the realms of bliss."

They were then hurried off to the stake, the executioners of the King being fearful of an insurrection of the people. Small fires were kindled under their feet. "This hellish torture was borne with fortitude and resignation, without cries or groans, imploring the mercy of God and maintaining the innocence and purity of their beloved Order to the last. At length De Molay, when his body was almost consumed, having yet command of his tongue, looking at the crowd before him, exclaimed:

"You who behold us perishing in the flames shall decide our innocence! I summon Pope Clement V. to appear in forty days, and Philip the Fair in twelve months, before the just and terrible throne of the ever-living God, to render an account of the blood which they have unjustly and wickedly shed!"[168]

The fires burned lower and lower, and in time became extinguished! The mortal parts of James de Molay and Guy had been reduced to ashes - their spirits had returned to their creator!

---

[167] "Addison," p. 279. Vertot gives this speech in different cords, though alike is substance, vol. i.,p. 219.
[168] Vertot, vol. i., p. 219.

Vertot and L'Histoire de l'ab. de l'Ord. both doubt the truth of this tradition. The manuscript of Knights Hospitalers, the manuscript of Knights Hospitalers of de la Hogue, and the degree of Novice of the Order of Unknown Phil. Judges state that De Molay made this prediction just before he was placed on the funeral piles.[169][170]

Vertot says that "In Germany the historians of that nation relate that Pope Clement having sent his bull for abolishing the Order to the Archbishop of Metey, for him to enforce, that prelate summoned all his clergy together, that the publication might be made with greater solemnity; and that they were suddenly surprised by the entry of Wallgruffer, Count Sauvage, one of the principals of the Order, attended by twenty other Templars armed and in their regular habits. The Count declared that he was not come to do violence to any body, but, having heard of the bull against his Order, came to insist that the appeal which they made from that decree to the next Council and successor of Clement should be received and published.

This he pressed so warmly that the Archbishop, not thinking it proper to refuse men whom he saw armed, complied. He sent the appeal afterward to the Pope, who ordered him to have it examined in a Council of his province. Accordingly a synod was called, and after a lengthy trial, and various formalities which were then observed, the Templars of that province were declared innocent of the crimes charged upon them. - Cole, " Masonic Library," pp. 288, 289.

Notwithstanding this verdict of innocence it does not appear that either their government or their possessions were restored to them as a distinct order. Their estates in the German Empire were divided between the Knights of Malta and the Teutonic Knights. Many of the Templars joined themselves to the Knights of Malta; and some writers hold this to be probable, for prior to this time the habit of the Knight

---

[169] "Orthodoxie Maconnerie," p. 393.

[170] Vertot, in his account of the origin of the Order of Knights Templars, states that "A Templar and a citizen of Breziers, having been apprehended for some crime, were committed together to a dungeon; for want of a priest, they confessed each other; that the citizen, having heard the Templar's confession, in order to save his own life, accused the Order to Philip, King of France; charging them, on the authority of what his fellow-prisoner had told him, with idolatry, sodomy, robbery, and murder; adding that the Knights Templars being secretly Mahomedan, each Knight, at his admission into the Order, was obliged to denounce Jesus Christ, and to spit on the Cross, in token of his abhorrence of it. Philip, on hearing these accusations, pardoned the citizen, and disclosed to the Pope this extraordinary confession, with a request that their Order should be suppressed." - Cole, " Masonic Library," p. 286.

Templar was originally white; but they now distinguish themselves by the same color as the Knights of Malta, viz., black.

"The fate of the persecutors of the Order is not unworthy of notice. A year and a month after the horrid execution, the Pope, Clement V., was attacked by a dysentery, and speedily hurried to his grave. His dead body was transported to Carpentras, where the Court of Rome then resided. It was placed at night in a church which caught fire, and the mortal remains of the Holy Pontiff were almost entirely consumed. His relations quarreled over the immense treasures he left behind him and a vast sum of money, which had been deposited for safety in a church at Lucca, was stolen by a daring band of German and Italian freebooters. Before the close of the same year, King Philip IV. died of a lingering disease which had baffled all the art of his medical attendants, and the condemned criminal, upon the strength of whose information the Templars were originally arrested, was hanged for fresh crimes.

"History attests," says Raynouard, " that all those who were foremost in the persecution of the Templars came to an untimely and miserable death. The last days of Philip IV. were embittered by misfortune. His nobles and clergy leagued against him to resist his exactions. The wives of his three sons were accused of adultery, and two of them were publicly convicted of that crime."

"The chief cause of the ruin of the Templars," justly remarks Fuller, "was their extraordinary wealth. As Naboth's vineyard was the chiefest ground of his blasphemy, and as in England Sir John Cornwall, Lord Fanhope, said merrily, not he, but his stately house at Ampthill, in Bedfordshire, was guilty of high treason, so certainly their wealth was the principal cause of their overthrow.

We may believe that Philip IV. would never have taken away their lives, if he might have taken their lands without putting them to death, but the mischief was. he could not get the honey unless he burnt the bees."

King Philip IV., the Pope, and the European sovereigns appear to have disposed of all the personalty of the Templars, the ornaments, jewels, and treasures of their churches and chapels, and during the period of five years over which the proceedings against the Order extended they remained in the actual receipt of the vast rents and revenues of the Fraternity. King Philip IV. put forward a claim upon their lands in France, to the extent of a million dollars, for the expenses of the prosecution, and Louis, his son, claimed a further sum of $300,000. "I do not know," says the celebrated Voltaire, "how much went to the Pope, but evidently, the share of the Cardinals, the Inquisitors delegated to make the process good, amounted to immense sums." The Pope, according to his own account, received only a small portion of the personalty of the Order, but others make him a large participator in the good things of the Fraternity.

Extracts from writings of Edward Manning, Cardinal Archs bishop of Westminster:

"The south of France, where a large Jewish and Saracenic element remained, was a hotbed of heresies, and that region was also a favorite one with the guild of Masons. It is asserted too that, as far back as the 12th century, the lodges of the guild enjoyed the special protection of the Knights Templars. It is easy in this way to understand how the symbolical allusion to Solomon and his Temple might have passed from the Knights into the Masonic formulary. In this way too might be explained how, after the suppression of the Order of the Temple, some of the recalcitrant, maintaining their influence over the Freemasons, would be able to prevent what had been hitherto a harmless ceremony into an elaborate ritual that should impart some of the errors of the Templars to the initiated.

A document was long ago published, which purports to be a charter granted to a lodge of Freemasons in England, in the time of Henry VII., and it bears the marks in its religious indifference of a suspicious likeness between Freemasons of then and now. In Germany the guild was numerous, and was formally recognized by a diploma granted in 1489 by the Emperor Maximilian. But this sanction was finally revoked by the Imperial Diet in 1707.

"So far, however, the Freemasons were really working stonemasons; but the so-called Cologne Charter (the genuineness seems certain), drawn up in 1535 at a reunion of Freemasons gathered at Cologne to celebrate the opening of the Cathedral Edifice, is signed by Melanchthon, Coligny, and other ill-omened. Nothing certain is known of the Freemasons - now evidently become a sect during the 17th century, except that in 1646 Elias Ashmole, an Englishman, founded the Order of Rose Croix, Rosicrucians, or Hermetic Freemasonry, a society which mingled in a fantastic manner the jargon of alchemy and other occult sciences with Pantheism. This Order soon became affiliated to some of the Masonic lodges in Germany, where from the time of the Reformation there was a constant founding of societies, secret or open, which undertook to formulate a philosophy or religion of their own.

"As we know it now, however, Freemasonry first appeared in 1725, when Lord Derwentwater, a supporter of the expelled Stuart

Dynasty, introduced the order into France, professing to have his authority from a lodge at Kilwinning, Scotland. This formed the basis of that variety of Freemasonry called the Scotch Rite. Rival organizations soon sprang up. Charters were obtained from a lodge at York, which was said to have been of a very ancient foundation."[171]

From this extract some of our recent writers have thought that "this connection exists just so far as the Templary of our own day clings to its knightly practices, and is true to its Templar Dogmas of the Christian faith and teaching."

The same spirit of Clement V. is here shown by this famous Manning.

From the various high-grade systems which sprang into existence in Europe during the middle and latter past of the 18th century came the Templary on the continent of Europe, for in each system there was to be found the Knight Templar degree. The Ancient and Accepted Rite of Twenty-five degrees. and its successor, the "Ancient and Accepted Scottish Rite," formulated at the close of the last century, are permeated with the Templar spirit.

The principles in all of the several rites wherein is to be found the Templar degree, are dogmatic utterances, and "squared with the words of that Ancient Landmark, God's Holy Word." The lessons of duty found in our modern Templarism are to be applied and practiced in our daily life, and he who follows faithfully all the teaching of our Order will be a "Christian in deed and in truth, and in whom there is no guile."

History says Philip died a few weeks after the martyrdom of De Molay, and Addison fixes the period of the death of the Pope a year and one month afterward, and he also says, "History attests that all those who were foremost in the persecution of the Ternplars came to an untimely and miserable death."[172]

By the execution of the principal officers of the Templar organization their enemies supposed that the Order was destroyed for all time; " but the Eagle of St. John was merely scorched - not killed. From the ashes of the old Phoenix has arisen another Order, more glorious in all its aspects than the original; and in the latter part of the 19th century,

---

[171] A Catholic Dictionary containing some "Account of the Doctrine, Discipline, Rites, Ceremonies, Councils, and Religious Orders of the Catholic Church." By William E. Addis, Secular Priest, sometime Fellow of the University of Ireland, and Thomas Arnold, M.A., Fellow of the same university. Second Edition, London. Large 8vo, 1884. In loco.

[172] "Addison," p. 280.

the Knightly Order of the Templars, clad in the Armor of Integrity, and armed with the sword of knowledge have waged, are still waging, and will ever wage eternal war against the three ancient enemies of the human race - Falsehood, Fanaticism, Superstition! Dieu le vent - 'The will of God.'"

After the execution of De Molay and the dispersion of the Templars, in all the nations of Europe, their possessions were confiscated and divided among various other Orders; the survivors were compelled to leave their homes, discard their garb of Templars, and mingle again with the world.

If traditions can be relied upon, some preserved their "Order of the Temple at Paris; " and some the "Templars in Scotland," of whom Charles Edward Stuart was chosen Grand Master. Some, it is said, sought refuge in the Society of Free and Accepted Masons, in order "that they might there enjoy with impunity the religious dogmas which they had brought with them from the East - the liberal sentiments of the Johannite Christians - the pure doctrines of the primitive Christian Church. Many entered the preceptories of the Knights Hospitalers, after a part of their lands had been granted to them." From this circumstance no doubt the modern degree of Knights of Malta has been incorporated into the Encampments of Knights Templars. The Knights of Malta were never anciently claimed to have been Freemasons. "In 1740 the Grand Master of the Order of Malta caused the bull of Clement XII. to be published in the Island of Malta, and forbade the meetings of Freemasons. On this occasion several Knights and many citizens left the Island." " In 1741 the Inquisition pursued the Freemasons at Malta. The Grand Master proscribed their assemblies under severe penalties, and six knights were banished from the Island, in perpetuity, for having assisted at a meeting."

From tradition, after the death of De Molay, in 1313, the Templars were divided into four parties, viz.:
1. The Templars in Portugal and Italy - known since as Knights of the "Order of Christ."
2. Those who accepted Peter d'Aumont as the successor of De Molay.
3. Those who asserted that John Marc Larmenius was his successor.
4. Those who refused to accept either Larmenius or D'Aumont.

Passing by the first, second, and third classes, our sketch need only to refer to the fourth - as Modern Templarism is supposed to be derived from the fourth class, which may be divided into two classes - the Scotch and English.

Edward having debarred the Templars from taking refuge either in England or Ireland, and who attempted to force them, as he had done their brethren, in those countries to enter the preceptories of the Knights of St. John, they were forced to join Bruce, who gave them ample protection; and it is said by their assistance he was enabled to defeat the forces sent against him by Edward at the battle of Bannockburn. He is said to have created, on June 24, 1314, the Order of St. Andrew du Chardin,' to which was afterward united that of Heredom (H.D.M.). He reserved to himself and to his successors forever the title of Grand Master; and founded the Royal Grand Lodge of the Order of H.D.M. at Kilwinning. As our object is, if possible, to trace the origin of our Templar Orders, we must here drop the history of the Royal Order and refer to the General History preceding - Chapter XXIX. - where a full [173]statement is made, according to all the light which could possibly be thrown on this difficult problem.

By the death of De Molay, the Order of the Temple was broken up, and the members scattered in all directions, as they had no common head. Those of them who had been leaders in each country were mostly imprisoned for life, or executed, the brethren, persecuted in all directions, and for concealment, wandered about and cast off the clothing of the Order, and again mingled with other men.

Addison says: " Papers and certificates were granted to men with long beards, to prevent them from being molested by the officers of justice as suspected Templars."

Their assemblies were forbidden under severe penalties, and at one time six Knights were banished from the island for having been at one of the meetings. There was no ritual of the Order, hence the ritual now used, which is a very beautiful and impressive one, is entirely modern. Gourdin says: " From ignorance of the true causes which forced some of the Templars to enter the Order of Malta has arisen the highly reprehensible practice of dubbing the candidate ' a Knight of the most valiant and magnanimous Order of Knights Templars and Knights of Malta of the Order of St. John of Jerusalem.' This ritual was once in force in the United States, and was incorporated in the diploma or patent."

1. The Order of Christ. When the Templars were suppressed in Portugal, their property, of all kinds, was assigned over to the Order of Christ, the equestrian militia, the latter name having been changed to the former. This Order, since its foundation in 1317, has been always

---

[173] This order was most probably created by James II. in 1440. - Mackey, in this work Chapter xxix., p. 259 et seq.

protected by the Kings of Portugal, and also by the Popes. They wear "a long and loose black mantle, turned up with ermine and thereupon the Crosses." They are called "Christian Militia," which is their motto. Thory says that "A Portuguese Mason founded at Paris, in 1807, in a Lodge, a chapter of this Order; he applied the formulas of reception to those of Freemasonry. It was the Templar system. He pretended to have received from Portugal the power to create Knights."[174] The same Order was in Italy. Pope John XXII. reserved the right of nominating those members called Pontifical Knights.[175]

2. The D'Aumont Templars. They professed the system of "Strict Observance," which its opponents declare to have been organized in Prussia by Baron Hund, who derived his knowledge of the doctrines in the Chapter of Clermont, in Paris, he being a member in 1754.[176] This system is exclusively used in Germany and Sweden. A long list of Grand Masters is produced who succeeded De MoJay, the first being D'Aumont, who is said to have been elected on an island of Scotland, December 27, 1313.[177] In Sweden it is said that the Grand Chapter of Stockholm has the last will and testament of De Molay, and that Beaujeau, his nephew, collected his ashes, interred them, and erected his monument with suitable inscriptions.[178]

3. The Larmenius Templars. James de Molay, foreseeing the evils by which the Order was threatened, nominated as his successor John Mark Larmenius, of Jerusalem, and invested him with the Patriarchal and Apostolic power. Larmenius transmitted this power to Brother Thibault of Alexandria in 1324.[179] The Order of Paris claim to have the Charter of transmission signed by Laminius and also the others who succeeded him in Office, down to the present time. They claim also to have the original statutes of the year 587 in manuscript, and several relics which formerly belonged to the martyrs. Some of the Templars were sent out in 1826 to Greece, to fight the Turks.[180]

---

[174] "Acta Latomorum," tome i., p. 299.
[175] "Encyclopedia of Heraldry," vol. i.
[176] "Acta Latomorum," tome i., pp. 68, 328. "Historical Landmarks," vol. ii., p. 45. The system of Ramsay was known in Germany before the Chapter of Clermont. "Orthodoxie Maconnerie," p. 222.
[177] "Acta Latomorum," tome i., p. 329. "Historical Landmarks," vol.ii., p. 13, note 26
[178] "Acta Latomorum," p. 339.
[179] "Manuel," p. 8.
[180] "Freemasons Magazine." vol. I p. 170.

There has been a difference of opinion among the brethren as to the authenticity of these legends relative to D'Aumont, Beaujeau, and Larmenius, and the relics. Some writers have asserted that De Molay had appointed four Grand Chiefs of the Order in Europe: at Edinburgh in the north; Paris in the west; Naples in the south, and Stockholm in the east.[181] According to the rules of the Order at that time it is very doubtful if De Molay appointed anyone as his successor, as the office had, up to that time, been elective, and no one appointed by De Molay or anyone else would have been recognized by the Order at large unless he had been regularly elected; hence we may be sure that De Molay had no successors.

4. The fourth were the Templars, who did not recognize either of the three above mentioned who assumed the authority of a Grand Master. Those may be divided into two classes: 1st. The Scotch Templars. These may be sub-divided into two sections: a. Those who fought with Robert Bruce; b. Those who entered the Order of Knights Hospitalers.

1. The Templars in Scotland, in consequence of the hostility of Edward III., King of England, were forced to join with Bruce, as he had refused to let them take refuge either in England or Ireland, and had endeavored to force them, as he had their brethren in those countries, to enter the preceptories of the Knights of St. John.

These Knights having joined Bruce and aided in the victory at Bannockburn, he created, June 24, 1314, the Order of St. Andrew du Chardon, to which was afterward united that of Heredom (H.D.M.).[182] He raised the Lodge of Kilwinning in Scotland, founded at the time of the constitution of the abbey of that name, in 1150, to the rank of Royal Grand Lodge of Heredom. These Scotch Templars are reported to have been expelled in 1324 by Larmenius, who had invented different signs and words to exclude them from the Order of which he was chief, because they had assisted Bruce, and of having joined the order of H.R.D.M. Some writers have conjectured that from this Royal Order had sprung the Ancient and Accepted Rite. The present writer feels confident that the third degree of Symbolic Masonry was originally derived from the H.R.D.M.

"From the General Regulations of Royal Arch Masons of Scotland, it may be inferred that the preservation of a remnant of the Templars in Scotland is chiefly to be attributed to the wars between Robert Bruce and Edward III. of England." It is confidently said that "the

---

[181] "La Maconnerie." tome I., p. 466.
[182] Chapter xix., ante.

25 degrees of Heredom were practiced at York, in 1784, by the College of Heredom Templars, being No. 1 under the Constitution of the Ancient Lodge at York, south of the river Trent, sitting at York."

In 1785 the Order of H.R.D.M. resumed its functions at Edinburgh, the presiding officer being styled Wisdom.[183] The body at Edinburgh established a Chapter at Rouen in 1786.[184] On January 4, 1787, a Chapter of Harodim was opened in London,[185] but it is not known whether this was a branch of the Royal Order. About the beginning of the present century there was a consistory at Hull and one at Grimsby.[186]

Rebold has it that the Grand Lodge of Heredom of Kilwinning united together with all the subordinates to the St. John Grand Lodge of Edinburgh.[187]

2. Those who entered the Order of Knights Hospitalers. In Scotland, in England and Ireland, many of the Templars joined the Order of the Knights of St. John. They resided amicably in the same preceptories at the end of the 14th and beginning of the 15th centuries, and continued thus until the Reformation.[188] But they did not, however, hold all their lands in common.[189] Many of these Knights of both Orders embraced Protestantism, and fraternized with the Freemasons. The Preceptor in Scotland, having become a Protestant, resigned the whole prosessions of the Preceptory, of the Hospitalers and Templars, received the same, as Lord Torphichen, ftom the Crown. Those Knights who remained Roman Catholics united with David Seaton. The Grand Master, Viscount Dundee, was slain at Killiekrankie. Charles Edward Stuart, who had been admitted, September 24, 1745, at Holyrood, became the Grand Master.[190] Mr. Oliphant, of Bachiltar, succeeded him. He died in 1745.[191] From the General Regulations of Royal Arch Masons of Scotland it may be inferred that the Masonic branch of the Order preserved the ceremonies which are used at a reception. The

---

[183] "Historical Landmarks," vol. ii., p. 86.
[184] "Acta Latomorum," tome i., p. 169.
[185] "Historical Landmarks," vol. ii., p . 86.
[186] "Historical Landmarks," vol. ii., p. 671, note 16.
[187] "Histoire Generale de la Francois Maconnerie," p. 151 Oliver, "Historical Landmarks," vol. ii., p. 16.
[188] "General Regulations of Royal Arch Masons of Scotland," Introduction, p. iii.
[189] "Historical Landmarks," vol. ii., p. 20, note 46.
[190] Gourdin, p. 25.
[191] "Historical Landmarks," vol. ii., p. 20, note 46. It is presumed that this portion of the Order is not connected with Freemasonry.

Sterling Ancient Lodge conferred the degree of Royal Arch, Red Cross, or Ark, the Sepulcher, Knights of Malta and Knights Templars, until the beginning of the last century, when two lodges were formed. The Ancient Lodge joined the Grand Lodge of Scotland in 1736, and the new one, called the Royal Arch, in 1759, when another division took place. And these degrees were conferred in an encampment until 1811, when the supreme encampmnent of Masonic Knights Templars was formed in Scotland.[192] Several encampments in Scotland, however, obtained, about 1795, charters from Ireland with the privilege of conferring the Royal Arch degrees, though the encampments in the latter country were merely private bodies. [193]

3. The English Templars. It is supposed, that with the exception of the Encampment of Observance, all the encampments in the United States and England owe their origin to the three original is Encampments of Baldwin," established at Bristol, Bath, and York.

[194]Oliver says: " In England and Ireland, as the Conciliae Magnae Britannicae show, the Templars were put down, and the Knights compelled to enter the preceptories of their opponents, the Knights of St. John, as dependants."[195] " Their lands were confiscated and given to the latter Order. But in treating of the manner in which a remnant of the Order was preserved in England, I must avail myself of information kindly furnished me by an eminent Brother who resides in Bristol."

"The Order of Knights Templars has existed in Bristol from time immemorial. The Templars held large possessions in this ancient city, and, with their House or Preceptory, and the Men of the Temple, are mentioned in many old charters and documents. The Temple Church and Parish of Temple point out the locality of their residence. About fifty years ago an active and respected member of the Craft, Brother Henry Smith, now deceased, introduced from France three degrees of the Ancient and Accepted Rite, which, with the degree of R.C., long before that time connected with the Knights Templars, were united into an Order or Community, called the Royal Orders of Knighthood. These were the degrees of the Nine Elect, the 9th degree of the Ancient and Accepted Rite, the Knights Grand Architects of Kilwinning, the 14th degree of that Rite, and the Knights of the East,

---

[192] "General Regulations of Royal Arch Masons of Scotland," Introduction, pp. ii., iii.
[193] "General Regulations of Royal Arch Masons of Scotland," Introduction, p. vii.
[194] "Lexicon," p. 265. Temp. chart, p. 47, by J. L. Cross.
[195] "Historical Landmarks," vol. ii., p. 20, note 46.

the Sword and Eagle, answering to the 16th degree, and the Knights R.C. or 18th degree, were, together with the order of the Knights Templars, held and practiced under one authority. In our oldest records the style or title of Knights Templars is given with the addition of K.-H., but that degree was, as far as I know, never given, and even the meaning of the title has fallen into oblivion."

"A candidate for admission into any one of the five degrees before mentioned must be a Royal Arch Mason. He may, however, take any one of the five degrees first, which may happen to be about to be given, at the time he seeks admission, as one general payment to the fund of the United Orders entitles him to admission to all. An attempt was made to enforce the proper progression through the five degrees, but failed.

"Nothing is known here of the Order of the Temple of Paris, but that is the real source of the present Grand Conclave of England, the late Grand Master, the Duke of Sussex, having been created at Paris in that body.

"I will shortly endeavor to explain the difference between the Encampment of Baldwyn and the Grand Conclave.

"The Duke of Sussex, having been installed as Knight Templar at Paris, I believe by Sir Sidney Smith, then Grand Master, was created Grand Master of the Knights Templars in England. From some cause or other, he never would countenance the Christian degrees connected with Masonry, and would not permit a badge of one of these degrees to be worn in a Craft Lodge. In London, of course, he ruled Supreme, and the meetings of Knights Templars there, if they continued at all, were degraded to the mere level of public-house meetings. A true descendant of the Knights of St. John of the Hospital was held, with all circumstances of ribaldry, at St.

John's Gate, Clerkenwell, and the degrees conferred at a weekly convivial meeting for the sum of 5s. On the death of the Duke of Sussex it was resolved to rescue the Order from its degraded position, and the Grand Conclave of England was formed, some of the officers of the Duke of Sussex's original Encampment, which he held once, and I believe once only, being then alive.

"In the mean time, of the three Original Encampments of England, the genuine representatives of the Old Knights of the Temple, two had expired, those of Bath and York, leaving Bristol the sole relic of the Order with the exception of those encampments which had been created in various parts of the country, not holding under any legitimate authority, but raised by Knights who had, I believe, without exception, been created in the Encampment of Baldwyn at Bristol.

"Under these circumstances, the Knights of Baldwin felt that their place was at the head of the Order, and though willing, for the common good, to submit to the authority of Colonel Tynte, or any duly elected Grand Master, they could not yield precedence to the Encampment of Observance (the Original Encampment of the Duke of Sussex) derived from a foreign and spurious source, the socalled Order of the Temple in Paris, nor could they consent to forego the privileges which they held from an immemorial period, or to permit their ancient and well-established ceremonies, costume, and laws to be revised by persons for whose knowledge and judgment they entertained a very reasonable and well grounded want of respect.

The Encampment of Baldwyn, therefore, refused to send representatives to the Grand Conclave of England, or to acknowledge its authority in Bristol, until such time as its claims should be treated with the consideration it is believed they deserve. I am, however, in hope that an arrangement will shortly be effected, and all the Templars in England united under one head."[196]

Gourdin, from whose admirable Historical Sketch of Knights Templars we have made many extracts, says, in continuation of the matters referred to in the above letter: "While we approve of the noble conduct of the Encampment of Baldwin, and trust that it may soon attain the eminent position to which it is entitled as the sole surviving preserver of our Ancient Mysteries in England, during many centuries of trial."

Some writers have contended that the Masonry of modern times "originated in the Holy Land during the Crusades, and was instituted by the Knights Templars." Laurie, or Brewster, who it is said wrote the work which bears Laurie's name, embodies the tradition as follows:

"Almost all the secret associations of the Ancients either flourished or originated in Syria and the adjacent countries. It was here that the Dionysian Artists, the Essenes, and the Kassideans arose. From this country also come several members of that trading association of Masons which appeared in Europe during the dark ages; and we are assured that, notwithstanding the unfavorable condition of that Province, there exists at this day, on Mount Libanus, one of these Syrian Fraternities. As the Order of the Templars, therefore, was originally

---

[196] Letter of David W. Nash, September 29, 1853, to Theo. S. Gourdin, Charleston, S. C., in his " Historical Sketch," 1855.

formed in Syria, and existed there for a considerable time, it would be no improbable supposition that they received their Masonic knowledge from the Lodges in that quarter. But we are fortunately, in this case, not left to conjecture, for we are ex pressly informed by a foreign author [Adler, de Drusis], who was well acquainted with the history and customs of Syria, that the Knights Templars were actually members of the Syriac fraternities There is no evidence of Freemasonry in Syria at that period.

It is very certain, from the best histories of the Templar Order, that, in addition to the open ritual for the reception of a candidate for the Order, there was a secret ritual, and no one was admitted within their quarters during the ceremony of reception.

This does not, however, prove that, whatever secret ceremonies were used, they were in any manner connected with the Freemasons. Recent examinations by our most advanced Masonic scholars, such as Wm.

James Hughan, Robert Freck Gould, and others too numerous to mention who are members of the Lodge Quartuor-Coronati in England, and the Grand Secretary of the Grand Lodge of Scotland, D. Murray Lyon, that, prior to the formation of the Grand Lodge of England in 1717, there was no ritualistic observance in the reception to Masonry. Nor have any indications been found anywhere in the world, that our modern rituals of the various degrees of the Lodge, Chapter, Council, and Templar Order, had any ancient formulas whatever. To the careful student, every one of these ritualistic formulas bears intrinsic evidence of the modern era in Masonry. In the three degrees of the Blue Lodge, the want of congruity and manifest errors as to the facts at the building of King Solomon's Temple, the topography itself of the site of the Temple, and the situation of the City of Jerusalem - all concur in the conclusion that the ceremonies are all symbolic and allegorical, and consequently so much the more valuable to the student of symbolism and the philosophy contained in these degrees - and this can be said also of all the other degrees.

The Knights of Malta being at the present day incorporated in the Order of Knights Templars, we deem it necessary that this sketch should include some important matters connected with that Order, which, from our preceding notices of them, it will be seen succeeded the Knights Hospitalers, or Knights of St. John, and so called Knights of Rhodes.

Pilgrims and traders from the West to Palestine were so numerous and constant, it became requisite to build in the city of

Jerusalem hospitals or places of entertainment during their stay in Jerusalem. In 870 Bernard, a monk, founded in the valley of Jehoshaphat, close to the Church of the Virgin, a hospital, consisting of twelve houses for pilgrims from the West, which held possession of gardens, vineyards, and fields for grain. There was a collection of books given by Charlemagne (in 768 to 800). A market was held in front of this place. When, in the 11th century, pilgrimage was greatly increased, a hospital was established in the city of Jerusalem, for the Latin pilgrims, which was erected by Amalfi and the Latin traders, about A.D. 1050. They also erected a church to the Holy Virgin, called St. Mary of the Latins. This hospital was the residence of the Benedictines, who devoted themselves to the necessities of the pilgrims, and contributed to the wants of those who were poor, or had been robbed by the banditti who infested all the roads leading to Jerusalem, and also aided them to pay the taxes required by the Moslems for permits to visit the Holy Places.

The great increase of pilgrims required another hospital which was raised near their church, having a chapel dedicated to St. John Fleemon (Almoner), a canonized Patriarch of Alexandria, who was the son of the King of Cyprus in the 6th century. He was elected Patriarch and founded a Fraternity in Jerusalem, whose object was to attend upon the sick and wounded Christian pilgrims to the Sacred Land. The Greek and also Roman Churches canonized this Archprelate by the name of St. John of Jerusalem.

Gerard, as before mentioned, presided over the Hospital of St. John at the time the Crusaders appeared at Jerusalem. When the city was taken (July 15, 1099), the wounded pilgrims were received, and "Duke Godfrey de Bouillon, some days afterward, visited them, to whom he personally administered aid and consolation, and, to mark his sense of the humane services rendered by the brethren, he endowed the hospital with his own Lordship of Montboire, in Brabant, and all its dependencies. Having enjoyed universal favor, Gerard and his brethren desired to be separated from the Monastery of St. Mary de Latina and become independent. There was no opposition to this, and they made a rule for themselves, to which they vowed obedience in the presence of the Patriarch, and assumed a black mantle with a white cross on the breast.

In 1130, from the Bull of Pope Innocent II., we have the first authentic notice of an intention of the Hospitalers to have any connection with military affairs. This Bull gives information that the Hospitalers retained, at their own expense, a body of foot- soldiers and horsemen to defend the pilgrims in going to and returning from the

Holy Places. The Hospitalers had resolved to add the protecting to the task of relieving pilgrims.

In 1168, the first year of Philip of Nablous as Grand Master of the Templars, the King of Jerusalem and Knights Hospitalers went forth on their memorable and unfortunate expedition to invade Egypt. The Templars refused to join this expedition, as it was in violation of all treaties.

From this period there was an entire change in the Order of the Hospital of St. John, and they became a great military body; their Superior was styled Grand Master, and he led in person the brethren into the field of battle. They, however, still continued their duties as attendants upon the sick and to relieve the indigent.

The Order of the Holy Sepulcher was instituted at the same period as the Knights of St. John of Jerusalem, and for the same causes.

The following is a list of the Patriarchs of Jerusalem, A.D. 1099 to 1187, from De Vogue:

Diambert (Arnulphe) 1099 to 1107
Ebremard (Gibelin) 1107 to 1111
Arnulphe 1111 to 11118
Gorman 1118 to 1128
Etienne (Stephen) 1128 to 1130
Guillaume (William) 1130 to 1146
Foulcher 1146 to 1157
Amanry 1157 to 1180
Eraclius (Heraclius)1180 to 1190

In 1847 the Pope re-established the Patriarchate of Jerusalem in the person of Bishop Velerga. He only had authority to confer the Order of Knights of the Holy Sepulcher. This was done in the apartment styled the Chapel of the Apparition, where Jesus is said to have appeared to Mary after his resurrection. The Candidate, kneeling before the Patriarch, is asked the traditional questions, and is then girded with the sword and spur of King Godfrey. We have in a former part of this sketch explained the union of the Knights of the Red Cross of Rome and Constantine with the Knights Hospitalers and Knights of the Holy Sepulcher, so that, when these Orders, after the Crusades had ceased, had been driven successively from Cyprus and Rhodes and found refuge in the island of Malta, Which was tendered to them by Charles V., King of Spain, and when the Order of the Templars was suppressed and many of them found a home with the Order of Malta, the junction of the two Orders was formed. We presume that when the modern Order of Knights Templars was formulated, the ritual of Malta was added to that of Knight Templar, and we consider the association much more consonant with the history of these two Orders than the degree of Knight of the Red Cross of Persia and Syria, which has evidently been mistaken for the Red Cross of Rome and Constantine, as before explained.

This Order has been known at different periods by the title of the Knights of St. John of Jerusalem, Hospitalers of St. John, Knights of St. John D'Acre, Knights of Rhodes, and finally Knights of Malta

In the year 1048 some pious merchant from Amalfi, in the kingdom of Naples, built a church and monastery at Jerusalem, which they dedicated to St. John the Almoner. The monks were hence called Brothers of St. John, or Hospitalers, and it was their duty to assist those sick and needy pilgrims whom a spirit of piety had led to the Holy Land. They assumed the black habit of the hermits of St. Augustine, distinguished only by a white cross of eight points on the left breast. They rapidly increased in numbers and in wealth and at the beginning of the 12th century were organized as a military order by Raymond du Puy, who added to their original vow of chastity, obedience, and poverty, the obligation of defending the church against Infidels. Raymond then divided them into three classes: Knights, who alone bore arms; Chaplains, who were regular ecclesiastics; and Servitors, who attended to the sick. After long and bloody contests with the Turks and Saracens, they were finally driven from Palestine in the year 1191. Upon this they attacked and conquered Cyprus, which, however, they lost after eighteen years' occupation. They then established themselves at the island of Rhodes, under the Grand Mastership of Fulk de Villaret, and assumed the title of the Knights of Rhodes.

It was here that the illustrious Villars died in the seventieth year of his age and the fourteenth of his Grand Mastership. In justice to his distinguished merit, the following epitaph was inscribed on his tombstone: "Here lies Virtue victorious over Fortune."

On December 15, 1542, after a tranquil occupation of this island for more than two hundred years, they were finally ejected from all their possessions by the Sultan Soliman the Second.

After this disaster they successively retired to Castro, Messina, and Rome, until the Emperor Charles V., in 1530, bestowed upon them the island of Malta, upon the condition of their defending it from the depredations of the Turks and the Corsairs of Barbary, and of restoring it to Naples, should they ever succeed in recovering Rhodes.

This island was formerly called Melita, from the vast quantities of honey which it produced. The Romans gained possession of it when they conquered Sicily; they were deprived of it by the Arabs in 828, who were expelled by Roger the Norman in 1190. From that period it continued under the dominion of the Kings of Sicily, till it fell, by the conquest of that island, into the hands of the emperor, Charles V.

The Order now took the name of the Knights of Malta, by which title they have ever since been designated. Here the organization of the Order was as follows: The chief of the Order was called "Grand Master of the Holy Hospital of St. John of Jerusalem and Guardian of the army of Jesus Christ." He was elected for life, and resided at the city of Valette. He was addressed by foreign powers with the title of "altezza eminentissima," and enjoyed an annual revenue of about one million guilders. The Knights were divided into eight languages, according to their respective nations. The languages were those of Provence, Auvergne, France, Italy, Aragon, Germany, Castile, and England. Upon the extinction of the language of England, that of Anglo-Bavaria was substituted The Grand Officers were also eight in number, and consisted of the chiefs of the different languages, as follows:

1. The Chief of the language of Provence was Grand Commander
2. The Chief of the language of Auvergne was Marshal.
3. The Chief of the language of France was Hospitaler.
4. The Chief of the language of Italy was Grand Admiral.
5. The Chief of the language of Aragon was Grand Conservators
6. The Chief of the language of Germany was Grand Bailiff.
7. The Chief of the language of Castile was Grand Chancellor.
8. The Chief of the language of England was Turcopolier, or Captain-General of the Cavalry.

The Knights, in time of war, wore over their usual garments a scarlet surcoat, embellished before and behind with a broad white cross of eight points. In time of peace, the dress of ceremony was a long black mantle, upon which the same cross of white linen was sewed.

From the time that the island of Malta was bestowed upon the Order, until the year 1724, the Knights were continually at war with the Turks; during which time the latter had expended vast quantities of blood and treasure, and the former had exhibited the most magnanimous examples of patience and undaunted heroism. A peace was at length concluded for twenty years, to be renewed at the expiration of that period, if the parties could agree.

In 1565 the island of Malta was beleaguered by Soliman II., on which occasion the Knights suffered immense loss, from which they never entirely recovered. Of the eight languages, the English became extinct in the 16th century; those of France, Auvergne, and Provence perished in the anarchy of the French Revolution; Castile and Aragon were separated at the peace of Amiens; and the remaining two have been since abolished. The Order, therefore, as respects its ancient constitution, has now ceased to exist.

On June 9, 1798, the island of Malta was taken by the French under Bonaparte. In the same year the Knights chose Paul I., Emperor of Russia, as their Grand Master, who took them under his protection.

Upon his death they elected Prince Carriciolo. Upon the reduction of the island by the English in 1800, the chief seat of the Order was transferred to Catanea in Sicily, whence, in 1826, it was removed, by the authority of the Pope, to Ferrara. The last public reception of the Order took place at Sonneburg in 1800, when Leopold, the present King of Belgium, and Prince Ernest, of Hesse Philippsthal Barchfeld, with several other Knights, were created.

In 1841 Ferdinand I., Ernperor of Austria, issued a decree restoring the Order in Italy, and endowing it with a moderate revenue. But the wealth, the power, and the magnificence of the Order have passed away with the age and the spirit of chivalry which gave it birth.

COMMENTARY REMARKS.

In Chapter XXIX. of this work, p. 258 et seq., Bro. Mackey reviews the history of the Templars in Scotland, and emphatically denies any claims of the Scottish Modern Templars to be the successors of the Templars who were dispersed after the death of De Molay. We shall not, in this sketch, attempt any defense of their claims or those of the Templars of the present day as to the legitimate succession. However, we must give our readers some extracts from Addison which will demonstrate that there were some reasons why such claims have been set up.

Lawrie, in his History of Freemasonry in Scotland, says that before 1153 King David I. introduced the Knights of the Temple into Scotland and established them at the Temple on the Southesk, and was greatly attached to them.

Little is known of the history of the Knights Templars from the time of Alexander II. until the 14th century, except that all their privileges (which we have omitted) were continued to them by succeeding kings, who directed their piety and their bounties toward the religious Orders. The possessions of the Fraternity were so extensive that their lands were scattered 'over the whole kingdom of Scotland toward England and over the whole kingdom to the Orchardis."

At the time of the persecution of the Order in other countries correspondently the Templars of Scotland suffered spoliation, but it is to be remarked, to the credit of the people of Scotland, that there is no account of any single member having suffered any personal torture. Their estates were transferred to their rivals the Hospitalers, and like their brethren in England a number very probably entered into that Order.

The Knights of St. John had also been introduced by David I. into Scotland, and Alexander II. had granted a charter to them soon after that granted to the Knights Templars. Their first Preceptory was at Torphicen, in West Lothian, which continued to be their principal residence, and after the acquisitions of the lands of the Templars and some others theIr possessions came to be immense and the date of the Reformation.

A union was effected, at the beginning of the reign of James IV., between the Knights Templars and the Knights of St. John, and their lands were consolidated. The precise period of this union is nor known. but the fact is established by the charter of King James, October 19, 1488, confirming the grants of lands made by his predecessors to these two Orders in Latin, which is thus translated: "To God and the Holy Hospitalers of Jerusalem and to their brethren of the Soldiers of the Temple of Solomon." Both Orders were then united and placed under the charge of the Preceptor of St. John, and there can be no doubt that such an arrangement was political and natural.

It was in Scotland alone that the Knights Templars owned independent property. The ban against them being yet in force throughout Europe, necessarily contracted their sphere of action.

The Knights of the Hospital, however, being entirely free of any obstruction, had great wealth and influence, and stood high in the favor of the sovereigns of Europe. Both Orders were represented by the Preceptor of St. John in the Parliament of Scotland, and the union continued down to the Reformation.

From the era of the Reformation these two Orders, combined, appear in Scotland only as a Masonic body; but the late Mr. Deucher averred that so early as 1590 a few of the brethren had become mingled with the Architectural Fraternity, and that a Lodge at Stirling, patronized by King Jamest had a Chapter of Templars attached to it, who were termed cross-legged Masons, and whose initiatory ceremonies were performed, not in a room, but in the old Abbey, the ruins of which are still to be seen in the neighborhood.

The first authentic notice we can find on the subject is in M. Thory's excellent Chronology of Masonry, wherein it is recorded that about 1728 Sir John Mitchell Ramsay, the well-known author of Cyrus, appeared in London with a system of Scottish Masonry, up to that date perfectly unknown in the Metropolis, tracing its origin from the Crusades, and consisting of three degrees, the Ecossais, the Novice, and the Knight Templar. For further notice of this subject we refer our readers to Chapter XXIX., ante.

During the 18th century the Scottish Order can be but faintly traced; though Mr. Deucher had, in 1836, the assurance of well-in formed Masons that, thirty or forty years previously, they knew old men who had been members of it for sixty years, and it had sunk so low at the time of the French Revolution that the sentence which the Grand Lodge of Scotland fulminated in 1792 against all degrees of Masonry except those of St. John, was expected to put a period to its existence. Soon after this, however, some active individuals revived it, and with the view to obtaining documentary authority for their chapters, as well as avoiding any infringement of the Statutes then recently enacted against secret societies, adopted the precaution of accepting Charters of Constitution from a body of Masonic Templars, named the Early Grand

Encampment, in Dublin, of whose origin we can find no account, and whose legitimacy, to say the least, was quite as questionable as their own. Several charters of this description were granted to different Encampments of Templars in Scotland about the beginning of the present century; but these bodies maintained little concert or intercourse with each other, and certainly were not esteemed in the country. Affairs were in this state when, about 1808, Mr. Alexander Deucher was elected Commander or Chief of the Edinburgh Encampment of Templars; and his brother, Major David Deucher, along with other Officers of the Royal Regiment, was initiated into the Order. A General Convocation of all the Templars of Scotland, by representatives, having taken place in Edinburgh, they unanimously resolved to discard the Irish Charters, and to rest their claims, as the representatives of the ancient Knights, on the general belief and traditions of the country.

They further determined to entreat the Duke of Kent, the Chief of the Masonic Templars in England, to become the patron protector of the Order in North Britain, offering to submit themselves to his Royal Highness in that capacity and to accept from him a formal Charter of Constitution. The Duke of Kent lost no time in complying with their request, and his Charter erecting them into a Conclave of "Knights of the Holy Temple and Sepulcher, and of St. John of Jerusalem. H.R.D.M. + K.D.S.M." bears date June 19, 1811.[197]

By a provision in it Mr. Deucher, who had been nominated by the brethren, was appointed Grand Master for life. [198]

Mills, Southerland, De Magny, Dumas, Burnes, Gregoire, and others show that the Order of Knights Templars, although suppressed, was never dissolved in France.

The persecution of the Templars in the 14th century does not close the history of the Order; for though the Knights were spoliated, the Order was not annihilated. In truth, the Cavaliers were not guilty, the brotherhood was not suppressed, and, startling as is the assertion, there has been a succession of Knights Templars from the 12th century even down to these days; the chain of transmission is perfect in all its links. James de Molay, the Grand Master, at the time of the persecution, anticipating his own martyrdom, appointed, as his successor in power and dignity, Johannes Marcus Larmenius of Jerusalem, and from time to time to the present there has been a regular, uninterrupted line of Grand Masters. The Charter of transmission, with the signatures of the various chiefs of the Temple, is preserved at Paris, with the ancient

---

[197] "Addison," p. 548.
[198] Ibid., p 549

statutes of the Order, the rituals, the records, the seals, the standards, and the early memorials of the early Templars.[199]

The brotherhood has been headed by the bravest Cavaliers in France; by men who, jealous of the dignities of knighthood, would admit no corruption, no base copies of the Orders of Chivalry, and who thought that the shield of their nobility was enriched by the impress of theTemplars' Red Cross. Bertrand du Guesclin was the Grand Master from 1357 till his death, 1380, and he was the only French commander who prevailed over the Chivalry of Edward III. of England. From 1478 to 1497 we may mark Robert Lenoncourt, a Cavalier of one of the most ancient and valiant families of Lorraine. Philippe Chabot, a renowned Captain in the reign of Francis I., wielded the staff of power from 1516 to 1543. The illustrious family of Montmorency appears as Knights Templars, and Henry, the first Duke, was chief of the Order from 1574 to 1614. At the close of the 17th century, James Henry de Duras, a Marshal of France, the nephew of Turenne, and one of the most skillful of the soldiers of Louis XIV., was Grand Master. From 1724 to 1776, three princes of the Bourbon family were Grand Masters, viz.: Louis Augustus, Duke of Maine, 1724-1737; Louis Henry Bourbon Conde, 1737-1741; and Louis Francis Bourbon Conde, 1741-1746. Louis Hercules Timoleon, Duke de Cosse Brissac, accepted the office of Grand Master in 1776 and remained in office until he died in the cause of royalty at the commencement of the French Revolution. The Grand Master at that time was Bernardus Fabre Palaprat. There are Colleges in England and in many of the chief cities in Europe.[200]

Grand Master Bernard Raymond died in 1838; he was succeeded in the regency of the Order by Admiral Sir William Sidney Smith, until his death in 1840. At that time, among the subjects of Great Britain who were office-bearers were the names of the Duke of Sussex, Grand Prior of England; the Duke of Leinster, Grand Prior of Ireland; the Earl of Durham, Grand Prior of Scotland; the Chevalier Burnes (Grand Master of Scottish Freemasons in India), Grand Preceptor of Southern Asia; the Chevalier Tennyson D'Eyncourt, Grand Prior of Italy; General George Wright, Grand Prior of India, etc. Among the functionaries of France were Prince Alexander de Wirtemberg, Dukes de Choiseul and Montmorency, and Counts Le Peletier, D'Aunay, De Lanjuinais, De Brack, De Chabrillan, De Magny, De Dienne, and others equally distinguished.[201] In consequence of the political changes in

---

[199] "Addison." p. 550.
[200] "Addison," p. 251.
[201] Ibid., p. 551.

France, an institution so much identified with ancient nobility and tradition naturally fell into abeyance; it, however, in 1874, is said by McCoy's Addison to number about thirty British Ministers, most of whom are in the Public Service in India, received by the Grand Preceptor of Southern Asia, under legative powers from the Grand Master, Bernard Raymond, sanctioned by the Duke of Sussex, without whose approval no British subject was admissible.[202]

The history of Sir William Sidney Smith's connection with the Order of KnightsTemplars is well substantiated, and is brought very near to our period, as will appear in the following extracts from John Barrow's Life and Correspondence of Admiral Sir W. Sidney Smith.[203]

From the end of 1815, Sir Sidney mostly made his residence in Paris, France. It was here, in fact, that he carried on the vast correspondence with the Knights Liberators, and also with another Order of Knighthood, of which he became a member, invested at the fountain-head, in a curious and romantic manner.

The following is Sir Sidney's own account of his obtaining this cross, which he wore during his life, and which is now in possession of the Convent of the Order of St. John of Jerusalem at Paris. The paper is in Sir Sidney's own handwriting, but has no address, though, judging by the appeal made on a point of conscience and religion, it was probably meant for the English Bishop resident in Paris at that time, viz., Dr. Luscomb.

Sir Sidney wrote a letter to a friend from Paris, dated October 28, 1839, saying:

"I am most anxious to leave Paris before another insurrection, though as Regent of the 'Order of the Orient' and the 'Milice du Temple,' denominated the Order of the Temple, I must always have a pied a terre (foot of ground) here, a residence magistral.

"In the exercise of my duty, representing the King in his dignity, as his Minister Plenipotentiary at the Ottoman Porte, and being decorated by Sultan Selim with his imperial Aigrette, and with a commission to command his forces by sea and land, on the coast of Syria and Egypt, consequently representing that Sovereign in his authority, in the absence of the Grand Vizier (his highness being the one to exert it, when present), and as the Captain Pasha was expressly put personally under my Orders, I thought it my duty to land at Cyprus, for the purpose of restoring subordination and the hierarchy of authority, on a sudden emergency, which arose from the bursting out of an insurrection

---

[202] Ibid., p. 552.
[203] London, 1848.

of Janissaries, Arnants, and Albanians, in the year 1799, after the raising of the siege of Acre.

"On visiting the Venerable Greek Archbishop afterward at the capital (Nicosia), to prevent him from disgracing himself by a visit to me, which I understood was his intention, his grace met me outside the city gates. I, of course, dismounted to receive his welcome and animated harangue, at the termination of which he embraced me paternally, and at the same moment adroitly threw the Templar's cross, which he wore as an Episcopal decoration on his breast, around file neck of his English guest, saying, 'This belonged to an Englishman formerly, and I now restore it. It belonged to Sr. Richard (Agio Ricardo), surnamed "Coeur-de-Lion," who left it in this church at his departure, and it has been preserved in our treasury ever since. Eighteen archbishops, my predecessors, have signed the receipt thereof, in succession. I now make it over to you, in token of our gratitude for saving all our lives, the archbishops ecclesiastics, laymen, citizens, and peasantry."

CONCLUSION.

In all writings, sketches, and theses upon any particularly important subject, it is eminently proper to draw conclusions there upon, that those who read may learn and duly appreciate the value of such examinations upon the subject-matter under consideration.

The old philosophers suggested that upon all valuable questions, or propositions, there should be, first, the affirmation; second, the denial; third, the discussion; fourth, the conclusion. We have, in preceding pages, endeavored, by quotations and deductions from the most approved authors, shown, we think, the history of the Organization, the progress, triumphal success, decline, and final destruction of the most glorious, chivalnc, and magnanimous Order of Knights which the world has ever witnessed[204]

In the day of their successful and triumphant battles of Truth against Error over their Saracen and Turkish opponents, they excited the wonder of their friends in the West and the highest admiration of their enemies. They were enthused by their zeal for the cause of Christ, as were also the Crusaders of every rank who suffered every inconvenience, toil, dangers, from their human foes, and the more insidious foes found in the climatic conditions of the countries through which they passed and were more than decimated by the peculiar local circumstances which accompanied and surrounded them, in their journeys, marches, and camping-grounds; yet they faltered not, nor ever ceased in their persistent efforts, which many times were so eminently successful in repelling all attacks, and in the forward movements to conquer and possess the strongholds of the Infidels. In the First Crusade, after untold misfortunes due to the special conditions of the country, diseases of the climate, and attacks of their foes, they, with a mere handful compared with the vast numbers with which they crossed the Hellespont, at length conquered and took Jerusalem, and finally, with the aid of the Templars and Hospitalers, succeeded in extending the Kingdom of Jerusalem over the whole country of Palestine. Their success, as is often the case in human affairs, caused their rulers to forget the circumstances of the "Crusade," and, exalting themselves above the great CAUSE for which they should be fighting, strove for dominion and empire for themselves each individual claiming rank and power, for human glory, and not for Christ's sake. Human history from time immemorial teaches the scholar this great lesson, that all things are by the direction of a Divine

---

[204] "Addison," p. 554

Providence. This is the true philosophy of all history; without that Providence we are driven to the evident conclusion of Fatalism of the Mohammedan, or Fortuity of the Infidel. These three conditions are alone possible. Which shall we choose? The vast majority of the world in all ages have chosen and acted under the "Faith" in a "Divinity above who shapes our ends, rough hew them as we may."

Does history repeat itself? What shall we say of the events at the close of the 19th century, as to the war between Spain and the Young giant of the West?" Can we perceive any parallel between the 11th, 12th, and 13th century Crusades and that of the 19th? Both have been impelled by a force beyond human conception. History has told us why the Old Crusades were undertaken - viz., for the Salvation, the conservation of the doctrines of Christ, which was for Humanity's sake. can any deny that the United States, almost unanimously, entered into the War for " Humanity's" sake and not for conquest or aggrandizement ?

Our limits will not admit of the many extracts from various writers, in continuation of the history of the Knight Templar Order in France, England, Scotland, and Ireland, which could be made to show that, up to the close of the 18th century, and some years in the present century, the Order was in a measure intact in Europe, and consequently, when Masonry was introduced into the United States, very many of the brethren belonged to the Templar Order, and from them we may surmise that the several encampments which are mentioned in the history of Masonry in this country can trace their origin. This particular matter will engage our attention when we write the history of the Knights Templars in the United States in the appropriate chapter.

LIST OF GRAND MASTERS OF KNIGHTS TEMPLARS[205]

1. Hugho de Payens, 1118.
2. Robert de Craon, 1136.
3. Everard des Barres or Barri, 1146.
4. Bernard de Tremelay, 1151.
5. Bertrand de Blanquefort, 1154.
6. Philip of Naplous (Native), 1167 to 1170.
7. Odo de St. Amand, 1170.

---

[205] The Templars, with Louis IX of France, took Damietta in 1249. Louis was taken captive; afterward released by paying ransom. In 1250, in a battle near the Tanitic branch of the Nile, the Grand Master lost one eye, but was enabled to cut his way through the lines of the enemy with only two knights; however soon after, on the first Friday in Lent, he lost the other eye and was killed.

8. Arnold de Torroge or de Troy, 1180, Chief Preceptor; while St. Amand was a prisoner the Chief Preceptor died at Verona, 1185.
9. Gerard de Riderfort, 1185. Taken captive near Brook Kishon, 1187; surrendered October 2, 1187; seat removed to ancient Tyre, successfully defended against Saladin; Grand Master released, 1188; eleven cities given up as a ransom; Grand Master fell at siege of Acre, October 4, 1189.
10. Brother Walter, 1189. During four years of siege of Acre, 100,000 Christians perished, among them Patriarch Heraclius. Third Crusade, preached by William, Archbishop of Tyre, Richard Coeur de Lion, and Philip Augustus, King of France, arrived in Palestine, 1191.
11. Robert de Sable or Sabloil, 1191. Great battle of Ramlah was gained and city of Gaza taken by Templars, 1191. About this time three encampments were established in England, at Bristol, Bath, and York.[206] Those in Bath and York were in existence in the early part of the present century, the one in Bristol in active operation in 1855. King Richard, in the guise of a Templar, left Palestine October 25, 1192. Bro. Richard John Bridges was the Eminent Commander of this Ancient and Venerable body, probably the oldest Encampment of Knights Templars in the world.
12. Gilbert Horal, or Erail, 1195. Many strong fortifications were built; most celebrated was Pilgrims' Castle, which would hold a garrison of four thousand men.
13. Philip Duplesseis, 1201. King John of England frequently resided at the Temple in London. He was there when he resigned England and Ireland "to his lord Pope Innocent the Third" and signed the "Magna Charta."
14. William de Charters became Grand Master. The Grand Master died at siege of Damietta, 1218.
15. Peter de Montague, Grand Preceptor of Spain, the Veteran Warrior, 1218. Damietta was surrendered to the Infidels, together with the prisoners of Tyre and Acre, and he obtained in return "the wood of the true Cross" and the prisoners at Cairo and Damascus; and the Sultan granted a truce for eight years.
16. Herrnan de Perigord, 1236. In this time a treaty was made with the Infidels to surrender again the Holy City to the Christians, 1242. In 1243 the Templars rebuilt the "formidable Castle of Saphet." In a great battle in 1243, near Gaza, with the Carizmians, a pastoral tribe of Tartars, which continued two days, the Grand Master was slain. Thirty-

---

[206] Letter of D.W. Nash, Secretary General H. E. for England and Wales, September 29, 1853. MS.

three Templars and twenty-six Hospitalers alone escaped. Pope Innocent IV. ordered a new crusade to be preached, but very little assistance was obtained 17. William de Sonnac, "A Veteran Warrior," 1245. The brethren in the Western Preceptories were summoned to Palestine The Carizmians, in 1247, were annihilated. The Grand Master presented to Henry III. "a magnificent crystal vase, containing a portion of the blood of our Lord Jesus Christ"
18. Reginald de Vichier, Grand Marshal, 1152. King Louis, after his release from captivity, aided in placing Palestine in a defensible condition.
19. Thomas Berard, 1256. The country was in a miserable condition.
The Bibars or Benocdar, the Sultan of Egypt, with 30,000 cavalry, had invaded Palestine (1262) The Infidels took all the strongholds with the exception of Pilgrims' Castle and Acre. When the Castle of Saphet capitulated (1266), Benocdar put the whole garrison to death, because of their refusal to become Mahomedans. Edward, afterward Edward I. of England, drove the enemy back to Egypt; a truce lasting ten years was made.
20. William de Beaujea was elected, May 13, 1273. Lists of Strict Observance give Robert , who died in 1277, and then Pierre de Beaujeu.

This closed the Seventh and last Crusade An effort was made by the Pope to raise another crusade; having, however, died in the meantime, with him all hopes of assistance from Europe died also.

In 1291 the city of Tripoli and fortress of Margat were taken by the Infidels, and very soon thereafter, in the third year from recommencement of hostilities, Acre and the Pilgrims' Castle were all that were left to the Christians.[207]

Acre was besieged on April 4th of the same year by Sultan Kahlil with 60,000 horse and 140,000 foot, and Acre had only 12,000 men under the Grand Master, "exclusive of the forces of the Templars and Hospitalers, with 500 foot soldiers and 200 cavalry commanded by the King of Cyprus."

Addison says: "so the garrison, which plainly saw they could not hold out long without a commander that was skilled in the art of war, elected Brother Peter Beauieu, Grand Master of the Templars, a general of great experience, who had grown old in the command of armies, to be Governor of the place Necessity of State, the truest interpreter of merit, made them offer the command to him and it was done even with the consent of the King of Cyprus himself, who on a juncture of such

---

[207] Gourdin. Hist. Sketch. p. 12.

importance and so full of danger was well contented to forget the title, which he had always affected, of King of Jerusalem."[208]

Beaujeu was killed on May 18, 1291, and the three hundred knights who had fought their way to the Temple appointed Theobald de Gaudini Grand Master (Addison fails to give his first name; the Manual calls him Theobaldus Gaudinius). [209]

The Grand Master, however, and a few companions, with the treasure of the Order and ornaments of the Churchs May 19th, at night, made their escape through a secret postern, and safely reached Cyprus.[210]

The rest of the Knights were buried beneath the ruins of "the Tower of the Master" when it fell, victims to their resolution to protect, at all hazards, the Christian women from insult and violation by the ruthless Infidels, and to their jealous devotion to the religion of the Cross. The power of the Latin Church in the East was extinguished by the destruction of the city of Acre.

Limisso, in Cyprus, became the chief seat of the Order. However, from Vertot, we learn that an anonymous writer says that Knight Roger succeeded Beaujeu as Grand Master, and that he established the seat of the Order at Ninove? a town of Cyprus, which belonged to the Order. He also says that Jean de Gaudin succeeded Brother Roger.[211]

James de Molay, Preceptor of England, was elected Grand Master by a general Chapter of the Order in 1297. He is thus described by an enemy of the Order, a French writer: "Molay was the younger brother of one of the most distinguished houses of the 'Comte' of Burgundy.

His elder brother possessed, in that country, a large property, and had a higher position. From his youth, Molay had been a member of the Order; in it he had acquired a great reputation. He had passed through all the degrees, and had become a Grand Prior.

He was a lord of true merit; brave, of high intellect, of a mild and amiable character; his morals were pure, and his character without a

---

[208] Vertot, vol. i., p. 171, says: "The Sultan tempted the Grand Master with offers of immense sums, to which the Templar made no answer but by showing a just indignation at the Sultan's fancying him capable of listening to him."
[209] "Manual," p. 252, and Lists of Strict Observances.
[210] "Addison " p. 395. Vertot (vol. i., p. 173) says: "Out of five hundred Templars that behaved themselves so bravely in the defense of Acre, only two escaped, who, getting into a boat, landed happily on the coast of Cyprus."
[211] Vertot, vol. i., p. 174. "Histoire de lab. de l'ord. des Templiers," p. 5. In another place he calls Gaudin, Monaoui de Gaudin. p. 21.

reproach. He had always appeared with distinction at the Court of France, and had been fortunate enough to merit the favor of the King, who, in 1297, had selected him to hold, at the baptismal font, M. Robert, his fourth son. He was still held in such high esteem, when all the lords of the Court, who were yet ignorant of the hatred of the King. and his fatal determination against the Order, concerning which he preserved the most profound secrecy, aided in the election of Molay, even believing that they were affording a pleasure to that prince."

An endeavor was made by the Grand Master to recover Palestine in 1302, which the Sultan of Egypt defeated, with a loss to the Knights of one hundred and twenty. This closed the efforts for the recovery of the Holy Land, and the usefulness of the Knightly Orders as military organizations ceased. No longer did the people of the several nations in Europe manifest any zeal in the Crusades.

The Templars, by many grants, from time to time, had become possessed of large estates and they were very rich, and consequently very powerful. Instead of Christendom having now any use for these military Orders, who were so prosperous from the donations of the lords and princes, they were jealous of them.

The clergy were also in constant dispute with them, and the Pope had been compelled to intervene. By some means Philip had become manifestly displeased with the Templars, and it is asserted that his need of money, and his own avarice, prompted him to suppress the Order, that he might enjoy the benefits to be derived from the confiscation of their riches and estate.

GRAND MASTERS OF THE ORDER OF ST. JOHN, RHODES, AND MALTA, A.D. 1099 TO 1799.

1. Gerard Tunc, installed, 1099; died, 1118.
2. Raymond du Puys, installed, 1118, died, 1160 3. Otteger Balben, installed, January, 1160.
4. Arnaud de Comps, installed, 1162.
5. Gilbert d'Ossaly (De Sailly), installed, 1163; drowned 1170.
6. Castus, installed, 1170 7. Joubert (De Osbert), installed, 1175; died, 1177 8. Du Moulin (Roger de Moulin), installed, 1177; killed, May 1, 1187 9. N. Gardiner, installed, 1187; died at Askalon, 1187.
10. Godfrey de Duison, installed, 1192; died, 1201.
11. Alphonsos installed, 1202; abdicated.
12. Godfrey Lo Rath, installed, 1205; died, 1208.
13. Gawen de Montacute, installed, 1208; died, 1231.

14. Bernard de Texis, installed, 1231.
15. Girino, installed, 1232; died, 1236.
16. Bertrand de Comps, installed, 1236; slain in battle, 1241 17. Peter de Villebride, installed, 1241; slain in battle, 1243 18. William de Chateau-neuf. installed, 1243; died, 1259, 19. Hugh de Revel, installed, 1259; died, 1278 20. Nicholas de Lorgne, installed, 1278, died broken-hearted, 1289.
21. John de Villiers, installed, 1289; died, 1297 22. Otho de Pins, installed, 1298 23. William Villaret, installed, 1300; died, 1306 24. Fulk de Villaret, installed, 1307; deposed, 1319 25. Helion de Villannoba, installed, 1319; died, 1346 26. Deodate de Gozon, installed, 1346; died, December, 1353 27. Peter de Cornillan, installed, 1354; died, 1355 28. Roger de Pins, installed, 1355 29. Raymond de Berenger, installed, 1365; died, 1374.
30. Robert de Julliac, installed, 1374; died, 1377 31. Heredia Castellan d'Emposta, installed, 1377 32. Richard Caraccioio, installed, 1383; died, 1395 33. Philip de Naillac, installed, 1396; died, June, 1421 34. Antony Fluvian, installed, 1421; died, October 26, 1437.
35. John de Lastic, installed, 1437; died, May 19, 1454 36. James de Milly, installed, 1454; died, August 17, 1461 37. Peter Raymond Zacosta, installed, 1461; died February 14, 1467 38. John Orsini, installed, 1467; died, 1476 39. Peter D'Aubusson, installed, 1476; died, June 30, 1503 40. Almeric Amboise, installed, 1503; died, November 8, 1512.
41. Guido de Blanchefort, installed, 1512; died, 1512 42. Fabricius Carretto, installed, 1512; died, January, 1521.
43. Philip Villers de l'Isle Adam, installed, 1521; died, August 22, 1534 44. A. del Ponte, installed, 1534; died, November, 1535 45. Desiderio di s. Jalla, installed, 1536; died, September 26, 1536.
46. Homedez, installed, 1536; died, September 6, 1553 47. Claudius de la Sengle; installed, 1553, died, August, 1557 48. John de Valetta, installed, 1557; died, August 21, 1568 49. Peter del Moate, installed; 1568; died, January 20, 1572.
50. Cassiere, installed, 1572 51. Verdale, died, 1595 52. Garzes, installed, 1595; died, February, 1601 53. Wignacourt, installed, 1601; died, 1622 54. Vasconcellos, installed, 1622 55. De Paul, installed, 1622; died, 1636 56. Paul de Lascaris Castellar, installed, 1636; died August 14, 1657 57. Redin, installed, 1657; died, February 6, 1660 58. Clermont de Chattes Gessan, installed, 1660; died, June 2, 1660 59. Raphael Cotoner, installed, 1660; died, 1663 60. Nicholas Cotoner, installed, 1663; died, April 29, 1680 61. Caraffa, installed, 1680.

62. Wignacourt, installed, 1690; died, September 4, 1697.
63. Perrellas, installed, 1697; died, February, 1720.
64. Zondadari, installed, 1720; died, 1722.
65. Anthony Manoel de Vilhenas installed 1722; died, 1742.
66. Pinto de Fonseca, installed, 1742.
67. Ximenes, installed, 1773; died, November, 1776 68. Rohan, installed, 1776, died, 1797.
69. Hompesch, installed, 1797.

LIST OF RULERS OF THE LATIN KINGDOM OF PALESTINE, A.D. 1099 - 1205

I. Godfrey de Bouillon, crowned, 1099; died, July 11, 1100 II. Baldwin I., crowned, 1101; died, 1118.
III. Baldwin II., crowned, 1118; died, 1131.
IV. Foulques (Fulk), Count Anjou, crowned, 1131, died, 1144.
V. Baldwin III., crowned, 1144, died, 1162.
VI. Almeric, crowned, February 18, 1162; died, 1174.
VII. Baldwin IV., crowned, abdicated, 1184.
VIII. Baldwin V., crowned, 1184; died, 1186.
IX. Sibylla and her husband, Guy de Lusignan, crowned 1186; Sibylla died, 1192; Guy abdicated, 1192.
X. Henry, Count of Champagne, crowned, 1192, killed by accident, 1194.
XI. Amauri, King of Cyprus, crowned, 1194; died, 1205
The following lists of Popes of Romey A.D. 1088 to A.D. 1316, will be found; useful for reference. The authority is Haydn's Dictionary of Dates.
Urban II., 1088. Promoted the First Crusade from 1096-1099.
Pascal II., 1099. Council of Clermont, 1095 Gelasius II., 1118.
Calixtus II., 1119.
Honorius II., 1125.
Innocent II., 1130.
Celestine II., 1143.
Lucius II., 1144.
Eugenius III., 1145. Promoted the Second Crusade, 1146.
Anastasius IV.,1153.
Adrian IV., 1154.
Alexander III., 1159.
Lucius III., 1181.
Urban III., 1185.
Gregory VIII., 1187.
Clement III., 1188. Promoted the Third Crusade, 1188.
Celestine III., 1191. Promoted the Fourth Crusade, 1195-1197.
Innocent III., 1198. Promoted the Fifth Crusade, 1198.
Honorius III., 1216.
Gregory IX., 1227. Promoted the Sixth Crusade.
Celestine IV., 1241.
Innocent IV., 1243. Promoted the Seventh Crusade Alexander IV., I254.

Urban IV., 1261.
Clement IV., 1265. The eighth and last Crusade.[212] Gregory X, 1271.
Innocent V., 1275.
Adrian V, 1276.
Vicedominus, John XXI., Nicholas III., 1277.
Martin IV., 1281 Honorius IV., 1285 Nicholas IV., 1288, Celestine V., Boniface VIII
1294 Benedict XI., 1303.
Clement V., 1305.
John XXII., 1316
As a comment upon the chronological confusion of the times we append from Dr. Barclay's City of at Great King, a second Table of the Crusades:
Crusade I., 1096 - 1099. Capture of Jerusalem.
Crusade II., 1147.
Crusade III., 1189.
Crusade IV., 1202.
Crusade V., 1217.
Crusade VI, 1238.
Crusade VII., 1245.
Crusade VIII. 1270.

Dr. Barclay wisely adds: "The cessation of the Crusades was not produced by any abatement of the love of arms, or of the thirst of glory to the chivalry of Europe. But the union with these martial qualities, of that fanatical enthusiasm which inspired the Christian warriors of the 11th century, had been slowly but almost thoroughly dissolved."

---

[212] After the Seventh Crusade and the surrender of all the places in Syria, there were several expeditions inaugurated, but the seventh was the last crusade.

CHAPTER LII

THE INTRODUCTION OF KNIGHT
TEMPLARISM INTO AMERICA

HAVING given in Chapter LI. a short history or the Knights Templars during the Crusades, and the suppression of that magnanimous and Christian Order by the Church of Rome, aided by its wretched and villanous adherents, the various sovereigns of Europe; and having also shown the remnants of the Order down to recent times, in England and France, it becomes a pleasing task to trace, as nearly as possible, the connection between those noble spirits, who gave their fortunes and their lives for the cause of Christianity against the Infidels and Mohammedans of Asia, and our modern Templars, who do not use the material implements of a carnal warfare, but employ the legitimate symbols of the Knightly Armor, to contend against the world, the flesh, and the devil.

All of our recent writers on the Order of the Temple agree, that there can not be found any direct connection between the ancient and present Templar systems; yet, like the sunken rivers found in many parts of the world, where we can trace the waters thereof, after they disappear on one side of a mountain, and discover where these same waters again appear, and proceed onward to the sea; the same flowing spirit which was manifested in the lives of the original Templars, from their origin in the 12th century until they disappeared beneath the obstructions placed in their path by the monarchies of Europe, and the succeeding prejudices of the peoples of each, we can now clearly trace in the Templar rituals of England and the United States the fundamental principles of the ancient Order, of ' Fidelity, Zeal, and Obedience," without those superstitions which always have been the accompaniments of the Priestly Orders of the Romish Church. Those superstitions of the early Templars were abolished by them after the close of the Crusades. The Templars, very soon thereafter having learned the deceptions of priestcraft, failed to pay the required respect and obedience to the hierarchy; and, consequently were antagonized by the Church, and their existence as an Order soon thereafter terminated. The modern Templars pay due allegiance to, and worship, the risen Saviour, in spirit and in truth, with no unmeaning ceremonies.

We learn from hilarious writers thats in the progress of Freemasonry in the American Colonies, somewhere about the latter half of the 18th century, some of fixers of an Irish regiment claimed to be possessed of the Knight Templar Order, and through them, several of our own Masons received the several appendant degrees and the Order of Knight Templar. Patents issued to such Knights, bearing dates as early as 1783, are now extant, notably one from Charleston, South Carolina. Toward the close of that century there appeared several appendant degrees, unknown to earlier times, such as Excellent, Superexcellent, Royal Arch Masons. In some of the New England States these degrees were promulgated and conferred under the charters of Blue Lodges; such as the body in the City of Washington in 1794 - two record books of which the present writer had the honor of discovering among the old papers in the office of the Grand Secretary of the Grand Lodge of the District of Columbia in 1875, which no living Mason in the District could give an account of. This body was called the "Excellent, Superexcellent, Royal Arch Encampment." The first book ran from 1795 to 1799; and then the body closed its labors and divided their funds. The second book was commenced in 1804 when the same body, under the charge of Companion Philip P. Eckles, of Baltimore, resumed its labors and continued until August 21, 1808, when the book ends abruptly after the annual election of officers.

A book was published by Cornpanion Joseph K. Wheeler, of Connecticut, which gave an account of similar bodies, bearing the same title, in the State of Connecticut. From these came the first independent particular Royal Arch Chapters, and from which Thos. Smith Webb and John Hanmer, both from Temple Chapter of Albany, New York, formed the first Grand Chapter of New England and New York in 1798, the history of which will be found under Capitular Masonry (Chapter XLIX.). Also under the chapter relating to the history of the Ancient and Accepted Scottish Rite will be found the writer's views as to what was the reason for these degrees being brought into the Masonry of the Blue Lodge, which we here casually mention as having been part and parcel of the very many appendant degrees communicated to the Brethren who had passed through the curriculum of the twenty-five degrees of the Rite of Perfection, or the Ancient and Accepted Rite of 1762-65, which was, in 1802, at Charleston, enlarged into thirty-three degrees of the Ancient and Accepted Scottish Rite by the Mother Council. It is well known to all well-read and advanced Masonic scholars, that all degrees of Masonry above the third degree, or so-called Master Mason's degree, are the outcome of the "thousand and one degrees" promulgated and sometimes worked in France and Germany from the middle to the close of the 18th century. Until the emperors of the East and West formulated the regular twenty-five degrees of the A.'.A.'.A.'.R.'. in 1762, those various degrees were communicated to all who desired, and were willing to pay for them. Within the regular twenty-five degrees were found the Arch and Templar degrees. Also from two of them the present Red Cross of the Commandery was formulated, which degree has no connection with the primitive Red Cross of " Rome and Constantine," attributed to Constantine the Great.

As to the Templar degree ritual, it is entirely different from the English ritual, as the latter, at the present day, is different from the ritual of the last century at its close and the commencement of the present. We have a certified copy of that ritual made as early as 1801 from an older ritual, which is also a copy from a much older one, which was sent to Brother General Albert Pike, and by him given to the present writer.

The first authentic information that we have of the Templar Order in the United States, is found in the history of St. Andrew's Royal Arch Chapter, which held its first recorded meeting, August 28, 1769, in the Mason's Hall in Boston, under the charter of St.Andrew's Royal Arch Lodge, from the Grand Lodge of Scotland, and the record of that date shows that the degree of Knight Templar was conferred.[213] At that time, and somewhat later, the bodies were termed "Excellent, Superexcellent, Royal Arch Encampments," as before stated. The records of that Chapter show that " Brother William Davis came before the Lodge, begging to have and receive the parts belonging to the Royal Arch Masons, which being read, was received, and he unanimously voted in, and was accordingly made by receiving the four steps, that of Excellent, Superexcellent, Royal Arch, and Knight Templar."[214] In all the histories of the chapters in the New England States, the above titles were first used; as also in the Chapter organized in the City of Washington, under

---

[213] Oration of Companion W. Sewall Gardner, at Centennial of St. Andrew's Chapter, pp. 42, 43.
[214] Oration of Companion W. Sewall Gardner, at Centennial of St. Andrew's Chapter, pp. 42, 43.

the Charter of Federal Lodge. The Red Cross does not appear in any of those old bodies. It has occurred to the writer that after the Templar degree had been dropped by Thos. Smith Webb, when in 1796 the movement had been inaugurated to institute the General Grand Chapter of New England and New York, that some of the Brethren formed a separate body for the Templar Order; and wishing to have the "Red Cross of Constantine" united with the Templar degree, as was the case after the Crusades, they must have mistaken the united degrees of the 15th and 16th for the "Constantine Red Cross." At all events, there is considerable difficulty in accounting for the curious mixture of the Persian Mysteries with the solemn ceremonies of the Christian Order of the Temple. Some writers say that "the records of Kilwinning Lodge, of Ireland, warranted 8, in 1779, show that its Charter was used as the authority for conferring the Royal Arch, Knight Templar, and Rose Croix degrees as early as 1782; but the Red Cross and the Rose Croix are two different degrees, and should not be confounded. It is thought possible that the Irish lodges, having the High Knight Templar degree, communicated it to their American Brothers prior to the Revolution, though there is no evidence of it; on the contrary, the records show that it was conferred first (1769) in America, and afterward in Ireland, 1779."[215]

Bro. Theo. S. Parvin says: " In 1766 there were two Military Lodges stationed at Boston: No. 58 on the register of England, connected with the Fourteenth Regiment, and No. 322, register of Ireland, attached to the Twenty-ninth Regiment. As early as 1762 St. Andrew's Lodge, of Boston, applied to the Grand Lodge of Scotland, from which it had received its Warrant, for leave to confer the Royal Arch degree; and subsequently, under this Warrant, it conferred both the degrees of Royal Arch and Knight Templar.

Even prior to this, as early as 1758, Lodge No. 3, at Philadelphia, working under Warrant as No. 359, granted by the Grand Lodge of All England, also worked as a chapter, and conferred the Royal Arch degree; but, as previously stated we do not find that this Chapter ever conferred the degree of Knight Templar."[216]

Some writers suppose that it was possible "that the degree of Knight Templar was conferred in Military Lodges and perhaps in other Lodges prior to the Revolutionary War."[217]

---

[215] Bro. Fred. Speed in "History of Freemasonry," p. 704.
[216] Bro. Fred. Speed in "History of Freemasonry," p 703
[217] Ibid.

From about the years 1776 to 1783, during the War of Independence, but little attention was given to Masonic organization except in the military lodges After peace had assumed her sway and the country began to thrive in all material interests, and the various Grand Lodges of the separate States were organized, what were termed the "higher degrees," which had been, up to that period always conferred in the lodges under the sanction of their Warrants, became the subject of a more independent character. We find from the various histories of the Royal Arch Chapters, especially in the New England States, that in various towns and cities independent bodies were organized, wherein the degrees of Royal Arch, Excellent, and Superexcellent Masters were attached to the Templar degree; and in some instances, the Red Cross, whatever ritual of that degree may have been used in its conference, was given.

"Few of these organizations have continued until the present time, and still fewer have left any records of the earlier years of their existence. An occasional discovery of an ancient diploma, or other fragment, has revived previously formed opinions as to which is the elder organization; but for the reason that bodies were self- constituted, and consisted of individuals who, being in possession of a degree, called to their assistance the requisite number of other qualified brethren, and gave the degrees to certain chosen spirits and then dissolved never to meet again, it is manifest that there can be no gathering together of the facts; and that beyond an occasional hint, received from the meager record of some old lodge- book, as it may be unearthed from its hiding-place, nothing further is to be looked for. As time passed on, and these occasional gatherings became more frequent, when the number of Templars had increased sufficiently, and more permanent organizations began to be made, out of these emergency bodies grew permanent ones."[218]

There has been much discussion in the various older jurisdictions as to the first duly organized encampment (commandery), and we do not know if the question has been finally settled. From the Proceedlngs of the Grand Encampment of 1883 we learn from the Address of Grand Master Dean that there was "Indisputable evidence that the degrees of Knight of the Red Cross and Knight Templar were

---

[218] Fred. Speed, " History of Freemasonry," etc., pp. 703, 704.

conferred in Charleston, South Carolina, in a regularly organized body as far back as the year 1782."[219]

"The South Carolina Encampment, No. 1, of Knights Templars and the Appendant Orders was established in 1780, as is evident from the old seal in our archives. But it does not appear from what source our ancestors derived their first Charter, all of our records previous to November 7, 1823, having been lost or consumed by fire.

It is clear, however that this encampment was in active operation in 1803, and continued so until long after the date of our oldest record, for, on December 29, 1824, it was "Resolved that, in consideration of the long and faithful services of our Most Eminent Feast Commanders Francis Sylvester Curtis, who regularly paid his arrears to this Encampment for more than twenty years, he is considered a life-member of this Encampment, and that his life- membership take date from November, 1823."[220] In artist of various Masonic degrees," in Cole's Ahiman Rezon, extracted from a publication in 1816, the Knight of the Red Cross is termed the ninth degree, the Knight of Red Cross is termed the ninth degree, the Knight of Malta the tenth, and the Knight Templar the thirteenth, and they are said to be conferred in the Sublime Grand Lodges in Charleston, S.C., in the City of New York, and in Newport, R.I.[221] on November 7, 1823, that encampment, which was then regularly working at Sir Knight Roche's Asylum, under the command of the M.E. Sir Moses Holbrook, M.D., Grand Commander, received "the authority from the G.G.E." to work. At the following meeting (November 15th) Moses Holbrook was reselected to the office which he then held John Barker was elected an honorary member, January 16, 1824. It was, at this time, the practice to introduce the candidates separately in both degrees. On January 18, 1824, James Eyland was created a Templar. The encampment met January 30, 1824, at Sir Knight H.G. Street's Asylum, and the meetings, which had hitherto taken place on every Friday evening, were changed, February 15, 1824, to the last Wednesday in each month, and the last Wednesday in November was fixed for the annual election. March 31, 1824, SirJohn

---

[219] Proceedings of the Grand Encampment of the United States, 1883, p. 59, Grand Master Dean's Address.
[220] Gourdin (MS. Records of South Carolina Encampment, No. 1), pp.29, 30.
[221] "Freemason's Library," p. 317.

Barker was voted to be recommended to be Grand Visitor for the Southern States.[222]

June 24, 1824, M.E. and M.W. Henry Fowle, Deputy General Grand Master of the G. G. Encampment of the United States of America, granted a Charter at Boston (S. C.), countersigned by John G. Loring, G. G. Recorder, to Benjamin Thomas Elmore, and eleven others, to form, open, and hold Columbia Encampment, No. 2. Brother Elmore was appointed the first Grand Commander, E. H. Maxey, Generalissimo, and John Bryce, Captain General. The Charter is in the Archives of Richland Lodge, No. 39, A.'. F.'. M.'. at Columbia, S. C., with some "rough sketches of their meetings," which were held in the hall of that lodge. [223]

The number of members increased to thirty or more, their meetings continued about four years, and from some cause ceased to exist. [224]There was at that time no Grand Encampment in South Carolina, as we find from the following:

"February 23d, 1825, the Encampment was informed that the three first officers had, in accordance with a previous resolution giving them discretionary power in the matter, recommended Georgetown Encampment to the G. G. Encampment for a charter." [225]

As an interesting incident in the history of this encampment, we make the following extract:

---

[222] MS. Records of South Carolina Encampment, No. 1.
[223] Gourdin, p. 30.
[224] Ibid.
[225] Ibid., p 31

"LA FAYETTE.

"The members of South Carolina Encampment, No. 1, were summoned to meet at Sir H.G. Street's, on the 16th of March, 1825, to wait on General La Fayette agreeably to a previous arrangement with him. The following Officers and Members attended precisely at half-past 2 o'clock."[226]

In consequence of a gap in the minutes from this time until January 26, 1827, no further information could be obtained concerning this very interesting occasion.

September 18, 1826, the Grand Encampment of the State of South Carolina was represented in the G. G. Encampment at New York by Sir John Barker, proxy for M. E. Moses Holbrook, Grand Master, and Sir William H. Jones, proxy for the M. E. Sir William E. Lathrop, G. Capt. Gen'ls, and the Committee, to whom were "referred the proceedings of the Officers of the G. G. Encampment since the last Meeting" (September 16, 1819), reported. "That these have been established, with the approbation of the G. G. Officers, Grand Encampments in the following States; to wit: New Hampshire, Vermont, Virginia, North Carolina, South Carolina, and Georgia."[227]

During the year 1819, Beaufort Encampment of South Carolina, at Beaufort, was established, which continued about four or five years. The records were burned up.[228]

Jos. M'Cosh, who was afterward an Ins. Genl. of the thirty-third degree, resigned November 28, 1827. He was the Recorder, November 7, 1823. During the year 1828, Sir James Eyland was Grand Commander. Many resignations took place.

In 1829, Sir James Eyland, G. Master, represented the Grand Commandery in the G.G. Encampment. He was elected that year G.G. Capt. General, and in 1832 was elected G.G. Generalissimo.[229]

About this time the meetings of the S.C. Encampment were very poorly attended. May 12, 1830, there was not a quorum, nor in October 11, 1830. The encampment was adjourned to the stated meeting of December. The following note appears:

---

[226] MS. Records of South Carolina Encampment, No. 1, Gourdin, p.31.
[227] B. B. French. "The Grand Encampment of Knights Templars, and the Appendant Orders, in the State of South Carolina," was incorporated for fourteen years, by A.A. of 20th December, 1826, viii Stats. p. 350.
[228] J. M. Barker.

[229] B. B. French.

I certify that no quorum ever after assembled. I met one or two only after the above note of an attempted meeting. Sir J. W. Rouse handed me over the books and papers all for me to deliver up to this Encampment, some time in 1832, with a letter of resignation at the same time. The books and papers of Grand Encamp ment of S.C. and all were flooded when Sir John May's workshop was burned. I received the remains in 1840.

(Signed) MOSES HOLBROOK, P. Gr. Commander.

I.W. Rouse died 23 April, 1834 Past Gr. Master of Gr. Encampment of South Carolina. The record of the G.G. Encampment does not show any representation from the G. Encampment of South Carolina subsequent to 1829.[230]

October 14, 1841, seven of the former members of South Carolina Encampment, among them the Grand Commander J. S. Burges, met at Rame's Hall, in Meeting Street, for the purpose of reviving it, after its long nap of eleven years and more.[231]

January 27, 1842, it was Resolved that the degree of Red Cross should be conferred upon Sr. Knight Benjamin Greer, on his paying $5, with the condition of his becoming a member of this encampment, he having received the other degrees before in Europe.[232]

A dispensation was issued to the encampment by Sir Jos. K. Stapleton, D. G. G. Master, May 17, 1843, to continue their labors, the Warrant having been burned up. This dispensation was brought to the notice of the encampment only on October 19, 1843, by Rev. A. Case, the G. Chaplain. In 1844, the G.C., Sir A. Case, represented South Carolina Encampment in the G.G. Encampment, and during this session a charter was ordered to that encampment free of charge, in consequence of the loss by fire of a former one. This charter was reported to the meeting, March 15, 1845, as having been received.

February 9, 1853, Joseph Hunter, P.D.G.M. of Savannah, Gag, was made a K.R.C. and K.T., and in token of respect his fees were returned to him, and he was elected a life member.

In 1853, M.'.E.'. A. G. Mackey represented the encampment in the G.G. Encampment, and was elected G.G. Warden.[233]

---

[230] B. B. French.
[231] MS. Records of South Carolina Encampment, No. 1. The last meeting held was March 9, 1830.
[232] Ibid.
[233] B. B. French.

December 27, 1854, the encampment acted as an escort to the Grand Lodge of South Carolina at the celebration of the Centennial Anniversary of the formation of a Provisional Grand Lodge.[234]

In 1855, South Carolina Encampment was the only one in existence in the State.[235]

Continuing the interesting history of this, one of the oldest organizations of Knights Templars, we refer to the Proceedings of the Grand Encampment of the United States for 1883:

The Grand Master states in his address that "on 8th of December, 1880, I issued a dispensation to South Carolina Commandery, No. 1, to appear in public in full Templar costume on the twenty-ninth day of December, 1880, for the purpose of celebrating the one hundredth anniversary of its organization. I also issued dispensations for a like appearance in public, to join in the celebration to Columbia Commandery, No. 2, Georgia Commandery, No. I, and Palestine Commandery, No. 7." [236]

As the question of when the first encampment in the United States was regularly organized is of great interest, we continue our notice of the introduction of the Templar Order of Knighthood into South Carolina, and show what Brother A. G. Mackey says of it in his History of Freemasonry in South Carolina. [237]He quotes from Gourdin what we have already copied, and then continues: "I have been unable to find any reference in the cotemporary journals of the day to the existence of South Carolina Encampment, No. 1, at that early period. I have, however, been more successful in obtaining indisputable evidence that the degrees of Knight of the Red Cross and Knight Templar were conferred in Charleston, in a regularly organized body as far back as the year 1783, and I have no doubt that the seal with the date 1780, to which Gourdin refers, belonged to that body and afterward came into the possession of South Carolina Encampment.[238]

"The proofs of what I have stated is contained in a small compass but the testimony is irrefutable. I have in my possession a diploma, written in a very neat chirography on parchment, with two seals in wax attached, one in red, of the Royal Arch, and the other in black, of

---

[234] MS. Records of South Carolina Encampment, No. 1.
[235] Gourdin, p. 33.
[236] Proceedings of the Grand Encampment of the United States, 1883, p. 58.
[237] Ibid., p. 58.
[238] Ibid., p. 59

the Knights Templar. The upper part of the diploma contains four devices within four circles, all skillfully executed with the pen. The first device, beginning on the left hand, is a star of seven points, with the ineffable name in the center, and the motto, 'Memento Mori,' the second is an arch on two pillars, the all-seeing eye on the Key-stone, and a sun beneath the arch, and 'Holiness to the Lord' for the motto; the third is the cross and brazen serpent, erected on a bridge, and 'Jesus Salvador Hominum' for the motto; and the fourth is the skull and crossbones, surmounted by a cross, with the motto, 'In hoc signo vinces.' The reference of the three last devices is evidently to the Royal Arch, the Red Cross, and Templar degrees. The first is certainly a symbol of the Lodge of Perfection, and hence, connectedly, they show the dependence of the Order of Templarism in the State at that time upon the Ancient and Accepted Rite." In the Proceedings is a heliotyped copy of the diploma, which is here shown. The original was placed in the possession of the Grand Master, Benjamin Dean, by the son of Bro. A. G. Mackey, the Hon.Edw. Mackey, to be presented, in his name, to the Grand Encampment of the United States. The expense of this and other plates in the volume was paid for by the Grand Master. As a matter of considerable interest, we subjoin further remarks of the Grand Master in connection with the subject.

"On the 6th of May, 1881, Sir Knight W. J. Pollard, because of a conversation with him in Boston, wrote me a long and interesting letter on the history of Freemasonry in South Carolina and Georgia, in which he says: 'I find in Charleston, from the South Carolina Gazette, that at some period, not clearly defined, there was a Lodge established in West Florida called St. Andrew's Lodge, No.40, and that it was moved to Charleston about 1783, and was Chartered as a York Lodge in the city of Charleston July, 1783, by the Grand Lodge of Pennsylvania.'"

"He also called my attention to the recovery by Sir Knight Jennison of valuable papers relating to the Encampment. Sir Knight Jennison also sent me copies of the papers. . . . A careful examination of the old diploma discovered on the Seal the words 'Lodge No. 40' These words and figures were not so prominent as the other legends on the Seal, and seemed to have escaped the attention of Brother Albert G. Mackey.

"A careful examination disclosed the remains of two ribbons, under those in sight, showing that there were originally four seals attached to the diploma; one of these ribbons is quite rotten."

From an address delivered December 10, 1878, before the Grand Lodge of South Carolina by M. W. Wilmot G. De Saussure,

P.G.M. of South Carolina, we quote "that the Warrant for No. 40 was granted to Brethren formerly of St. Andrew's Lodge No. 1, West Florida, and then of Charleston, on the 12th of July, 1783."

Brother Frederick Speed says:

In summing up the evidence, this writer is compelled to regret the conclusions of Fratres Dean and Mackey, that there is "Indisputable evidence that the degrees of Knight of the Red Cross and Knight Templar were conferred in Charleston in a regularly organized body as far back as the year 1783." He then continues: "St. Andrew's Lodge No. 1 was not a Templar body at any time in its history. Like St. Andrew's Lodge of Boston, it was a Master's Lodge and the degrees were conferred, as evidenced from the diploma, under the sanction of its warrant as a Blue Lodge; but it seems to be established beyond a reasonable doubt, by the resolution relating to the membership of Francis Sylvester Curtis, that South Carolina Encampment No. 1 was a regularly organized Templar body as far back as the year 1804, and probably earlier. It was, like all older encampments, self-created, and worked without a charter, until the year 1823, when it was "reopened in conformity with the Constitution" of the General Grand Encampment of the United States, at which time, it appears from the petition - and resolution of the encampment embraced therein -

"That on diligent search being made in the archives, it clearly appears that this encampment was in full operation under the sanction of a warrant of 'Blue' Lodge, No. 40, upwards of thirty years ago, and continued in operation many years subsequent; and has, time out of mind, caused to be made and used a common seal. It also further appears that the said encampment has lain dormant for several years past.

"Resolved, That the M.'. E.'. Sir James C. Winters, together with the Recorder, be authorized to forward the necessary documents to prove the existence of this encampment prior to the year 1816, and obtain the desired recognition.'

Extract from the minutes.
(Signed) JOSEPH McCOSH,
Recorder pro tem.[239]

The question of in "Regularity" here presents itself as to the "Validity" of the Templar organizations as it does as to the "Vailidity" of

---

[239] Grand Encampment Proceedings, 1883, p. 172.

the Capitular degrees, not only in the United States, but originally in Europe.

From the very first organization of the Grand Lodge of England in 1717, all Masons agree that no single individual has any prescriptive right or prerogative to communicate any knowledge of a "Rite" or any part of its ritual, unless so authorized by the "Constitution" under which said ritual is promulgated. The Altar obligations, of all the Rites, provide against any such violation of the "Constitution." In the Section VIII. of the New Regulations of 1738 we find the following as an amendment to the Section VIII.

Of 1723, viz.:

"VIII. Every Brother concerned in Making Masons clandestinely shall not be allowed to visit any Lodge till he has made due submission, even though the Brother so admitted may be allowed.

"None who make a stated Lodge without the Grand-Master's Warrant shall be admitted into regular Lodges, till they make due submission and obtain Grace.

"If any Brethren form a Lodge without leave, and shall irregularly make Brothers, they shall not be admitted into any regular Lodge, no not as Visitors, till they render a good Reason or make due submission.

"Seeing that some extraneous Brothers have been lately made in a clandestine manner; that is, in no regular Lodge, or by any authority or Dispensation from the Grand Master, and upon small and unworthy considerations to the Dishonour of the Craft:

"The Grand Lodge decreed, that no person so made, nor any concerned in making him, shall be a Grand Officer, nor an officer of any particular Lodge; nor shall any such partake of the General Charity, if they should come to want."

We have here the general principles upon which to base a judgment as to all legitimacy of Masonic work. The innocent parties; upon whom Masonic work has been commenced, are to be held blameless, and are to be admitted to fellowship, and those only are to be punished who were guilty of the irregular and clandestine work.

In the matter of the various parties, who without competent authority attempted to confer the degrees of the Commandery upon innocent Brethren, it appears, from all that we can learn from recent writers, that the several degrees of Red Cross, Knight Templar, and Knight of Malta were conferred, whatever may have been the severai rituals, at that early period, and they were assumed to be correct. These germs, however obtained, came in time to be the veritable means for establishing the bodies, by which finally, and however irregularly conducted, the several State Grand Commanderies were organized. We have seen that from these have grown up, in the United States, a system of Masonic Templarism which is the most extensive and influential body of men anywhere in the world, as we shall be able to demonstrate in the conclusion of this sketch.

We have carefully read and pondered over nearly all, if not quite all, the writings of reliable authors who have, as far as possible, culled from authentic documents and every source of legitimate information every item which could add to our knowledge of the introduction of the Templar and appendant orders into the United States; and we must deal with the subject as we have found it. It is barely possible that the fountain was impure at the beginning; but taking the system, as it is at the very close of the 19th century, where else in the world can we find such a body of United Fraters, Masons, distinguished gentlemen, of all the useful professions, arts, sciences, and trades, as compose the Officers, Constituencies, and Members, scattered as they are, in all the States, Territories, cities, towns, and hamlets of this vast country? What is now the true status of Masonic Templary in the United States - with its total membership of 114,540 at the close of 1898?

In the admirable history of the Order by Lieutenant-Colonel W. J. B. MacLeod Moore, he is very persistent in challenging the Masonic Templary of the United States. He says: "I may appear to have frequently indulged in fault-finding with the system of purely Masonic Templary practiced in the United States of America, and am fully alive to the fact that the popularity of the degrees there among its most enlightened members is an argument stronger than all the criticism that can be brought against it; but in order to explain my objections, it was necessary to refer to the glaring discrepancies and inconsistencies existing, which prove the system to be not only false, but a perversion of the principles of the true Templar Order, from which it derives its name - merely an imitation Military Masonic degree - a parody upon the pure doctrines of the Ancient Templars."

Several pages are devoted to his view of these inconsistencies and discrepancies - too lengthy for our columns - and hence must refer our readers to his sketch.[240]

In many things we must, of course, concur with him; but suppose we apply his method of criticism to our Modern Masonry,

---

[240] "History of Masonry and Concordant Orders," p. 742 et seq.

beginning with the early rituals of 1725 by Anderson and Desaguliers, all the way through the various Modifications of Martin Clare, Hutchinson, Dunckerley, and Preston, to the very last formed by the union in 1813 of the Modern and Ancient work of Hemmingway, which isthe present ritual of the United Grand Lodge of England, - and compare all of the various forms with well-known facts as we have them in the sacred writings and history - and where will the ritualism of the three degrees of the Blue Lodge stand? where the ritualism of the Mark degree, where that of the R A. Chapter?

We say, let the question, as to Orthodoxy of American Templarism, settle itself; all in good time; very very few Templars in the United States know anything whatever of this controversy and Where ignorance is bliss, twere folly to be wise

We have among our Members distinguished Clergymen of all our Christian denominations, but we are not aware of a single descendant of Jacob who is a Knight Templar. Our ceremonies all conduce to the idea of a pure Christianity. Let us therefore be content to let matters remain as they are; that each individual Member shall for himself interpret the ceremonies, and apply him self to the consideration of Christianity as his instructions in Christianity have dictated, according to his "FAITH."

It appears from all accounts of the introduction of the Order of Knights Templars into the United States, prior to the period of the War of Independence, that where there was any attempt to confer the Order, the same was mingled with the "Excellent, Superexcellent, and Royal Arch," the Templar degree following the Royal Arch. We have concluded that the Templar Order with appendant degrees of Red Cross, St. John's of Jerusalem, and Knights of Malta, were as legitimately conferred, and by the same authority, as were the degrees now constituting "Capitular" Masonry.

We will endeavor, in our list of Commanderies, which were subsequently organized as such in the different jurisdictions, to give authentically the first efforts to establish the Encampment degrees chronologically, until the firm establishment of State Grand Commanderies (Encampments) and the General Grand Encampment in 1816. We may make some errors, but trust that in the main we shall be found quite accurate in dates. In the preceding pages of this chapter, we have quoted vanous writers as to the workings of the Order in the different States; but there have been vagueness and uncertainty as to the dates given.

M.E. William B. Hubbard, General Grand Master of the General Grand Encampment of the United States, said:

"It is to be regretted that we have no authentic and reliable history of the first formation of the first Encampments, with the governmental rituals, as we now have them. For these, if I may be allowed the expression, are somewhat Americanized. I suppose that we owe the origin of the introduction of Templar Masonry into the United States to a distinguished Sov.'.Ins.'. of the.Scottish Rite."[241]

The first notice of the Templar degree being conferred is found in the history of St. Andrew's Chapter of Boston, and the dates given are August 28th and September 17th, 1769, by the Grand Master of the Grand Lodge of Massachusetts, Wm. Sewall Gardner, in his oration at the centennial celebration of that chapter, September 29th, A. L. 5869.

We will now give the dates referred to in the preceding pages, in Chapters LI. and LII., and the States wherein the Templar degree was conferred.

1769. Massachusetts - authority, Wm. Sewall Gardner.
1780 } 1783 } South Carolina, Patent.
1785. New York, McCoy
1790. Maryland
1793. Pennsylvania, Creigh
1794. District of Columbia Ceased in 1799, renewed in 1804, ceased in 1898
1796. Connecticut
1797. Pennsylvania first Grand Encampment
1802. Pennsylvania
1802. Rhode Island, St. John's Encampment, No. 1.
1812.} 1814.} Pennsylvania
1816. Organization of General Grand Encampment at New York

---

[241] MS. Letter. March 16, 1855 (from Gourdin, p. 29, Note A).

CHAPTER LIII

THE GENERAL GRAND ENCAMPMENT OF KNIGHTS TEMPLARS IN THE UNITED STATES

THE true origin of the Grand Encampment of Knights Templars of the United States is involved in some uncertainty. In the first volume of the "Proceedings" of the Grand Encampment of the United States, from the Preface we learn that from its formation in 1816 the proceedings, and also those of the Second Conclave in 1819, were not printed until 1859; and at that session the Grand Recorders Sir Knight Benj. B. French, presented the following paper:

"I have found it impossible to obtain a single set of the printed proceedings of this Grand Body from its origin. By the aid of our respected and distinguished former General Grand Recorder, Sir Charles Gilman, I succeeded in obtaining two printed copies of the proceedings of 1826, and more or less of these of each year up to 1847. By writing out from the original records the proceedings of 1816 and 1819, I succeeded in making two perfect copies of the proceedings up to and including those of 1856. One of these I sent to our M. E. Grand Master and the other I retained myself. These are, probably, the only perfect copies of our proceedings in existence, except the original written records in the office of the Grand Recorder. I respectfully suggest the propriety of having the proceedings up to and including 1856 reprinted. There are now no copies of the proceedings in my office anterior to 1847; only two of 1847, twenty-six copies of 1850, one hundred and four copies of 1853, and one hundred and thirty copies of 1856.'

In pursuance of instructions given to the General Grand Recorder, " What purport to be the Minutes of the 'Formation of the General Grand Encampment of Knights Templars of the United States,' was printed and distributed among the members of the Grand Body."

The statements published were accepted as authentic, until within very recent years, when great doubts arose as to the correctness of the statements made as to those who constituted the membership of the Convention in 1816.

At the conclave in 1889, Past Grand Master James H. Hopkins presented a paper, showing the result of his examination as to the origin of the General Grand Encampment. This paper was ordered to be printed in the is "Proceedings," and that, in a reprint of the older "Proceedings," the history of the formation should be corrected, in accordance with his statement. The committee, how.

ever, who had charge of the reprint, deemed it advisable to print the formation," as it was first printed, and as it appears in manuscript in the Minute Book of the General Grand Recorders and to publish in the Preface the facts as discovered in the paper referred to. This report was signed by James H. Hopkins, W.P. Innis, and Wm. B. Isaacs, names well known and highly tlonored, as worthy of all credence, by every true and valiant Knight Templar.

We subjoin a few extracts from Knight Hopkins's paper, for a better understanding of the "Formation of the General Grand Encampment." That record states that "at a convention holder at Mason's Stall in the City of New York on the 20th and 21st June, 1816, consisting of Delegates or Knights Companions from eight Councils and Encampments of Knights Templars and Appendant Orders, viz. :[242]

"Boston Encampment, Boston; St. John's Encampment, Providence; Ancient Encampment, New York; Temple Encampment, Albany; Montgomery Encampment, Newport; Darius Council, Portland, the following Constitution was formed, adopted, and ratified."

"Anyone investigating the history of the Order in this country, without any other information than this, would be bound to believe that this official record was entirely accurate and to be accepted as absolute verity. It can scarcely be doubted that those who, in 1859, caused the first 'proceeding' to be disseminated, had implicit faith in the correctness of the statements." . . .

"I have recently had occasion to look more fully and deeply into the facts connected with the early history of the Order in this country, and with the formation of the Grand Encampment, and I submit some of the results of that investigation. None but the weak, or worse, will

---

[242] Proceedings of the General Grand Encampment of the United States, 1891, Prefaces pp 3, 4

hesitate to make a frank admission of error of opinion, when discovered rather than obstinately adhere to a position proved to be untenable."

"The Minutes of the Convention which formed this Grand Encampment, as first published in 1859, are a correct transcript from the manuscript on file in the Office of our Grand Recorder. How or why this entry was made. no living man can tell. That it is wholly inaccurate is perfectly demonstrable.

"The Official Minutes declare that the delegates from eight different Councils and Encampments, therein specified, met in New York on June 20 and 21, 1816 and formed the Grand Encampment.

"I have caused diligent search to be made for the records of the different subordinates mentioned. Some of them can not be found of a date early enough to throw any light on the subject; and of those still preserved there is no mention of any appointment of any delegates for the purpose named, nor any action indicating that the Council or Encampment had any part in the Work. The absence of any positive, affirmative Minute in matter of such importance is strong evidence that no such participation was had. But there exists not only negative proof that the subordinate sent no delegates to the Convention, but direct evidence that they did not.

"The Minutes of the Boston Encampment (Commandery), show that on May 28, 1816, the Treasurer was authorized to lend to the Grand Encampment (Commandery), the money in his hands to pay the expenses of the delegates from said Grand Encampment (Commandery) to the Convention referred to. Saint John's Encampment (Commandery), of Providence, by a vote, declined to make a loan to the Grand Encampment for the same purpose. Here is evidence on the records of two of the Commmanderies that they did not, but that the Grand Commanders of that jurisdiction did, send delegates to the Convention. Of the other Subordinates of Massachusetts and Rhode Island mentioned as participating, the Minutes of the one at Newburyport can not be found; those of Newport and Portland are silent.

"Then we have the positive testimony of the Minutes of the Grand Commandery of Massachusetts and Rhode Island, wherein it appears that on May 15, 1816, three delegates were appointed to confer with delegates from other Grand Encampments (Commanderies) upon the subject of a general Union of all under one head. On June 25, 1816, there is the report of these delegates and the action of the Grand Encampment (Commandery) of Massachusetts and Rhode Island approving of their action and changing the local Constitution so as to bring it into harmony with that of the General Grand Body.

"Although this official record is of no greater weight than that of our Grand Encampment, the corroborating and circumstantial evidence renders it conclusive that our record is wrong and that of Massachusetts and Rhode Island is correct.

"In addition to the Minutes referred to, more conclusive evidence has been discovered amongst the papers of Thomas Smith Webb. These papers were examined by our late Grand Master, W. Sewell Gardner, and by him vouched for as authentic and in Webb's handwriting. They consist of the Credentials of the delegates appointed by the Grand Bodies of Massachusetts and Rhode Island, New York and Pennsylvania, to represent them at a Convention in Philadelphia, a Minute of adjournment to New York with a copy of the Constitution there adopted.

"The Encampments (Commanderies) of New York which are reported to have had representatives in the Convention which formed this Grand Encampment were Ancient Encampment, New York; Temple Encampment, Albany; Montgomery Encampment, Stillwater.

"None of the early records of these bodies can be found, and the history of two of them is mainly traditional. It is quite certain, however, that neither of them belonged to the Grand Commandery of New York in 1816.

The truth of history requires of us to mention some things which may prove of interest, yet it will be found not to be very agreeable; yet like very much of the Ancient history of Masonry in all its branches, we will find great irregularities, according to our present ideas of how Masonic bodies should be organized.

"In 1802, Boston Encampment was organized by ten Knights of the Red Cross without a Warrant from any competent power.

"In the same year St. John's Encampment, of Providence, was formed without authority from any source by six Sir Knights.

"Darius Council of Portland was organized by three Knights of the Red Cross in 1805, when after admitting two more members, they applied to Massachusetts for recognition."

In 1795 at Newburyport an Encampment was organized without any authority. In Newport, several Royal Arch Masons deputed Companion Shaw to visit New York, where the Orders of Knighthood with other degrees were conferred upon him. The Consistory there gave him a Warrant authorizing him to confer the Orders. Joseph Cerneau presided over the Consistory which he had organized in 1807, without any authority whatever. The only authority ever produced to show that he was more than a Master Mason is the following well- authenticated patent from Mathew Dupotet, which, it will be perceived, emanated from an Inspector General of the A.'.A.'.A.'.R.'. on the Island of Cuba, viz.:

[TRANSLATION.]

TO THE GLORY OF THE GR: ARCH:
OF THE UNIV: Lux ex Tenebris.

From the Orient of the Very Great and Very Puissant Council of the Sublime Princes (of the Royal Secret), Chiefs of Masonry, under the C: C: of the Zenith (which responds) to the 20d 25' N: Lat:
To our Ill: and Very Valiant Knights and Princes, Masons of all the Degrees, over the surface of the two Hemispheres:
HEALTH !

We, Antoine Mathieu Dupotet, Grand Master of all the Lodges, Colleges Chapters, Councils, Chapters and Consistories, of the higher degrees of Masonry, Deputy Grand Master of the Grand Orient of Pennsylvania, in the United States of America; and of the Grand Lodge and Sovereign Provincial Grand Chapter of Heredom of Kilwinning, of Edinburgh, for America, under the distinctive title of the Holy Ghost, Grand Provincial of San Domingo in the Ancient Rite, Grand Commander or Sovereign President of the Th: Puissant Grand Council of the Sublime Princes of the Royal Secret, established at Port au Prince, Island of San Domingo, by constitutive patent of 16 January and 19 April, 1801, under the distinctive title of The Triple Unity; transferred to Baracoa, Island of Cuba, on account of the events of war, Do declare, in the name of the Sublime and Th: Puissant Grand Council, do certify and attest, that the Very Resp: Gr: Elect Knight of the White and Black Eagle, Joseph Cerneau, Ancient Dignitary of the Lodge No. 47, Orient of Port au Prince Grand Warden of the Provincial Lodge, same Orient, Venerable founder of the Lodge of the Ancient Constitution of York, No. 103, under the distinctive title of the Theological Virtues, Orient of the Habana, Island of Cuba, has been regularly initiated in all the Degrees of the Sublime Masonry, from that of Secret Master to, and including that of Grand Elect Knight of the White and Black Eagle; and wishing to give the strongest proofs of our sincere friendship for our said Very Dear Bro: Joseph Cerneau, in recognition of the services which he has rendered to the Royal Art, and which he is rendering daily, we have initiated him in the highest, in the most eminent and final Degree of Masonry; we create him our Deputy Grand Inspector, for the Northern part of the Island of Cuba, with all the powers that are attached thereto, giving him full and entire power to initiate the Bros: Masons, whom he may judge (Worthy ?), to promote them to the Sublime Degrees, from the 4th up to and including the 24th; provided however, that these Masons shall have been officers of a Lodge regularly constituted and recognized, and in place only, where there may not be found Sacred and Sublime and regularly constituted Asyla; from which Bros: he will receive the obligation required and the authentic submission to the Degrees of the Sublime Princes; consulting, however, and calling to his aid the B: B: whom he shall know to be decorated with the Sublime Degrees; we give him full and entire power to confer in the name of our aforesaid Grand Council, the highest Degree of Masonry on a Kt: Prince Mason, one only each year, whose virtues he shall recognize, and the qualities required to deserve this favor; and to the end that our dear Bro: Joseph Cerneau, so decorated, may enjoy, in this quality, the honours, rights and prerogatives, which he has justly deserved, by his arduous labors in the Royal Art, we have delivered to him these presents, in the margin whereof he has placed his signature, that it may avail him everywhere, and be useful to him alone.

We pray our Resp: BB: regularly constituted, spread over the two Hemispheres, with whatever Degree they may be decorated, whether in Lodge, Ch:, Col:, Sovereign Council . . . . Sublime, to recognize and receive our dear Bro:, the Very Illustrious Sov: and Subl: Prince, Joseph Cerneau, in all the Degrees above mentioned; promising to pay the same attention to those who, in our Orients shall present themselves at the doors of our Sacred Asyla, furnished with like authentic titles.

Given by us, S: Sublime Princes, G: C: G: I: G'al: of our aforesaid Grand and Perfect Council, under our Mysterious Seal, and the Grand Seal of the Princes of Masonry, in a place where are deposited the greatest treasures, the sight whereof fills us with consolation, joy and gratitude for all that is great and good.

At Baracoa, Island of Cuba anno 5806, under the sign of the Lion, the 15th day of the 5th month called Ab, 7806, of the Creation 5566, and according to the Common Style the 15th July, 1806.

Signed, MATHIEU DUPOTET, President, Sev:.....G'al:
[A true copy :] Signed MATHIEU DUPOTET, President, S: G: I: G'al:

I certify that what is transmitted above and the other portions are conformable to my Register.

TIPHAINE, S∴P∴R∴S∴,D∴I∴G'al∴G∴Comm:

The foregoing translation of the ancient copy in French has been correctly and faithfully made by me.

ALBERT PIKE
March 20, 1882.

The Grand Commandery of New York was organized in the following manner, as ascertained from the Official Proceedings. On January 22, 1814, the Sovereign Grand Consistory, Joseph Cerneau's body, decreed the establishment of a Grand Encampment of Sir Knights Templars and appendant Orders for the State of New York, and immediately proceeded to its formation by choosing the Grand Officers thereof[243] who were all members of said Consistory. This was done solely by the action of the Consistory, without the concurrence of any Commandery, nor of any Knights Templars. This body, which it has often since been proved to have had no legal Masonic authority for its existence, as a Consistory, having been established by Joseph Cerneau alone, in 1807, a few months only after his patent from Mathieu Dupotet had been issued to him which gave him permission to confer one degree, the 25th of the A∴A∴A∴R∴. upon one person only each year, who was qualified by having received all the lower degrees of that Rite, in Cuba only, made his appearance in New York, and finding a total ignorance on the part of all Masons in New York as to the "Rite of Perfection," induced a large number to receive, at his hands, degrees which he had no authority to give. From this beginning, he organized his Consistory. In 1816, Columbian Commandery in New York received a Warrant; and a Warrant on the same day was issued to a new commandery in New Orleans. These two were the only Commanderies who recognized the Grand Encampment of New York. All the other encampments in the State refused to recognize the Grand Body, and remained independent for many years.

It is not certain that any of those members, who formed this Grand Commandery of New York, had ever received the degrees of the Commandery in a regular body of Knights Templars, but that they assumed the degrees of the Consistory as being the same as those in the Commandery. There is no evidence whatever that Cerneau, who went

---

[243] Proceedings of the Grand Commandery of New York, 1800, PP. 5, 6, from the paper by Sir Knight James H. Hopkins.

from Port Republican in San Domingo to Cuba, and from Cuba to New York, in 1807, ever saw a regular Knight Templar Mason, or ever was anywhere in the vicinity of a Commandery; hence we draw a fair inference, that the Knight of the Red Cross, and also of the Temple, were derived from the rituals of the 15th and 16th and 24th degrees of the A.'.A.'.A.'.R.'. The ritual of the Templar degree in the United States differs so essentially from the old ritual of England of 1801, now in the possession of the writer, and also from the present English one, that nave can presume that it was invented in the United States by those who took the degree from the possession of the Lodges and constituted the semblance of Commanderies (Encampments).

A Grand Convention of Knights Templars was held in the Masonic Hall in the city of Philadelphia, Tuesday, February 15, 1814, for the purpose of forming a Grand Encampment of Knights Templars in Pennsylvania, with jurisdiction belonging thereto, and also over all such Encampments in other States as may agree to come under the jurisdiction of the same. Sir Knight John Sellers, of Wilmington, Del., was called to the Chair, and Sir Knight Henry G. Keatinge, of Baltimore, Md., was appointed Secretary.

It was "Resolved, That the Delegates and Proxies from the Several Encampments to be represented in the Convention from the respective States be called over. The following named Sir Knights produced their Credentials under Seals of their respective Encampments as Delegates and Proxies, and were admitted to take their seats in the Convention: Encampment No. 1, Philadelphia, Delegates, Sir William M. Coxkill, Sir Alphonso C. Ireland, Sir Nathaniel Dilhorn.

"Encampment, City of New York, Proxies, Sir Thomas Black, Sir James Humes.

"Rising-Sun Encampment, City of New York, Delegate, Sir James M'Donald; Proxies from same, Sir Thomas Armstrong, Sir Anthony Fannen.

"Encampment No. 1, Wilmington, Del., Delegates, Sir John Sellers, Sir Archibald Hamilton, Sir John Patterson.

"Encampment No. 1, Baltimore, Md., Delegate, Sir Henry G. Keatinge.

The Grand Convention being duly organized, proceeded to form a Constitution which was agreed to February 16, 1814, and signed by the Delegates and Proxies as above named. Also the Grand Officers were elected and installed.

"The Most Eminent Sir William McCorkle, of Philadelphia, General Grand Master.

"Most Eminent Sir Archibald Hamilton, of Wilmington, Del., Grand Generalissimo.
"Most Eminent Sir Peter Dobb, of New York, Grand Captain General.
Right Eminent George A. Baker, of Philadelphia, Grand Recorder."

The foregoing account of the formation of this Freemason's Grand Encampment in Philadelphia is taken from The Freemason's Library and General Ahiman Rezon, by Samuel Cole, P.M., Edition of 1826, and we do not find any notice whatever of the Convention held in June, 1816, by those celebrities, viz.: Thomas Smith Webb, Henry Fowle, and John Snowe, who went to Philadelphia to confer with the above-mentioned Grand Encampment of Pennsylvania, "upon the subject of a general Union of all the Encampments in the United States under one head and general form of government," pursuant to the resolution of the "Grand Encampment of the United States," Massachusetts and Rhode Island Encampment being known as such.

Having failed in their mission to Philadelphia, they repaired to New York and being there joined by Thomas Lowndes, who had been appointed by the Grand Encampment of New York as its delegate to represent that body at a Convention of Knights Templars from different States of the Union, to be held in the City of Philadelphia, on Tuesday, June 11th, on the 20th and 21st of June.

at Masons' Hall. held "a Convention." The records of this quartette's proceedings describe them as " delegates from eight Councils and Encampments," all of which we have mentioned on page 1386 of this chapter.

GRAND MASTERS,CONCLAVE,YEAR.NAME.

I. 1816 De Witt Clinton, New York, N. Y.
II. 1819 De Witt Clinton, New York, N. Y.
III. 1826 De Witt Clinton, New York, N. Y.
IV. 1829 Rev. Jonathan Nye, Claremont, N.H
V. 1832 Rev. Jonathan Nye, Claremont, N. H
VI. 1835 James Madison Allen, Cayuga, N. Y.
VII. 1838 James Madison Allen, Cayuga, N. Y.
VIII. 1841 James Madison Allen, Cayuga, N. Y.
IX. 1844 Archibald Bull, Troy, N. Y.
X. 1847 Wm. Blackstone Hubbard, Columbus, Ohio.
XI. 1850 Wm. Blackstone Hubbard, Columbus, Ohio

XII. 1853 Wm. Blackstone Hubbard, Columbus, Ohio
XIII. 1856 Wm. Blackstone Hubbard, Columbus, Ohio
XIV. 1859 Benj. Brown French, Washington, D. C.
XV. 1862 Benj. Brown French, Washington, D. C.
XVI. 1865 Henry L. Palmer, Milwaukee, Wis,
XVII. 1868 Wm. Sewall Gardner, Newton, Mass.
XVIII. 1871 J. Q. A. Fellows, New Orleans, La.
XIX. 1874 James Herron Hopkins, Washington, D. C.
XX. 1877 Vincent Lombard Hurlbut, Chicago, Ill.
XXI. 1880 Benjamin Dean, Boston, Mass
XXI I. 1883 Robert Enoch Withers, Wytheville. Va.
XXIII. 1886 Charles Roome, New York, N. Y.
XXIV. 1889 John P. S. Cobin, Lebanon, Pa.
XXV. 1892 Hugh McCurdy, Corunna, Mich.
XXVI. 1895 Warren La Rue Thomas, Baltimore, Md
XXVII. 1898 Reuben Hedley Lloyd, San Franctsco, Cal.
XXVIII 1901 Henry Bates Stoddard, Bryan, Texas
XXIX. 1904 George M. Moulton, Chicago, Ill
XXX. 1907. Henry Warren Rugg, Providence, R. I.
XXXI . 1910 William B. Melish, Cincinnati, O

CHAPTER LIV.

HISTORY OF THE INTRODUCTION OF FREEMASONRY INTO EACH STATE AND TERRITORY OF THE UNITED STATES

The First Lodges and the Grand Lodges.

THE Institution, in its modern system of Speculative Masonry, having been established in Great Britain first, and then upon the Continent of Europe, early in the 18th century, we may well assume that among the various colonists from Europe who made their homes in the Western Hemisphere, there must have been many Operative Masons who had been initiated prior to their emigration.

From the various writers on this subject which we have consulted, we learn it is recorded that as early as 1680 there came to South Carolina one John Moore, a native of England, who before the close of the century removed to Philadelphia and in 1703 was commissioned by the King as Collector of the Port. In a letter written by him in 1715 he mentions having spent "a few evenings in festivity with my Masonic Brethren." This is perhaps the earliest mention we have of there being members of the Craft residing in Pennsylvania or elsewhere in the Colonies.

We must bear in mind that this was several years prior to the organization of the Mother Grand Lodge of Speculative Masonry, which occurred June 24, 1717.

Roger Lacy's deputation of 1735, given by Lord Weymouth, Grand Master of the Grand Lodge of England, was the second American lodge on the English Roll.

Gould's History of Freemasonry[244] says of this lodge: "The Charity of the Society was solicited in the Grand Lodge of England,

---

[244] Gould, vol. vi., p. 456.

December 31, 1733, to enable the trustees of the new Colony to send distressed Brethren to Georgia, where they may be comfortably provided for." In 1735 a Deputation to Mr. Roger Lacy for constituting a lodge (No. 139) at Savannah was granted by Lord Weymouth. It was doubtless the body referred to by Whitfield in his diary, where he records, " June 24, 1738 (Savannah), was enabled to read prayer and preach with power before the Freemasons, with whom I afterwards dined"

Brother Wm. S. Rockwell, of Georgia, has said that a lodge organized by Roger Lacy existed earlier than 1735, possibly 1730.

No certain evidence has been discovered confirming this statement.

Hayden, in his Washington and His Masonic Compeers, says: "King Solomon's Lodge at Savannah, which had commenced its work under an old oak tree in 1733, when the first settlement in Georgia began, had belonged to the branch of Masons denominated Moderns, but in February, 1785, it was proposed by Major Jackson, who was then one of its members, that they form themselves into a Lodge of Ancients.

The proposition was referred to a Committee, and was subsequently agreed to, and the brethren were duly constituted, by the usual ceremonies, a Lodge of Ancient York Masons."[245] The Grand Lodge of the "Ancients" never warranted any lodges in the State of Georgia.

There was a tradition that this old lodge was instituted by General James E. Oglethorpe.

With this short introduction we shall now proceed to present the histories of the first Lodges and of the Grand Lodges in the several States and Territories of the United States. We commence with Pennsylvania for the reason that the evidence is conclusive that St. John's Lodge in Philadelphia was the first lodge duly organized of which there is any record, and we may, with some degree of assurance, say that Masonry in an organized form existed in Pennsylvania some time prior to 1730, because, as shown in the plate opposite this page, the fac-simile copy of "Liber B" indicates very conclusively that there must have been a prior Liber A.

Pennsylvania.

Up to the discovery of "Liber B" by Bro. Clifford P. McCalla, in 1884, of this original lodge, dated June, 1731, everyone had accepted as a fact that Henry Price, of Boston, was the first commissioned officer in

---

[245] Hayden, p. 348.

charge of Freemasonry in the Colonies, and that St . John's Lodge, in Boston, was the first regularly constituted lodge ins any of the Colonies. Our Brethren of Massachusetts yet contend that the lodge in Boston was the first duly constituted lodge by the authority of the deputation to Henry Price (and they refer with much force to the correspondence which occurred between Benjamin Franklin and Henry Price).

Bro. John Dove, in his reprint of the proceedings of the Grand Lodge of Virginia, in his "Introduction" claims the first lodge "derived directly from the Mother Grand Lodge of England, was No.172, the Royal Exchange in the Borough of Norfolk, Virginia, Dec.1733." He also says:

"During the above period, dating from 1733 and extending to 1792, the Masons of Massachusetts worked under the authority of Provincial Grand Masters appointed by, and deriving their authority from, the Grand Lodges of England and Scotland in 1733, at which period Henry Price was first appointed, by the Grand Lodge of England, Grand Master of the St. John's Grand Lodge of Massachusetts, in 1734, and upon petition, his authority was extended to all North America, and under his power, thus extended, Benj. Franklin applied for and obtained a Charter for a Lodge at Philadelphia, Pennsylvania."

From all that we can gather in the various sketches of this formation period in the history of Freemasonry in the Colonies, it appears to us that the weight of testimony is in favor of the worliing of Masonry, first in Philadelphia, secondly in Massachusetts by secondary constituted authority, and thirdly in Norfolk, Va., by direct charter, emanating from the Grand Lodge itself.

At the period of the working of St. John's Lodge in Philadelphia, the Brethren exercised their prescriptive privilege to open a lodge without a charter, because there was no Grand Lodge to issue one so far as they knew. The lodge may have existed some considerable time prior to 1731, which latter date, it must be remembered; was only eight years after the publication of the Anderson Book of Constitutions, and eight years was a short period in which to fill up a " Liber A."

From all the historical data now available our conclusion is that we must give Pennsylvania the preference, by placing that colony foremost, as having started Freemasonry in an original prescriptive, organic form; followed by Massachusetts, as second, in a lodge, chartered by constituted authority of a Provincial Grand Master; and thirdly, by giving to Virginia the first lodge chartered by the Grand Lodge itself; each of these being authoritative, accordlng to the circumstances governing those who instituted the proceedings.

Thus, in Pennsylvania, Freemasonry is presented as having been organized in an original prescriptive lodge, with proper officers, working for some indefinite time prior to June, 1731, as shown by their ledger.

The present records of the Grand Lodge commence July 29, 1779, and have continued up to the present time. It is thought that during the Revolutionary War, as Philadelphia was a great center of the troubles during that war, all the records and papers of the Grand Lodge were either lost or destroyed, and tradition only gives any idea of the transactions up to the above date. The oldest minutebook now known is of Lodge No. 3, which goes back to November 19, 1767, and comes up to the present time; and it refers to an older book.

December 28, 1778, the Grand Lodge, with the Brethren, about three hundred, celebrated St. John's Day, and Brother William Smith, D.D., preached a sermon. General Washington was present on that occasion. Bro. Rev. Wm. Smith, having abridged and digested the Ahiman Rezon, it was adopted by the Grand Lodge, November 22, 1781.

At the quarterly Communication of Grand Lodge, September 25, 1786, steps were taken to sever the official relations between the Grand Lodge and the Grand Lodge of England, by the following:

Resolved, That this Grand Lodge is and ought to be, a Grand Lodge independent of Great Britain or any other authority whatever, and that they are not under any ties to any Grand Lodge except those of brotherly love and affection, which they will always be happy to cultivate and preserve with all lodges throughout the globe.

The Grand Lodge having, up to this time, been under a Warrant from the Grand Lodge of England, was closed finally. A convention was held the next day, September 26, 1786. Thirteen different lodges under warrants of the preceding Grand Lodge of Pennsylvania having full power from their constituent members, therefor:

Resolved, That the Lodges under the jurisdiction of the Grand Lodge of Pennsylvania, lately held under the authority of the Grand Lodge of England, Will, and do now, form themselves into a Grand Lodge, to be called the Grand Lodge of Pennsylvania and Masonic jurisdiction thereunto belonging, to be held in Philadelphia; and that the late Grand Officers continue to be the Grand Officers of Pennsylvania, invested with all the powers, jurisdictions, preeminence, and authority thereunto belonging, till the usual time of the next election; and that the Grand Lodge and particular Lodges govern themselves by the Rules and Regulations heretofore established, till other rules and regulations shall be adopted.

June 24, 1834, the Grand Lodge celebrated "the Centennial annniversary of the establishment of the first lodge in Pennsylvania, of which Lodge Brother Benjamin Franklin was the first Master." This antedated the claim made by Massachusetts of the first lodge having been established by Price in 1733. The date was evidently mistaken, as the "Liber B," since having been discovered, shows the date of June, 1731.

On June 24, 1734, Franklin was elected Grand Master, and it was in November of that year his letter to Price was written, asking for a copy of his deputation as Provincial Grand Master. etc.

December 4, 1843, the change was permanently made whereby all the business of the lodge, also the opening and closing of the lodge, must be in the Master's degree. It was at this time also that, under the lodge Warrant, those possessing the higher degrees could confer them. Several of the lodges, as many as four, worbed the Royal Arch degree. In 1849, Franklin Lodget No. 134, was authorized to loan its Warrant to confer the Order of the Temple on Encampment No. 29 in Philadelphia. Also Union Lodge, Not 121, was authorized to loan its Warrant to organize Union Encampment, No. 6. This resolution of the Grand Lodge was rescinded on February 15, 1857.

Massachusetts.

In consequence of an application from several Brethren, reading in New England, Free and Accepted Masons, to the Right Honorable and Most Worshipful Anthony, Lord Viscount Montaguei Grand Master of Masons in England, he was pleased. in the year 1733, to constitute and appoint Right Worshipful Henry Price Provincial Grand Master of New England aforesaid.

Upon the receipt of this commission, the Brethren assembled July 30th; and the Charter of Constitution being read, and the Right Worshipful Grand Master duly invested and congratulated, a Grand Lodge was formed under the title and designation of "St. John's Grand Lodge," and the following officers chosen and installed:

Right Worshipful Andrew Belcher, Deputy Grand Master; Right Worshipful Thomas Kennelly, Senior Grand Warden; Right Worshipful John Quann, Junior Grand Warden pro tempore.

A petition was then presented by several worthy Brethren residing ln Boston, praying to be constituted into a regular lodge, and fit was voted that the same be granted.

Thus was Masonry founded in Massachusetts.

The anniversary of St. John the Baptist was celebrated June 24, 1734, in ample form.

A petition being presented from Benjamin Franklin and several Brethren residing in Philadelphia for a constitution holding a lodge there, the Right Worshipful Grand Master, having this year received orders from the Grand Lodge in England to establish Masonry in all North America, was pleased to grant the prayer of the petitionerse and to send them a deputation appointing the Right Worshipful Benj. Franklin their first Master.

A petition from the Brethren resident in Portsmouth, in New Hampshire, for the erection of a lodge there was also granted.

At the usual celebration of the festival of St. John the Evangelist, December 27, 1735, the Right Worshipful Grand Master appointed the Right Worshipful James Gordon his Deputy.

About this time sundry Brethren going hence to South Carolina, and meeting with Masons thereg formed a lodge at Charleston; from whence sprung Masonry in those parts, December 27, 1736. At the celebration usual on this day, the Right Worshipful Robert Tornlinson was appointed Deputy Grands Master; all the other officers were continued in their respective trusts.[246]

The Right Worshipful Robert Tomlinson having received a commission from the Right Honorable and Right Worshipful John Earl of Loudon, Grand Master of England, appointing him Provincial Grand Master of North America in the stead of the Right Worshipful Grand Master Henry Price, resigned, he was properly installed and invested, and duly congratulated, April 20, 1737.

At the usual celebration, on June 24th following, he was pleased to nominate and appoint the Right Worshipful Hugh McDaniel his Deputy. On the next December festival, the Right Worshipful James Gordon was re-chosen Deputy Grand Master.

In the year 1738 the Right Worshipful Grand Master went to England via Antigua, where, finding some old Boston Masons, he formed them into a lodge, giving them a Charter of incorporation; and initiated the Governor, and several gentlemen of distinction there, into the Society.

The Right Worshipful Lodge of Masters, in Boston, was founded January 2, 1739. In the year 1740, the Right Worshipful Grand

---

[246] "Constitutions, History, and General Regulations of Massachusetts," by Rev. T. Mason Harrison 1798.

Master granted a deputation, at the petition of several Brethren, for holding a lodge at Annapolis in Nova Scotia; and appointed the Right Worshipful Erasmus James Phillips Deputy Grand Master there, who afterward erected a lodge at Halifax, and appointed his Excellency Edward Cornwallis their first Master.

The Right Worshipful Thomas Oxnard having received a deputation dated London, September 23, 1743, from the Right Honorable and Most Worshipful John, Lord Ward, Baron of Birmingham in the County of Warwick, and Grand Master of Masons in England, appointing him Provincial Grand Master in the room of the Right Worshipful Grand Master Tomlinson, deceased; which being communicated March 6, 1744, he was properly acknowledged, invested, installed, and congratulated. He then proceeded to nominate and appoint:

The Right Worshipful Hugh McDaniel, Deputy Grand Master; Right Worshipful Thomas Kelby, Senior Grand Warden; Right Worshipful John Box, Junior Grand Warden; Charles Pelham, Grand Secretary.

The following Grand Officers were chosen and installed at the festival of St. John the Evangelist, holden December 27, 1744:

Right Worshipful Hugh McDaniel, Deputy Grand Master; Right Worshipful Benj. Hallowell, Senior Grand Warden; Right Worshipful John Box, Junior Grand Warden; Charles Pelham, Grand Secretary.

The petition of several Brethren in Newfoundland, for constituting a lodge there, was granted December 24, 1746, and a Charter transmitted.

December 27, 1749, a Charter was granted to a lodge in Newport, R I. The Right Worshipful Grand Master, assisted by his Grand Officers, February 15, 1750, constituted and consecrated "A Second Lodge" in Boston; March 7th following, he also constituted and consecrated "The Third Lodge in Boston."

At the Quarterly Communication in August, 1750, he granted a Charter for a lodge at Annapolis, Md., and also a Charter for "Hiram Lodge" at New Haven, Conn.

At the festival of St. John the Evangelist, December 27, 1750, the Brethren attended divine service in Christ's Church, Boston, where Rev. Brother Charles Brockwell delivered a sermon, which was afterward printed in Boston and reprinted and passed through several editions in England, and was added to the Pocket Companion and History of Freemasonry, London, 1754.

Lord Colvill having been appointed Deputy Grand Master, summoned the Brethren to attend him at the Grey Hound Tavern in Roxbury,.January 24, 1752, where he held a Grand Lodge in due form, and the day was celebrated as usual, and Grand Officers were duly chosen.[247]

Lord Colvill having returned to England, October 30th, R. W. Hugh McDaniel was again appointed Deputy Grand Master.

A dispensation was granted to erect a lodge at New London, in Connecticut, January 12, 1753.

A Grand Lodge was held at Graton's, in Roxbury, June 26, 1754, " but by reason of the death of Worshipful Grand Master Thomas Oxnard, this morning at 11 o'clock, the celebration was rather sorrowful than joyous."

"In honor of their Right Worshipful Grand Master, whose loss was sincerely lamented by all who had the pleasure and honor of his acquaintance, and more especially by the Society over which he had for eleven years presided with dignity, they voted to attend his funeral, in mourning, with the honors of Masonry; and to invite the several Lodges in Boston to assist on this mournful occasion."

October 11, 1754, at the Quarterly Communication, the Brethren petitioned the Right Honorable and Right Worshipful Grand Master of Masons in England, for a new deputatiox to fill King Solomon's Chair, vacant by the death of their late Grand Master; and recommended the Right Worshipful Jeremy Gridley to him for that Important and honorable trust.

June 24, 1755, the Right Worshipful Deputy Grand Mastet summoned the Brethren to attend him at Graton's Tavern, in Roxbury, to observe the Festival of St. John the Baptist. The Grand Officers were chosen and present August 21st. At a special meeting the Right Worshipful Jeremy Gridley informed the Brethren that the Right

---

[247] A year or two since, a clergyman of the Church of England, who is probably more Conversant with that church in America than any other individual living, politely furnished us with a document wherein it appeared that the first regular Lodge of Freemasons in America was holden in King's Chapel, Boston, by a dispensation from the Grand Lodge of England, somewhere about the year 1720. It produced great excitement at the time, and the Brethren considered it prudent to discontinue these meetings.
"Masonic Mirror and Mechanics' Intelligencer," by Bro. Chas. W. Moore, January 27, 1827.

Honorable and Right Worshipful Grand Master James Brydges, Marquis of Caernavon, Grand Master of Masons in England, had sent a deputation appointing him Provincial Grand Master of North America, where no Grand Master is appointed.

In 1767, Jeremy Gridley, the Provincial Grand Master of North America, died on September 10th; his funeral took place on the 12th, and the members of St. Andrew's Lodge, sixty-four in number (Joseph Warren being the Senior Warden), walked in the procession.

After this, however, when every generous effort on the part of St.Andrew's had completely failed, and when it became evident that no "Union of Love and Friendship could be effected" the members of that lodge changed their ground. Men like Warren, Revere, Hancock, and others of illustrious name, felt their patience exhausted and determined not to quietly submit to be any longer denounced as clandestine Masons and imposters. The early proceedings of St.Andrew's were indeed as irregular as it is possible to conceive.

Originating in the Association of Nine Masons who had been made clandestinely, it was chartered by the Grand Lodge of Scotland in 1756, and then numbered twenty-one members, exclusive of the original nine, who had left Boston in the interval. Its Charter did not arrive until 1760, at which time the lodge had been increased by eighteen additional members, so that in all thirty-one candidates were initiated before the lodge received its Charter.

At a conference held April 28, 1766, between committees of St.John's Grand Lodge and St. Andrew's Lodge (Richard Gridley being a member of one and Joseph Warren of the other), the representatives of the latter fully admitted the illegality of their early proceedings, but contended that it was in the power of the Grand Lodge of Scotland to "make irregular Masons regular." Against this tfle other committee formulated their belief "that the language of the Constitution for irregularities was submission."

We have quoted this circumstance to show the fallacy of those who refer to the facts connected with the irregularity of the formation of St. Andrew's Lodge.

We have brought the history of Masonry in Massachusetts from its commencement in 1733 to the beginning of the political troubles which finally ended in the independence of the Colonies. Soon thereafter Masonry resumed its wonted character, and after some years of struggle the various warring interests of the Brethren of the different constitutions on March 5, 1792, were united by the organization of but one Grand Lodge, which has continued with prosperity and wonderful success until the present time.

The following copies of two letters from Benjamin Franklin to Henry Price, in which we find acknowledgments of the relative Masonic positions of Massachusetts and Pennsylvania, will be found interesting.

Right Worshipful Grand Master and Most Worthy and Dear Brethren, We acknowledge your favor of the 23d of October past, and rejoice that the Grand Master (whom God bless) hath so happily recovered from his late indisposition; and we now, glass in hand, drink to the establishment of his health, and the prosperity of your whole Lodge.

We have seen in the Boston prints an article of news from London importing that at a Grand Lodge held there in August last, Mr.Price's deputation and power was extended over all America, which advice we hope is true, and we heartily congratulate him thereupon and though this has not been as yet regularly signified to us by you yet, giving credit thereto, we think it our duty to lay before your Lodge what we apprehend needful to be done for us, in order to promote and strengthen the interest of Masonry in this Province (which seems to want the sanction of some authority derived from home, to give the proceedings and determinations of our Lodge their due weight), to wit, a Deputation or Charter granted by the Right Worshipful Mr. Price, by virtue of his Commission from Britain, confirming the Brethren of Pennsylvania in the privileges they at present enjoy of holding annually their Grand Lodge, choosing their Grand Master, Wardens and other officers, who may manage all affairs relating to the Brethren here with full power and authority, according to the customs and usages of Masons, the said Grand Master of Pennsylvania only yielding his chair when the Grand Master of all America shall be in place. This, if it seems good and reasonable to you to grant, will not only be extremely agreeable to us, but will also, we are confident, conduce much to the welfare, establishment, and reputation of Masonry in these parts. We therefore submit it for your consideration, and we hope our request will be complied with: we desire that it may be done as soon as possible, and also accompanied with a copy of the Right Worshipful Grand Masters first Deputation, and of the instrument by which it appears to be enlarged as above mentioned, witnessed by your Wardens and signed by the Secretary; for which favors this Lodge doubt not of be ing able to behave as not to be thought ungrateful.

We are, Right Worshipful Grand Master and Most Worthy Brethren,

Your affectionate Brethren and obliged humble Servts,
Signed at the request of the Lodge,
Philadelphia, Nov. 28, 1734.

B. FRANKLIN, G. M,
DEAR BROTHER PRICE I am glad to hear of your recovery. I hoped to have seen you this fall, agreeable to the expectation you were so good as to give me; but since sickness has prevented your coming, while the weather was moderate, I have no room to flatter myself with a visit from you before the spring, when a deputation of the Brethren here will have an opportunity of showing how much they esteem you. I beg leave to recommend their request to you, and to inform you that some false and rebel Brethren, who are foreigners, being about to set up a distinct Lodge in opposition to the old and true Brethren here, pretending to make Masons for a bowl of punchs and the craft is like to come into disesteem among us, unless the true Brethren are contenanced and distinguished by some such special authority as herein desired. I entreat, therefore, that whatever you shall think proper to do therein may be sent by the next post, if possible. or the next following

I am Your Affectionate brother & humble Serv't,

B. FRANKLIN, G. M.
Pennsylvania
Philadelphia. Nov. 28. 1734

P. S. If more of the Constitutions are wanted among your please hint it to me.

These letters were addressed as follows:

To Mr. HENRY PRICE,
At the Brazen Head,
Boston N.E. Georgia

Solomon's Lodge, No. 1, received a Warrant for Savannah is 1735; a Warrant for Unity Lodge, No. 2, was issued in 1774, and a Warrant was issued for Grenadier's, No. 386, in 1775. All of these were granted by the Grand Lodge of England.

Roger Lacy's deputation of 1735, given by Lord Weymouth, Grand Master of the Grand Lodge of England, was the second lodge on the English Roll for America. On October 29, 1784, a lodge was chartered by the Grand Lodge of Pennsylvania for Savannah.

On December 16, 1786, the Grand Lodge of Georgia was organized in that city, when the permanent appointments made by the Grand Master of England were solemnly relinquished by the Right Worshipful Samuel Elbert, Grand Master, and the other officersls of the Grand Lodge; and regulations were adopted by which the Grand Officers were to be elected annually. Then the last Provincial Grand Master resigned his position, and William Stephens was elected the first Grand Master under the new and present formation. A notable event occurred March 21, 1824. The cornerstone of the monuments to Greene and Pulaski were laid, General Lafayette acting as Grand Master for the occasion.

As there are those still interested in the search for the origin of Masonry in Georgia, and who believe that a lodge existed there prior to 1735, the date of the Warrant of Solomon's Lodge, which has been lost, it is well to note the following, for reference, as coming from the records: In England a Grand Lodge was holden "by virtue and in pursuance of the right of succession legally derived from the most noble and Most Worshipful Thomas Thyre, Lord Viscount Weymouth, Grand Master of England, 1735, by his Warrant directed to the Right Worshipful Roger Lacy; and by the renewal of the said power by Sholto Charles Douglass Lord Aberdour, Grand Master of Scotland for the year 1755-56 and Grand Master of England for the years 1757-58; as will appear in his Warrant directed to the Right Worshipful Grey Elliot."[248]

---

[248] The lodges which formed the Grand Lodge were Solomon's, No. 139 (1735), at Savannah; Unity, No. 2 (1774), Savannah (371, English Register); Grenadier's, No. 386 (English Register), (1775), Savannah.

Masonry was somewhat prosperous in Savannah, yet in the county outside of the city generally, Masonry had nearly disappeared by the year 1820. The Grand Lodge in that year adopted a new constitution; and the quarterly meetings of March and June were to be held in Savannah, and those of September and December were to be held at Milledgeville, the State Capital. This change was designed to accommodate the wishes of the conflicting parties of the two parts of the State, North and South.

In December, 1826, a convention was held which adopted a new constitution dispensing with the quarterly meetings, and made Milledgeville the permanent place of meeting. The Grand Lodge, however, which met at Savannah at the usual times March, 1827, refused to concur with the alteration and chose their Grand Officers

The Milledgeville body met on December 3, 1827, and elected their Grand Officers. As this was a very interesting period in the history of Masonry in Georgia, we must give the final result of this division. The New Grand Lodge appointed committees to possess themselves of the property of the Savannah or old body, and they declared the election held in March of no effect; and all the members of the lodges adhering to the Old Grand Lodge were expelled. Lodge No. 8, one of the Savannah lodges, held to the Milledgeville body; all the others in Savannah held to that body.

Union No. 3 of these lodges was the first lodge which adopted Royal Arch Masonry. In the hall of this lodge, the Grand Lodge of Savannah met. Finally, all the lodges in Savannah left the Grand Lodge except Solomon's Lodge, and united with the new body at Milledgeville. January 5, 1837, efforts were made for a reconciliation, which ended at the Grand Communication held November 6, 1839. Solomon's Lodge was admitted to the Grand Lodge by her representatives, and Masonry resumed a united front.

Prosperity followed, which was only checked by the Civil War from 1861 to 1865. Since 1866 prosperity has again visited that jurisdiction, and no Grand Lodge in the country can boast of a greater increase proportionally than Georgia.

New Hampshire.

Solomon's Lodge was reorganized October 29 1784, Savannah.
Grenadier's Lodge and Solomon's Lodge ceased working, leaving no record.

On February 5, 1736, a petition (the original of which has been preserved) was addressed by six Brethren at Portsmouth, N. H., to Henry Price, whom they styled "Grand Master of Free and Accepted Masons held in Boston." The petitioners described themselves as "of the holy and exquisite Lodge of St. John," and for power to form a lodge "According to order as is and has been granted to faithful Brothers in all parts of the World," and they declared that they had their "Constitution both in print and Manuscript as good and ancient as any that England can afford." The favor was asked because they had heard there is a "Superiour Lodge held in Boston." Be it noted this was early in 1736, when no lodge had been warranted in Portsmouth; and as the Brethren stated they possessed "Constitutions" in manuscript - which it is hardly possible could have been anything else than a copy of the "Old Charges" - as well as in print the evidence is consistent with the supposition that, while at the date named the lodge must have been some years in existence, its origin may have reached back even to the 17th century.

I am anxious not to lay too much stress on the precise meaning attached by me to the mention of manuscript constitution; nevertheless, I think the petition may be taken as fair evidence that in 1736 there were Brethren in New Hampshire (meeting as Masons in a lodge) who possessed a copy (or print) of the English Constitutions published in 1723, as well as a version of an older set of laws in MS., thus pointing to the possible existence of the lodge at even an earlier period than the Grand Lodge era of 1716-17.

The granting of the authority, which was a written instrument, was, in connection with that granted to Philadelphia, the first written Masonic authority known to have been issued by a Provincial Grand Lodge.[249]

It will be observed that, in like manner, as Grand Master, Henry Price issued authority to warrant a lodge to the eighteen Masons in Boston who petitioned in behalf of themselves and "other Brethren;" therefore the Brethren had been meeting as a lodge anterior thereto and discharging Masonic duties: convening and working as Masons without other authority than that of ancient immemorial right, which the Craft had many decades before exercised, of meeting when and where circumstances permitted or required, and choosing their own temporary Master; it is probable that thus many of the old Masons in America had been admitted to the Mystic Rites.

---

[249] C. McClenachan

Portsmouth was the first settlement by Europeans in New Hampshire (1623). Several lodges were many years afterward constituted within that territory by authority of the Grand Lodge of Massachusetts.

In a letter from Joseph Webb, Grand Master of the Grand Lodge of Massachusetts, in reply to one received from William Smith, Grand Secretary of the Grand Lodge of Pennsylvania, dated Boston, September 4, 1780, occurs this paragraph:

"I have granted a dispensation to New Hampshire, till they shall appoint a Grand Master of their own, which I suppose will not be very soon, as there is but one Lodge in that State."

A "convention" of delegates from two or more lodges was called at Dartmouth in 1787, but the Grand Lodge of New Hampshire was not organized until July 8, 1789. It was in the last of the three years' service of General John Sullivan as Governor of the State that he was elected the first Grand Master of the independent Grand Lodge. It is true there were but five lodges in the State, and but one, St. John's of Portsmouth, that antedated the Revolution; of this General Sullivan was the Master. In October, 1790, the Grand Master, from ill health, was compelled to decline re-election, and Dr. Hall Jackson was elected Grand Master in his stead.

The title assumed by the Grand Body is "The Most Worshipful Grand Lodge of the Ancient and Honorable Fraternity of Free and Accepted Masons of the State of New Hampshire"

South Carolina.

A Warrant was granted in 1735 by Lord Weymouth, Grand Master of England, for the establishment of a lodge in the city of Charleston, which was organized on October 28, 1736, by the name of Solomon's Lodge.

Brother Sidney Hayden, in Washington and his Masonic Compeers,[250] states that Grand Master Henry Price of Massachusetts, having received an extension of his authority in 1734, from the Grand Master of England, giving him jurisdiction over all North America, granted a Warrant on December 27, 1735, for a lodge at Charleston, S. C.

The St. John's Grand Lodge of Boston, Mass., warranted a lodge in Charleston, S. C., in 1738; this was followed by a grant from the Grand Lodge of England establishing Prince George's Lodge at

---

[250] Hayden, p 240

Winyaw, in 1743; and Union Lodge, by the same authority, at Charleston, May 3, 1755, and, again, a "Master's Lodge" at the same place, on March 22, 1756, and a lodge at Beaufort on September 15th of the same year.

The Grand Lodge of Scotland then appeared in the Province, and warranted Union Lodge, No. 98, in 1760.

St. Mark's Lodge was warranted by the Grand Lodge of England in 1763.

With regard to powers delegated to Provincial Grand Masters, we have first of record, John Hammerton, appointed by the Earl of Loudoun in 1736.

A second Provincial Grand Lodge was established by a deputation of the Marquis of Carnarvon to Chief Justice Leigh in 1754. Dr.Mackey, in his Encyclopedia, says upon this subject that, in 1777, this Grand Lodge, deputized by the Marquis of Carnarvon, assumed independence and became the "Grand Lodge of Free and Accepted Masons," Barnard Elliott being the first Grand Master. As early as 1783 the Athol or "Ancient " Masons invaded the jurisdiction of South Carolina, and in 1787 there being then five lodges of the Ancients in the State, they held a convention, and on March 24th organized the "Grand Lodge of Ancient York Masons." Between the Moderns and the Ancient Grand Lodges there was always a very hostile feeling until the year 1808, when a union was effected, which was but temporary, for a disruption took place in the following year. However, the Union was permanently established in 1817, when the two Grand Lodges were merged into one, under the name of the "Grand Lodge of Ancient Freemasons."

New York.

From the quotations of authorities herein following, it will be evident that Freemasonry must have existed in the Province of New York prior to the year 1737. The advertising notices and newspaper squibs are convincing that secret communications were being held either among the residents or the sojourning soldiery. By what authority these assemblies were held we are not yet able to disclose; whether under powers granted by Daniel Coxe, by reason of the deputation held by him from June 5, 1730, until the expiration of his personal investment, to wit, until June 24, 1732, or those of his successors, who were to be elected every other year on the feast of St. John the Baptist, when the Provincial Grand Master was to be installed. No testimony has been found of the exercise by Bro. Daniel Coxe of his delegated powers; perhaps no action was had by him; yet "it was a rare thing for any reports to be made by the Provincial Grand Masters abroad of their doings." We incline to the belief that no power was exercised by Brother Coxe pending the period during which he was deputized.

It is not impossible that warranted power existed among the soldiery who were or had been stationed in the Province; nor is it an impossibility that there was an immemorial Charter, or even an inherent or self-born power of constitution the exercise of which would not have been masonically illegal when we consider the condition of the Society, the period, the locality, and Masonic custom, or at least in following the precedent in other lands and of former days.

THE FIVE MASONIC DEPUTATIONS GRANTED TO PROVINCIAL GRAND MASTERS FOR NEW YORK BY THE GRAND LODGE OF ENGLAND

1. Colonel Daniel Coxe, June 5, 1730. Time of service, 2 years
2. Captain Richard Riggs, November 15, 1737. Time of service, 14 years
3. Francis Goelet, 1751. Time of service, 2 years
4. George Harrison, June 9, 1753 Time of service, 18 years
5. Sir John Johnson, 1781. Time of service, 10 years

The date of transition of the Grand Lodge from a Provincial to an independent State Masonic organization might be a subject of difference of opinion: herein the date of the summary retirement of the Grand Master and most of the other Grand Officers with the King's troops is assured as a data, to wit, September 19 and October 1, 1783. It might be urged with considerable force that as a definite date, June 6, 1787, should be given, inasmuch as on that date the Grand Lodge accepted and confirmed the Athol Warrant, and declared its establishment under it.

The Grand Lodge "Resolved, that next Grand Lodge be appointed for all the Lodges in the State to give in their Respective Warrants or Constitutions, or copies of them properly authenticated, that the Rank and Precedency of the whole may be then determined."

A more direct resolution from St. John's Lodge, No. 2, proceeded further to question the Grand Warrant under which the Grand Lodge existed. This was referred to next Grand Lodge.

Accordingly, on March 7, 1787, "The Resolution of St. John's Lodge, No. 2, referred for consideration to this evening, was read, and debates arising, it was resolved, on motion of Worshipful Brother Malcom, that a Committee be appointed to consider the propriety of holding the Grand Lodge under the present Warrant, and the proper measures to effect a change if it should be thought constitutional and expedient, and report their opinion, with the reasons on which it is founded, to the Grand Lodge, at their next Quarterly Communication."

The committee on June 6, 1787, reported their consideration of the propriety of holding the Grand Lodge under the present Warrant. The report was read, accepted, and confirmed.

The subject of the Grand Warrant being disposed of, the Grand Lodge, on the following September 5, 1787, adopted this recommendation:

"That as soon as the Committee appointed to establish the precedency of Rank of the Lodges of this City do report, that then all the Lodges in the State be required to take out new warrants and deliver up the old ones, the dues to the Grand Lodge being previously paid."

The report on lodge precedency and the determination of this subject was finally made June 3, 1789.[251]

Rhode Island

In Rhode Island, as in other localities, we find traces of a pre historic age of Freemasonry. The earliest date when, according to tradition, the Masonic system was known and practiced within the limits of Rhode Island and Providence plantations goes far back of authentic records. There are hints and intimations, with plenty of unverified legends, pointing to a 17th century expression of Freemasonry in Newport, R. I.; but the documents and records which ardent explorers have searched for, to support the theory that Freemasonry was planted in Rhode Island before the Institution was known either in Philadelphia or Boston, have not been found. As the case now stands, there is only a supposition that such may have been the fact.[252]

The organic life of Freemasonry in Rhode Island, as we trace its existence by historic records, goes back to the warranting or St.

John's Lodge, Newport, December 27, 1749. This lodge was authorized by St. John's Provincial Grand Lodge of Boston, Mass., Thomas Oxnard, Grand Master. Caleb Phillips was the first Master of the lodge thus authorized. Some unpleasantness having been caused by

---

[251] At the meeting of the Grand Lodge, held June 3, 1789, this subject was duly taken up and the several lodges presented their warrants, and were duly assigned their numbers, according to dates of charters. St. John's Lodge (1757), No. 29 was given No. 1.
[252] Memorial. by Henry W. Rugg, D.D.

the Master's withholding from the lodge the dispensation thus granted, a second Warrant was issued dated May 14, 1753. Under these warrants the Newport Brethren were only authorized to confer the first two degrees of Masonry. They did not recognize the limitation, however, and proceeded to confer the Master's degree as supplementing the degrees of Entered Apprentice and Fellow-craft.

On being called to account for thus extending the authority granted them, they made so good an explanation of the causes that had led them to transcend their powers, that the Grand Lodge confirmed them in the exercise of such powers by granting them a Charter to hold a Master's Lodge.

This lodge - the first organized in Rhode Island - was given additional powers, and we may assume that the ordinary lodge, having control over the degrees of Entered Apprentice and Fellowcraft, was united with or merged into the Master's Lodge, so that two separate organizations were not maintained.

As throwing some light upon the misapprehension pertaining to the conferring of degrees by St. John's Lodge of Newport, during this first period of its history, it is important to keep in mind the fact that the third degree was not then, as now, closely united with and expected to follow the two preceding degrees. Candidates for Freemasonry often went no further than the degree of Fellowcraft; those who did advance to the Master's grade were required to pay an additional fee.

A little more than two years before the granting of the confirmation Charter to the Brethren of Newport, a Masonic lodge had been organized in Providence, also taking the name of St.John's. A Warrant for this lodge was issued by the same authority that created the body established at Newport.

By the terms of this Charter the Providence Brethren were required to observe the constitution, make returns to the Grand Lodge, and annually keep or cause to be kept the feast of St. John the Baptist, and to dine together on that day, or as near that day as shall be most convenient, and that they send to the Grand Lodge in Boston contributions for poor Brethren.

The Charter of St. John's Lodge in Providence was one of sixteen similar authorizations which, up to that time, had been granted by the Provincial Grand Lodge of Massachusetts to sixteen lodges in eleven different provinces or colonies.

The Charter was issued by the direct authority of the eminent and patriotic Jeremy Gridley, then Provincial Grand Master of North

America. He was a lawyer of excellent reputation and a devoted member of the Masonic Fraternity.

Freemasonry in Rhode Island at the close of the War of the Revolution was represented by St. John's Lodge in Providence and King David's Lodge in Newport. The first lodge (St. John's) in Newport was inactive, as it had been for a long time. The lodge in Providence, after its revival, had greatly prospered under the efficient leadership of Bro. Jabez Bowen, its Worshipful Master from 1778 to 1790, and had received among its new members a large accession of influential citizens. One of these, William Barton, initiated in 1779, is deservedly remembered and honored for his heroic exploit in making a prisoner of the British General, William Prescott, on the island of Rhode Island, and for other patriotic services. Another, John Carlile, initiated in 1783, served the Craft with exceptional skill in many important offices for a long term of years.

On Monday, June 27, 1791, "being the day affixed on for the celebration of the Feast of St. John the Baptist" (St. John's Day having occurred on the previous Friday), a number of Brethren representing the two lodges met in the State House at Newport and proceeded to organize a Grand Lodge in accordance with the plan that had been approved. The Right Worshipful Moses Seixas presided and installed the officers who had been previously designated for the several stations. When the organization had been completed, the newly installed officers, with members of Grand Lodge and visiting Brethren, marched in procession to Trinity Church, where a discourse, having appropriateness to the occasion, was delivered by the Rector, Rev. Wm. Smith, and a collection was taken amounting to 11 9s. 4d., which sum it was ordered "should be invested in wood and distributed to the poor of this town during the ensuing winter."

By attending as a body on divine service, and making their offering in the house of worship for a benevolent purpose, the Brethren who formed the Grand Lodge of this State, and those masonically associated with them at that time, plainly signified their respect for religion and for that practical charity so much emphasized by the teachings of Freemasonry.

Maryland.

Masonry was introduced into Maryland, during the Colonial period, from three sources, viz.: by the Grand Lodge (Moderns) of Massachusetts, Grand Lodge (Moderns) of England, and the Grand

Lodge (Ancients) of Pennsylvania. Traditions indicate that it was also introduced here from Scotland and Germany.

The earliest lodge of which we have any reliable evidence in Maryland, was held at Annapolis. It was chartered by Thomas Oxnard, Provincial Grand Master of the St. John's Grand Lodge of Massachusetts, and Provincial Grand Master of North America. There are no records of this lodge known to be in existence, and the only reference to it, on the records of the Grand Lodge of Massachusetts, is the following, courteously furnished by Brother Sereno D. Nickerson, Grand Secretary : [253]

"1750, Aug. 12. At the Petition of sundry Brethren at Annapolis in Maryland, Our Rt. Wors'l Grand Master, Bro. Thos. Oxnard, Esqr. Granted a Constitution for a Lodge to be held there, and appointed The Rt. Worstl — first Mas'r.

"Fryday, July the 13th, 1750. For the Lodge at Maryland, Bro. McDaniel, D. G. M. app'd & pd. for their Constit'n 13.9.

"In the lists, the Lodge is sometimes described as ' Maryland Lodge' and sometimes as 'the Lodge at Annapolis.'"

Among the archives of the Grand Lodge of Maryland, fortunately preserved, are the books of three of the old Colonial lodges, viz.: one located at "Leonardtown, St. Mary's County," in 1759; one at "Joppa, Harford, then Baltimore County," in 1765, and at "Queenstown, Queen Anne's County."

The records of the Leonardtown Lodge extend over a period of three years, and although they appear to be the full and complete minutes of the lodge for that period, there is not the slightest mention by which can be discovered the authority under which it was held, or from whence it emanated.

Upon one of the calendars of the "Modern" Grand Lodge of England, there is the following entry: "Lodge No. 198, Chartered in foreign parts, June 6th, 1759." As this date corresponds exactly with the date of the first meeting of the Leonardtown Lodge, it is probable that the entry refers to it. It may, however, have been a branch of the lodge at Annapolis. It was not an unusual thing in this country in the early days for one lodge to have branch lodges in other towns or districts. Forty years subsequently a branch lodge was held at this same town.

---

[253] From History of Maryland, by E. T. Schultz. We are indebted to Bro. Schultz for all the information we have in that jurisdiction.

The records of the Leonardtown Lodge, with one exception, those of the St. John's Lodge, Boston, are the oldest original lodge proceedings discovered in this country, the old ledger of St.

John's Lodge, Philadelphia, recently discovered, being simply the secretary's account with the members.

On June 17, 1783, two months after Congress had issued the peace proclamation, we find the lodges on the "Eastern Shore" convened at Talbot Court-house, for the purpose of organizing a Grand Lodge of Free and Accepted Masons for the State of Maryland. There were five lodges represented by deputies, one lodge more than participated in the formation of the Grand Lodge of England in 1717.

There were present at this convention, as a deputy from Lodge No.7, of Chestertonvn, the Rev. William Smith, who was at the time Grand Secretary of the Grand Lodge of Pennsylvania, although residing in this State; and Bro. Dr. John Coates, Past Deputy Grand Master of Pennsylvania, a member of Lodge No. 3 of Philadelphia, but then a resident of the Eastern Shore of Maryland. It was unanimously Resolved, " That the several Lodges on the Eastern Shore of Maryland consider it is a matter of right, and that they ought to form a Grand Lodge independent of the Grand Lodge of Philadelphia." When the convention prepared to go into an election of officers for a Grand Lodge, Bro. Smith, Deputy from No. 7, stated that "he was not authorized to elect such officers." Whereupon the convention adjourned until the 31st day of July following. " The Rev. Bro. Smith was asked and promised to prepare a sermon against their next meeting."

It was determined to petition the Grand Lodge in Philadelphia for a Warrant for a Grand Lodge to be held on the Eastern Shore of Maryland.

The convention re-assembled at Talbot Court-house on July 31, 1783, agreeably to adjournment, the Rev. Dr. Smith, being a Grand Officer, took the Chair. The same lodges were in attendance as at the former session, with the exception of No. 37 of Somerset County, which was not represented, but No. 6 of Georgetown (Eastern Shore) was in attendance, and was represented, as were all the other lodges, by their Masters and Wardens, and not by deputies, as at the former session.

The resolution adopted at the previous session, regarding the right to form a Grand Lodge, independent of the Grand Lodge of Pennsylvania, was unanimously reaffirmed. It was further determined that the Grand Lodge should be a moving lodge: "that is to say, it shall sit at different places at different times; also that said Grand Lodge shall have quarterly communications."

A vote of thanks was then given to Bro. Dr. Smith "for the Sermon preached this day," and a copy asked for publication. They then proceeded to ballot for Grand Officers, when Bro. Coates was elected Grand Master, and Charles Gardner, Grand Secretary. Other officers were elected, and the convention adjourned, to assemble again at Chestertown, on December 18th following, (1783).

The Grand Lodge assembled according to adjournment, December 18th, but on account of the severe weather a number of the Brethren were prevented from attending, and the meeting was not organized until next day.

"From accident and other causes" there was no meeting on that days nor was there any meeting held, as far as the records show, until nearly three years subsequent. The subordinate lodges, however, maintained their organization and doubtless considered their allegiance to the Grand Lodge of Pennsylvania severed, as they were not thenceforth represented in that body.

Connecticut.

Masonry in Connecticut derived its organic life from the Grand Lodge in Massachusetts, the St. John's of which Paul Revere was subsequently Grand Master, but also Massachusetts Grand Lodge.

The charters granted by St. John's were:

August 12, 1750, Hiram, at New Haven, David Wooster as Master.

January 12, 1753, at New London, ceased before 1789
February 4, 1754 St John's, Middletown.
April 28, 1762, St. John's, Hartford.
April 28, 1709, Compass, Wallingford
July 10, 1771, St. Alban's, Guilford; became dormant in 1776 revived May 17, 1787.

March 23, 1780, Union, Danbury.

Provincial Grand Master of New York (Geo.) Harrison, under Grand Lodge of England, granted a Charter to "St. John's," in Fairfield, and afterward Bridgeport, in 1762; "St. John's," in Norwalk, May 23, 1765; "Union," at Greenwich, November 1864; and "St. John's," at Stratford, April 22, 1766.

The Massachusetts Grand Lodge (Scotland) granted a Charter to Wooster,"in Colchester, January 12, 1781; "St. Paul's," at Litchfield, May 27, 1781; the Charter dated June 21, 1781; "King Hiram," at Derby, January 3, 1781; "Montgomery" at Salisbury, March 5, 1783 (no record of the Charter to this lodge being granted).

"Columbia," at Norwich, June 24, 1785; and "Frelleich," at Farmington, September 18, 1787 - seventeen lodges.

The Army Lodge, "American Union," chartered by St. John's Grand Lodge at Boston, February 13, 1776, and attached to a Connecticut regiment, frequently met in the State.

It is said that these lodges, chartered by different Grand Lodges, continued to be harmonious as far as was possible.

A convention of lodges met April 29, 1783, in pursuance to the action of a convention held March 13th preceding; thirteen lodges were represented; the formation of a Grand Lodge was duly discussed, and on January 14, 1784, a Grand Master and other officers were chosen, but no progress was made until May 14, 1789, when another convention was called, and this adjourned until July 8, 1789; a constitution was then adopted, officers elected, and the present Grand Lodge of Connecticut was duly organized.

Twelve lodges were then represented, which are all existing at the present date and were at the centennial of the Grand Lodge, 1889.

When the Grand Lodge was organized, Stamford, Norwalk, Derby, New London, Guilford, and Waterbury were not represented; Norwalk, Derby, and Stamford, however, were subsequently connected with the Grand Lodge.

The new Grand Lodge chartered the first lodge at Windham viz. v Norwich, No. 13, October 18, 1790, which is at work at the present time.

The growth of the Fraternity and its popularity are shown in the fact that to the year 1800 the lodges had increased to fortyfour, with three thousand members. About this time one Joash Hall established clandestine lodges, one in Middletown, one in New London, and one in Wallingford. These, however, soon died out.

When the proposition to establish a Supreme Grand Lodge was started among the various Grand Lodges, Connecticut deemed the project inexpedient.

This Grand Lodge granted two charters to form new lodges in Ohio, viz.: "Erie," No. 47, now "Old Erie," No. 3, at Warren; the other "New England," No. 45, afterward New England, No. 4, at Worthington, and now belonging to the spurious and clandestine body calling itself a Grand Lodge in Ohio, and the names of all the bodies which constituted that affair have been published by the Grand Lodge of Ohio in 1898. The above two lodges, with "American Union," the Army Lodge, mentioned above, assisted in forming the Grand Lodge of Ohio in 1808.

Jeremy L. Cross was appointed Grand Lecturer in 1816 for the State of Connecticut.

In 1821 an act of incorporation was passed by the Legislature. In 1823 the Grand Lodge refused to divide the State into Masonic districts. The Grand Lodge made an appropriation, in 1826, of $500 for a monument to Brother George Washington.

At this period the anti-Masonic movements had reached Connecticut, the Brethren generally neglected to attend their lodges and many charters were surrendered and revoked; and such was the condition of the Craft at the annual session of 1831, that all the officers of the Grand Lodge, except the Grand Treasurer, resigned their offices, and new officers, except the Grand Treasurer, were chosen.

Yet at the next annual session only the Grand Master and Grand Treasurer were present; at that time they adopted the "Declaration of Masonic Principles," and this, in some measure, allayed the anti-Masonic sentiments. Twenty-five lodges were represented at the session in 1841. There was an improvement up to 1845. and to the present time Masonry, in that jurisdiction, has kept even pace with all the other States in New England.

The Civil War was the cause of several applications for army lodges. June 6, 1861, a dispensation was issued to twelve Brethren of the 4th Connecticut Regiment for a lodge to be named "Connecticut Union." No. 90.

Another dispensation was asked for "Ensign" Lodge, No. 91, in the 5th Connecticut Regiment, but was refused.

Several years since (1887) quite a difficulty occurred between Hiram Lodge, No. 1, and the Grand Lodge, in consequence of the Grand Lodge having by statute changed the mode of giving the due-guard of the third degree, which resulted in the arrest of the Charter of the lodge and expulsion of several of the officers After some time better counsel prevailed, and the members, being satisfied that they were wrong in their action, they made all proper acknowledgments, and matters were duly arranged and the Charter was restored, and the utmost harmony has prevailed ever since.

Virginia.

From the Freemason's Pocket Companion, by Auld and Smellie, published in Edinburgh, Scotland, in 1765, appears "An Exact List of Regular English Lodges;" therein we find "No. 172, The Royal Exchange in the Borough of Norfolk, in Virginia; 1st Thursday Dec., 1733;" "No. 204 in York-Town, Virginia; 1st and 3d Wednesday, Aug.1,

1755." This is corroborated by the Pocket Companion published in London, England, in 1759, by John Scott, under the head of "Lodges in Foreign Parts;" "Norfolk, in Virginia, 1st Thursday; York-Town, Virginia, 1st and 3d Wednesday."[254]

The date calf 1733 is challenged by several of our recent writers as being a misprints and they say it should have been 1753. We have seen no cogent reason for this correction, but must submit to the weight of authority as we have no corroborative evidence to sustain the earlier date of Bro. John Dove, the Grand Secretary of the Grand Lodge of Virginia, who was very sure that it was correct, and in the first volume of his History of the Grand Lodge of Virginia says: "Thus it will be seen from reliable data, that Masonry was practised in Virginia under chartered privileges in 1733, derived from the Mother Grand Lodge of England." Very soon after these two lodges were chartered, eight other charters were applied for and obtained from the several Grand Lodges existing in Great Britain in the following localities: Norfolk Lodge, No. 1, in the Borough of Norfolk; Port Royal, No. 2, in Caroline County; Blandford, No. 3, Petersburg; Fredericksburg, No. 4, Fredericksburg; St. Tammany, No. 5, Hampton; Williamsburg, No. 6, Williamsburg; Botetourt, No. 7, Gloucester Court-house; Cabin Point, No. 8, Prince George Court-house; York Town, No. 9, York Town.

The work of these lodges was continued legally and masonically under their independent charters, until the course of time and the eventful period of the Revolutionary War caused them to organize a convention, which was called to meet at the request of Williamsburg Lodge, No. 6, at Williamsburg, May 6, 1777, and which resulted in the establishment of the Grand Lodge of Virginia, October 13, 1778, at Williamsburg, by the election of John Blair as the first Most Worshipful Grand Master of Ancient York Masons in America. He was at that time Past Master of Williamsburg Lodge, No. 6. This Grand Lodge was held in Williamsburg until 1784, when it was removed to Richmond.[255]

Charters were continuously granted to new lodges, until their numerical denomination, being derived from various sources, had become too complicated for discrimination; at the meeting in October, 1786, a resolution was adopted that a committee be appointed to regulate the rank of the several lodges then under the jurisdiction of the

---

[254] John Dove's "History of the Grand Lodge of Virginia."
[255] Removed from Port Republican, Island of San Domingo, when insurrection of blacks occurred

Grand Lodge of Virginia. We make the following table for future reference:

No. Charter.	Name of Lodge.	Constitution under which Chartered.	Date of
1	Royal Exchange 172	England	5733
	Norfolk	Norfolk(old #142)	June 1, 5741
2	Kilwinning Cross Scotland	Caroline County.	December 1, 5755
3	Blanford Scotland	Petersburg.	September 9, 5757
4	Fredericksburg Scotland,1757	Fredericksburg.	July 21, 5758
5	Tammany...............	Hampton.	February 2, 5759
6	Williamsburg	Williamsburg	November 6, 5773
7	Botetourt	Gloucester Court-house.	November 6, 5773
8	Cabin Point Royal Arch	Prince George Court-house	April 15, 5775
9	Swan (204) Scotland	York Town.	July 1, 1755 February 22, 5780
10	Richmond	Richmond.	December 28, 5780
11	Northampton	Eastville, N. H. Co.	July 8, 5785
12	Kempsville	Princess Ann Co.	October 1, 5785
13	Staunton	Staunton.	February 6, 5786
14	Manchester	Manchester.	February 28, 5786
15	Petersburg	Petersburg.	May 6, 5786
16	Portsmouth	Portsmouth.	June 15,

	Wisdom G. Orient, La Sagasse France		5876
17	Charlotte Virginia	Charlotte	July 6, 5786
18	Smithfield Union Virginia	Richmond	October 29, 5787
19	Richmond Randolph Virginia	Richmond[256]	October 29, 5787

---

[256] The Capital of the State having been changed from Williamsburg to Richmond.

FREEMASONRY IN THE UNITED STATES

By reference to the Pocket Companion before mentioned, it will be seen that York Lodge, No. 204, was chartered for York Town, Va., August 1, 1755. The conclusion is that it became dormant (and was revived in 1780), as was probably the case with Royal Exchange, No. 172 of date December, 1733, which became No. 1 of June, 1741.

Although it is evident from authentic history that the Masons of Virginia had the right to open and hold a Provincial Grand Lodge under and by authority of Cornelius Harnett as Provincial Grand Master by right of his deputation as such, yet it was deemed by them more in accordance with Masonic law to obtain their charters from the Grand Lodge itself. The Masons of Norfolk petitioned for and obtained the Charter for the Royal Exchange, as we firmly believe with Brother Dove, in 1733. The records of Virginia show that a second lodge was chartered for the same place as Norfolk Lodge June 1, 1741, and held their meetings the same night every month; we therefore think that Royal Exchange had ceased to exist, and Norfolk Lodge took its place and was represented in Williamsburg at the conventions held May 6, 1777, and October 13, 1778.

In the autumn of 1784, Lafayette came to America, and visited Washington at Mount Vernon. Of all the generals of the Revolution he had been the most beloved by Washington; and both to him and to his wife in France had the hospitalities of Mount Vernon been often tendered by Mr. and Mrs. Washington. Madame Lafayette had wrought with her own hands in France a beautiful Masonic apron of white satin groundwork, with the emblems of Masonry delicately delineated with needle-work of colored silk; and this, with some other Masonic ornaments, was placed in a highly finished rosewood box, also beautified with Masonic emblems, and brought to Washington on this occasion as a present by La fayette. It was a compliment to Washington and to Masonry delicately paid, and remained among the treasures of Mount Vernon till long after its recipient's death, when the apron was presented by his legatees to the Washington Benevolent Society and by them to the Grand Lodge of Pennsylvania, in whose possession the apron now is, while the box that contained it is in possession of the lodge at Alexandria. The apron presented to Washington by Messrs. Watson & Cassoul two years before, and which is still in possession of Lodge No. 22 at Alexandria, has been often mistaken for this; but the two aprons may be easily identified, by the Watson & Cassoul apron being wrought with gold and silver tissues with the American and French flags combined upon it, while the Lafayette apron is wrought with silk and has for its design on the frontlet the Mark Master's circle, and mystic letters, with a beehive as its mark in the center. The same device is beautifully inlaid on the lid of the box in which it was originally presented to Washington; and as this box is also in possession of Lodge No. 22 at Alexandria, and kept with the Watson & Cassoul apron, it has by many been supposed that this was the apron presented in 1784 by Lafayette. This mistake has also, perhaps, been perpetuated by a Statement that when Lafayette visited this lodge during his visit to America in 1824, he was furnished with the apron now in possession of Lodge No. 22, and in the box in which he had in 1784 presented one to Washington, to wear on the occasion; and that he there alluded to it as the one he had in former years presented to his distinguished American Brother. Even were this statement true, a lapse of forty years might have misled him in the identity of the apron, particularly as it was handed to him for the occasion in the well-remembered box in which he hadt in his early Masonic life, presented one to Washington. The historic descriptions of the aprons leave no doubt as to the identity of each, and both are among the valued memorials of Washington's Masonic history. The Watson & Cassoul sash and apron, and also the Masonic box in which the Lafayette apron was presented to Washington, were presented to Lodge No. 22 at Alexandria, June 3, 1812, by Major Lawrence Lewis, a nephew of Washington, in be half of his son, Master Lorenzo Lewis.[257]

North Carolina.
    The first organization of Masons in this colony was a lodge warranted by the Grand Lodge of England (Moderns) "at Wilmington, in Cape Fear River, in the Province of North Carolina, March, 1754 (Calendar says 1755); but was not Listed until 1756, although the Constitution was paid for June 27, 1754."[258]
    The Royal White Hart Lodge, No. 338, English Register, was warranted for Halifax N.C., August 21, 1767. It was retained on the register until 1813. The first is known as St. John's, No. 1, and the second retains its original name of Royal White Hart Lodge, No. 2[259]
    In the transaction of the St. John's Grand Lodge of Massachusetts a record states that on October 2, 1767, that body granted

---

[257] Hayden's Washington, etc
[258] John Lanets "Masonic Records," p. 67.
[259] John Lane's "Masonic Records," p. 108.

a deputation to Thomas Cooper, Master of Pitt County Lodge, as Deputy Grand Master of the Province.

In 1771, a lodge now known as St. John's, No. 3, was established at New Berne.

Judge Martin, in a discourse delivered on June 24, 1789, says that Joseph Montford was appointed, toward the year 1769, as Provincial Grand Master by the Duke of Beaufort, and in 1771 he constituted St. John's Lodge, above mentioned as No. 3; that this was probably the true date of the Provincial Grand Lodge of North Carolina, for on December 16, 1787, we find nine lodges in the territory; and that a convention was held at Tarborough and organized "The Most Worshipful Grand Lodge of Ancient Free and Accepted Masons of North Carolina."[260]

In 1771, a Grand Lodge was organized, which met at Newbern and Edenton. The records were destroyed by the English during the War of the Revolution.

December 9, 1787, an effort was made to reorganize the Grand Lodge by the representatives of the following lodges: Unanimity; St. John's, No. 2; Royal Edwin, No. 4; Royal White Hart, No. 403; Royal William, No. 8; Union at Fayetteville, Blandford, Bute, and Old Cone.

At a meeting of the Grand Lodge held June 25, 1791, the lodges were all renumbered and new charters were issued to them.

The General Assembly of North Carolina incorporated the Grand Lodge in 1797. Some of the lodges were also incorporated.

In 1856, St. John's College was established at Oxford, the present writer having furnished a design for the building. During the war, from 1861 to 1865, the college was vacated by the students. After the war the Grand Lodge converted the building and grounds into an orphans' home, and with varied success it has at last become permanently one of the best orphans homes in the country. Several additions have been made to the original buildings. This Grand Lodge stands among the first of the Southern States for its prosperity in all essential features.

Maine.

The first Masonic lodge organized in Maine was located at Falmouth, which was subsequently called Portland.

Jeremy Gridley, Provincial Grand Master for Massachusetts (St.John's Grand Lodge), granted authority to Alexander Ross to constitute this lodge. We learn that this "Constitution" was not acted

---

[260] Mackey's "Encyclopedia," p. 536

upon. Ross died November 24, 1768, and a petition was signed by eleven Brethren, and sent to John Rowe, who succeeded Gridley, and on March 30, 1769, he granted a new Charter, deputizing William Tyng to act as Master. The first meeting was held May 8th of that year. It seems that the two rituals, viz., the '*Modern" and "Ancient," were in conflict in this lodge, and in 1772 the lodge resolved for harmony's sake to use these rituals on alternate evenings.

June 5, 1778, an application, which did not have a sufficient number of signers, was made to the Grand Lodge of Massachusetts (acting under the Grand Lodge of Scotland), to be called Warren Lodge, to be located at Machias. This petition was returned, and when properly signed, September 4, 1778, the Grand Lodge granted a Warrant, September 10, 1778.

A lodge was warranted by the United Grand Lodge of Massachusetts, June 1, 1792, to be named Lincoln Lodge. The same Grand Lodge issued a Warrant for another lodge in Portland in 1806.

Maine was admitted into the Union of the States in 1819, whereupon Simon Greenleaf issued a call for a convention to be held October 14, 1819, for the purpose of organizing a Grand Lodge for that State. There were then thirty-one lodges in that State all warranted by Grand Lodges in Massachusetts. Twenty-nine of these unanimously agreed to constitute a Grand Lodge in Maine.

The committee appointed by this convention, in consequence of the determination of the late "Massachusetts Grand Lodge, in 1781," that all charters granted without the limits of this (Massachusetts) State shall be understood to remain in force until a Grand Lodge is formed in the government where such lodges are held; "requested that the connection with the Grand Lodge of Massachusetts should be dissolved, etc., which was finally granted, donating $1,000 as a foundation for a charity fund, and the District Deputy Grand Masters in Maine were directed to pay what funds they might have in hand belonging to the Grand Lodge of Massachusetts to the new Grand Lodge.

What a commentary this is upon the conduct of very many Grand Lodges, who fought frightfully against the organization of new Grand Lodges in territory where they held lodges under their obedience. The generosity and Masonic bearing of this grand old Commonwealth commend the Brethren thereof to our praise and admiration. We have had occasion in another place to mention this historical circumstance.

June 1, 1820, twenty-four bodies were represented and chose their Grand Officers. William King, the Governor of the State, was elected the first Grand Master.

The Grand Lodge, through the Grand Officers, was incorporated by the Legislature of Maine, June 24, 1824. The Grand Officers were installed, at the meeting-house of Rev. Mr. Payson, by the Grand Master of New Hampshire.

Simon Greenleaf succeeded William King as Grand Master.

At a meeting of the Grand Lodge, July 10, 1820, the following was proposed:

"To consider whether a person, who is conscientiously scrupulous against taking an oath, can be admitted to the benefits of Masonry by solemn affirmation."

This was fully considered, and on January 8, 1824, the following report of the committee was received and adopted by the Grand Lodge:

"Your committee deem this a question of no little importance as it bears on the interests of the Craft. On the one hand, if decided in the negative, there will be necessarily excluded from a participation of all the Mysteries, and very many of the benefits and advantages of Masonry a large class of Men, among the most respectable of our citizens, on account of their integrity, their conscientious regard for all those great moral principles which dignify human nature, and certainly not among the most backward in deeds of mercy and charity. On the other hand, if decided in the affirmative, it would seem at last to sanction a departure from what, for ages, has been deemed a form of sacred words, and what has not hitherto failed to bind the consciences of otherwise the most hardened offenders. It is impossible that your committee should not examine with mistrust a principle which should shut out from the Masonic Fraternity such men as Clarkson; and they can not close their eyes to the bad effect which sanctioning such principles must have on the moral sense of the Community. On the whole, your Committee conceive that no Masonic principle is violated in adapting the form of the Obligations to consciences of Men equally good and true, but on the contrary, that serious hurt would grow to the Institution of Masonry, by an adherence to the technical form of words, heretofore used, for the purpose of securing that fidelity on the Crafts Men which have never yet been violated, even when all other principles have been wrecked, in the vortex of unhallowed appetites, or the whirlwind of ungoverned passions."

The Grand Lodges of the United States commented upon this action.

Missouri, Tennessee, Kentucky, Delaware, Virginia, and Pennsylvania protested, and the last passed the following resolutions:

"That the Grand Lodge of Maine be respectfully requested to reconsider the resolution adopted by them on the 8th January, 1834, proposing a new mode in which the degrees of Masonry can he conferred.

"That this Grand Lodge feel themselves bound to refuse to recognize any person, as a Mason, known to be initiated in the Mode proposed by the Grand Lodge of Maine."

Soon after this the so-called "Morgan excitement" prevailed to such an extent over all the Northeastern States, that it had the same depressing effect as in New York and Pennsylvania.

In 1829 there were fifty-eight lodges. A large number of these suspended their labors.

At the annual meeting of the Grand Lodge in 1837, the oldest lodge at Portland was the only one represented. In 1844, sixteen lodges were represented. In 1849, Mount Hope was organized, the only one in twenty years. In 1860, there were ninety-six lodges, having four thousand three hundred and nineteen members. In ten years (1870) there were one hundred and fifty-four lodges with fourteen thousand seven hundred and twenty-six members.

New Jersey.

This colony was the home of the first Provincial Grand Master appointed by the Grand Lodge of England for any Province in America, to wit, that of Daniel Coxe, who received a deputation in 1729. Anderson mentions the issuing of this Masonic instrument in his History of Masonry. It was dated contemporaneously with one to Lower Saxony, and one to Bengal, India. Daniel Coxe appears never to have exercised any Masonic power in New Jersey. He was a resident of Burlington, and represented Gloucester County, N.J., in the Assembly of 1716, at which he was elected Speaker.

On May 13, 1761, a constitutional number of Master Masons in and about the town of Newark petitioned for and received from the hands of George Harrison, Provincial Grand Master of the Province of New York, a Warrant of Dispensation, Directed to William Tukey as Master, and others as officers, to meet and operate as a lodge, the first meeting-place being Rising Sun Tavern; after that the communications were held at the residences of the respective members. The lodge was called St. John's Lodge, No. 1, and preserves its original minutes to the present day.

"This Lodge observed Washington's Birthday as a Masonic Festival as early as 1792; and that venerable Lodge has, from that time to the present, yearly convened on that festive day to commemorate the Masonic Virtues of Washington."[261]

On June 24, 1762, Jeremy Gridley, Grand Master of Masons of the Province of Massachusetts, granted a deputation to Jonathan Hampton, Esq., to constitute a lodge by the name of Temple Lodge, No. 1, to be located in Elizabethtown, N. J.

On June 20, 1764, as set forth in an original document in the Archives of the Grand Lodge of Pennsylvania, the Grand Lodge of London (Ancients), Thomas Erskine, Grand Master, appointed Wm.Ball, Esq., Grand Master of Masons for the Province of Pennsylvania and the territories thereunto belonging: by virtue of this authority, three lodges were instituted in New Jersey, in the years 1767, 1779, and 1781.

In 1779 the headquarters of General George Washington were at Morristown, N. J. Numerous military lodges were organized in the American Army; and on December 27th of that year a festival was held by the "American Union Lodge" at Morristown, at which Bro.George Washington was present. The Minutes of the Proceedings of American Union Lodge are at the present time in the possession of the Grand Lodge of Connecticut.

On February 7, 1780, a convention lodge held at Morristown in accordance with a previous understanding, December 27, 1779, favored a Grand Lodge of America. This movement Pennsylvania also endorsed in 1780. New Jersey subsequently withdrew its assent.

A convention of Master Masons was held on December, 18 1786, for the preparatory consideration of, and to mark out the course to be adopted for, the formation of a Grand Lodge for the State. This resulted in the adoption of the constitution on April 2, 1787, from which period the Grand Lodge dates.

Michigan.

No written history of Masonic events prior to 1826 have as yet been discovered. From the "Historical Sketch," by Brother Foster Pratt, M.D., Past Grand Secretary of the Grand Lodge, Free and Accepted Masons, of Michigan, we are enabled to glean all the well established facts as to the early introduction of Masonry into that State: " From 1764 to 1844, historical material accumulated around our Mystic Temple, not in consecutive records, nor in permanent forms, but in fragmentary papers, and varying traditions; and it has required no little research and

---

[261] Sidney Hayden's "Washington," etc.

labor to dig up from 'the rubbish' and to establish beyond question, exact dates, historical landmarks, and the true order of Masonic events."

There has been no written history of Masonry in Michigan prior to 1844. Three Grand Lodges have been organized in that State. The first was in 1826. The first lodge, is "named Zion," was formed by a Warrant from Provincial Grand Master George Harrison, of New York, under the date of April 27, A.D. 1764, which was No 448 Register of England, and No. 1 of Detroit. It is most likely that the military and citizens of Detroit were combined in this lodge.

When the British troops at a later date were serving in Michigan, there were probably three military lodges - which were noticed in an English Masonic Register as No. 289 at Detroit in 1773, No. 320 at Detroit in 1783; and St. John's Lodge, No. 373, at Mackinaw in 1785. These were undoubtedly military lodges. The registry shows that their warrants came direct from England.

These lodges left no trace in Michigan, but they all went with their respective regiments, in 1796, when Michigan was surrendered to the United States.

The SECOND MASONIC PERIOD commenced in 1794. From the peculiar conditions of the country and the times it seems no records were preserved; yet there was some evidence that during a portion of that time, for thirty years, Zion Lodge maintained life and performed some labor. So long as Great Britain claimed Michigan as a part of Upper Canada, which was until 1796, the Masonic jurisdiction was therefore in the Grand Lodge of Canada, which had already been organized. On September 7, 1794, a Warrant was issued to Brethren in Detroit from the Provincial Grand Lodge of Canada, called Zion Lodge, No. 10. This lodge was instituted December 19, 1794, James Donaldson, Worshipful Master. In 1796 American troops planted the flag and institutions of the United States at Detroit.

The THIRD MASONIC PERIOD, A.D. 1806, New York jurisdiction. - The records of the Grand Lodge of New York show that September 3, 1806, a Charter was granted by DeWitt Clinton, Grand Master, to the Brethren of Detroit, by which Zion Lodge was reformed and-recorded as "No. 1 at Detroit." With their petition they surrendered to the Grand Lodge of New York the original Warrant of 1764. This lodge was "installed" July 6, 1807. We find no other records of interest..

The FOURTH MASONIC PERIOD, A.D. 1812 - 20, second war with England. - Until October 5, 1813, when the battle of the Thames occurred, there were no meetings, as the country was occupied by the British forces. In October, General Lewis Cass became Governor, and the American flag again waved at Detroit, the lodge having forfeited its Charter by the events of the war. Upon petition of its members the Grand Lodge of New Yorks, March 14, 1816, granted a Charter to Zion Lodge, No. 62, instead of former No. 1. By a new arrangement of numbers in 1819, according to the original charters, this lodge became No. 3.

The FIFTH MASONIC PERIOD, First Grand Lodge. - A dispensation was granted by the Grand Lodge of New York in 1821, and instituted December 26, 1821, by the name of Detroit Lodge, No. 337

March 7, 1822, in the town of Pontiac, County of Oakland, by the name and style of Oakland Lodge, No. 343, which had been previously organized under dispensation.

A Warrant was issued September 1, 1824, a dispensation having been issued on June 12, 1824, to form a lodge in Green Bay, in the county of Brown, by the name of Minomanie, No. 374, which is in Wisconsin at this time, as then it was in the territory of Michigan. December 1, 1824, at the town of Monroe, in the county of Monroe, territory of Michigan, by the name of Monroe Lodge, No. 375.

The Grand Lodge was Organized in 1826. - The convention met June 24, 1826. Were present by their representatives Lodges No. 3, No. 337, No. 374, and No. 375, all chartered by the Grand Lodge of New York. No. 343 of Pontiac was not present at this meeting, but appeared later and joined in its action. June 28th a constitution was adopted. July 31st Grand Officers were elected and installed.

This new Grand Lodge was duly recognized by the Mother Grand Lodge of New York by suitable and fraternal resolutions, June 11, 1827.

At the Institution of the Grand Lodge, General Lewis Cass was installed Grand Master. Four lodges were soon thereafter organized, viz.: Stony Creek, Western Star, St. Cloud, and Friendship. These made nine lodges in its jurisdiction. The meager official records of its proceedings have been published, yet all that the Grand Lodge accomplished soon came to naught.

The principal importance that attaches to the matter arises from the fact that it became the cause of four years of Masonic confusion, after eleven years of silence. The exact date of the suspension of life is not known, and the manner of it was unique; "and when dead it did not rest in peace."

As a Masonic curiosity, the dispensation granted by Grand Master Lewis Cass to Stony Creek Lodge, January 9, 1828, is yet in existence, which is the only lodge which maintained its existence during the dark days of the anti-Masonic excitement.

The SIXTH MASONIC PERIOD, A.D. 1840 - 44, Reconstruction. - Michigan attained to Statehood in 1837. The population increased from 1829, when Masonic labor ceased, with only about 30,000, to nearly 250,000 in 1840. The increase of population being mainly from States where Masonry had resumed its labors after the recent anti-Masonic crusade, the Institution began to revive in 1840, and on November 15th of that year a convention was held at Mt. Clemens.

Nothing definite was accomplished and it adjourned to May 5, 1841.

The history of the proceedings of the Brethren during the four years between 1840 and 1844 is very interesting but entirely too lengthy for our limits, and we refer our readers to the local history of the Grand Lodges of Michigan.[262]

On September 17, 1844, the Grand Lodge of Michigan was constitutionally organized and elected the Grand Officers - which Grand Lodge continues to the present time and has grown and prospered and is among the leading Grand Lodges of the United States.

Delaware.

There appears to be some uncertainty concerning the first lodge instituted in Delaware. It is said that the Grand Lodge of Scotland in 1764 warranted Union Lodge No. 121, at Middletown, for General Majoribank's Regiment. The Grand Lodge of Pennsylvania granted warrants to Lodge No. 5, at Cantwell's Bridge on June 24, 1765, and renewed March 5, 1798, and was surrendered, January 30, 1815, in order to unite in forming the Grand Lodge of Delaware. Hyneman's World's Masonic Register says: "The Grand Lodge of Delaware was organized June 6, 1806." Here is a difference of ten years in the date of organization of the Grand Lodge.

A Charter to Lodge No. 13, at Christiana Ferry, afterward Wilmington, was granted, December 27, 1769; surrendered and renewed, January 22, 1789; was vacated, September 15, 1806, for un-Masonic proceedings in the establishment of the pretended Grand Lodge of Delaware (Hyneman, ante); to Lodge No. 18 at Dover, Kent County, granted, August 26, 1775; surrendered and renewed, May 31, 1787; to Lodge No. 33, at New Castle and at Christiana Bridge, one year

---

[262] "Historical Sketch of Early Masonry in Michigan," by Foster Pratt, p. 42 et seq.

at one place and the ensuing year at the other, granted, April 3, 1780; surrendered and renewed, March 1, 1790; vacated, September 15, 1806, for un-Masonic conduct in the formation of the pretended Grand Lodge of Maryland; to Lodge No. 44, at Duck Creek Cross Roads; granted, June 24, 1785; surrendered and renewed, September 6, 1790; has ceased long since; to Lodge No. 63, at Lewistown; granted, May 28, 1794; vacated, April 7, 1806; to Lodge No. 96, the Delaware Hiram Lodge at Newark; granted, December 6, 1802; vacated, September 15, 1806, for un-Masonic conduct in the formation of the Grand Lodge of Delaware.

The Grand Lodge of Maryland granted a Warrant to St. John's Lodge in Laureltown, Sussex County, on September 18, 1792. It became delinquent to the Grand Lodge and its Warrant was forfeited, June 13, 1800. June 6, 1806, it petitioned to be revised but was refused. Grand Lodge warranted a new lodge named "Hope" at the same time and place. Nine Brethren, said to represent Lodge No. 31, Grand Lodge of Maryland, Nos. 33, 96, and 14, Grand Lodge of Pennsylvania, met at the town hall in Wilmington, and resolved that, as a matter of right, and for the general benefit of Masonry, they ought to form a Grand Lodge within said State, and did then proceed to form the Grand Lodge of Delaware. A committee of five was appointed to prepare a set of regulations. The meeting adjourned to June 7, 1806, when twelve Brethren were present. They proceeded to the appointment of Grand Officers, pro tempore, and thereupon, without any previous installation, opened the Grand Lodge of Delaware. Warrants were granted without any charge except the secretary's fees for executing them, etc. The Grand Lodge of Pennsylvania, to whom the proceedings had been referred, refused to recognize them, that five lodges at least were indispensably necessary to form a Grand Lodge (there were only five lodges at the formation of the pretended Grand Lodge), and that three of the lodges were indebted to the Grand Lodge of Pennsylvania for fees and dues. Accordingly, these warrants were vacated. The Grand Lodge of Maryland also refused to recognize the new Grand Lodge, and in 1808, the Charter of Hope was annulled. The action taken by Pennsylvania and Maryland did not seem to affect the new Grand Lodge, and in 1816 the Lodge No. 5, Cantwell's Bridge, under the Grand Lodge of Pennsylvania, joined the new Grand Lodge by permission of the Grand Lodge of Pennsylvania, thus making five.

Vermont.

In 1778, some of the towns in New Hampshire, near the Connecticut River, put themselves under the control of Vermont. The attention of the citizens was directed to this circumstance, and a petition from sixteen towns, including Hanover and some others, east of Connecticut River, was presented to the Legislature of Vermont, at the first session in March, 1778, with the request to receive them into Union and Confederation. At the next session of the Legislature an act was passed to authorize these towns to elect and send members to the Legislature at their next session. At the session of the General Assembly, in October, 1778, delegates from at least eight towns of New Hampshire took their seats in the Assembly.[263]

We have stated this much of the political history of that early period, to account for circumstances in the Masonic history, which would not be otherwise understood, viz.: that the original petition for a Charter for a Vermont lodge was dated at "Cornish, Vermont," and why the lodge met at Charlestown, N. H., in place of Springfield, Vt., which town was named in the Charter. Again: Ira Allen's History says that, "On the meeting of the Legislature of Vermont at Windsor, February 12, 1779, to get rid of a connection which had occasioned so much trouble and danger, the Assembly passed an Act dissolving the Union of the sixteen towns in New Hampshire."[264] For a period of four years ending February, 1782, both sides of the Connecticut River were to some extent common territory.[265]

November 8, 1781, a petition from Cornish, Vt., was presented to St. Andrew's Grand Lodge of Massachusetts, and a Charter was ordered to be issued November 10, 1781, the lodge to be located at Springfield, Vt.

This lodge, instead of meeting at Springfield, Vt., held the meetings in Charlestown, N.H. May 17, 1787, the lodge was in some doubt as to the propriety of their meeting in Charlestown, N. H.

A Charter was applied for, to St. Andrew's Grand Lodge, for a lodge at Charlestown, named Faithful, which was granted, February 2, 1788. The Vermont lodge was removed to its proper place at Springfield. On May 14, 1795, upon petition to the Grand Lodge, the said lodge was moved to Windsor, Vt., and the lodge met there until September 19, 1831, when it suspended its meetings, in consequence of the anti-Masonic or Morgan excitement. On January 10, 1850, upon petition, the present Charter was granted by the Grand Lodge of Vermont. The second lodge established in Vermont was chartered by St. Andrew's

---

[263] Ira Allen's History, in George F. Koon's "Freemasonry in Vermont."
[264] Ibid
[265] Ibid.

Grand Lodge of Massachusetts, January 20, 1785, and was named North Star, in Manchester, Bennington County, and was constituted, February 3, 1785.

Dorchester Lodge was the third lodge constituted in Vermont previous to the formation of a Grand Lodge in Vermont. This lodge was chartered by Sir John Johnson, May 5, 1791, Grand Master of the Province of Quebec.

Temple Lodge, at Bennington, was chartered by the Grand Lodge of Connecticut, May 18, 1793.

Union Lodge, at Middlebury, was the last lodge chartered prior to the organization of the Grand Lodge of Vermont. The Charter was issued by the Grand Lodge of Connecticut, May 15, 1794.

A convention was held at Manchester, August 5, 1794, and the following lodges were represented, viz.: North Star, Dorchester, and Temple. After appointing committees for several purposes, preliminary to a permanent establishment of a Grand Lodge, the convention adjourned, to meet at Rutland, October 14, 1794, at which time the Grand Lodge adopted the constitution. There were present, by representatives, the following lodges, viz.: North Star, Vermont Lodge, Dorchester, Temple, and Union. The Grand Officers were elected, Brother Noah Smith being Grand Master.

The Grand Lodge continued to hold the annual communications until during the anti-Masonic excitement in 1826. From 1828 to 1836 many of the lodges failed to be represented, and to pay their annual dues to the Grand Lodge. At the Annual Communication, October 11, 1831, a resolution, recommending an unqualified surrender by the Grand Lodge of the charters of the several secular lodges was dismissed by a vote of ayes 99 to noes 19.

Without dwelling upon the history of that time, which tried the souls and patience of all good Masons, we extract from the proceedings of the Grand Lodge held October 7, 1834.

At the session of October 7, 1834, the following transaction took place:

On motion of Bro. Joel Winch, a committee of three was appointed to examine the communications received from secular lodges and present the views of the Grand Lodge at this time. N.B. Haswell, Joel Winch, and Solomon Mason were appointed, who made the following report:

Whereas, The Grand Lodge of the State of Vermont has witnessed with regrets the assembling in different counties of the State of Masons called together by a notice or authority new and unknown to the usages of the craft and in opposition to the constitution of the order; therefore Resolved, That the Grand Lodge deem the assemblage of Masons in the manner above alluded to to be unmasonic and unconstitutional.

Resolved, That the resolution adopted by the Grand Lodge at its last session (whereby permission was given to the secular Lodges to surrender their charters and records, giving to said Lodges authority to retain and dispose of their property and funds as they see fit) was a measure calculated to relieve [all] who wished to retire from Masonry.

Resolved, That the Grand Lodge do hereby receive, and they instruct their Secretary to receive hereafter, such charters and records as may be surrendered by virtue of the resolution aforesaid, and they order the same whenever surrendered to be deposited among its archives.

Resolved, That this Grand Lodge feel it a duty they owe themselves as well as the whole Masonic fraternity to declare, that while its individual members are left to the free and unmolested enjoyment of their sentiments upon the various subjects connected with religion and politics, and the right to judge of men and their actions, they hereby most solemnly declare that Masonic bodies have not tile right to connect the institution with the sectarian or party views of eitherthat any attempt thereat is a gross innovation upon those principles which among good and correct Masons are universally acknowledged, and should be universally practised upon.

Resolved, That the Grand Lodge do at this time as they have hitherto done, declare to the world that the object of their association, and motives for continuing therein, are founded upon the principles of brotherly love, relief, and truth. They disclaim the right of Masons to inflict corporeal punishment and acknowledge no other right to enforce obedience from its members but reprimand, suspension and expulsion.

Resolved, That the Grand Lodge recommend to those brethren who incline still to adhere to the institution of Masonry, to continue to cultivate a spirit of good will towards those who may differ from them respecting the origin and continuance of Free Masonry; and while we are ready to forgive those whose fidelity has been shaken by one of those popular commotions incident to our free institutions, we are also ready to judge with candor the motives by which they have been governed.

In presenting the foregoing resolutions, your committee will close their report in the language of one of the late officers of this Grand Lodge whose labors on earth are finished; we ask you to gaze with us upon the ominous gathering, which to no eye can be viewless; we ask you to contemplate its swelling aspect, its various phases, and its multiform ramifications; listen to its busy notes of preparation and anticipate its maturity of strength, and then imagine its consummation to have taken place; then cast your eye around and see how many have quaked and quailed, how many have failed, how many have surrendered at discretion, and how many have renounced their faith and armed to batter us down; then complete the picture, and when you find the smoke and din of the conflict is passed, and the light streaming in upon us once more, not a heart flinching, not a hand palsied, but each and every one still invincible in defence of the mighty truth.

If Free Masonry falls, her monument will not crumble, nor her epitaph fade. It is erected upon the everlasting hills, it is firmly planted in the deepest vallies. The widow's prayer of joy, the orphan's tear of gratitude as they ascend, like the dew before the solar influence, bear with them its eulogy and its praise. So long as there remains a fragment of the temples of antiquity; so long as one stone of the edifices it has consecrated shall rest upon another; so long as brotherly love, relief, and truth obtain among men, so long will its mausoleum endure. The waves of popular prejudice may beat against it, the shouts of popular clamor may be thrown back in echoes from its base, the winds and weathers of time may press upon it, but still it will endure, glory will encircle it, honor will be yielded to it, and veneration will be felt for the hallowed recollections it quickens into action; and hereafter when he casts his eyes over the galaxy of social institutions among men, the philanthropist will involuntarily associate with his subject that other and celestial galaxy, and realize as now from the fiat that has effected the one, so then from the economy that controlled the other, that he will soon have to mourn for a lost Pleiad which can never more be visible in the moral constellation.

The few faithful Brethren in Vermont never surrendered their Masonry, but continued to hold their communications of the Grand Lodge, and adjourned from year to year, until all the excitement had died out, when the politicians discovered that they could no longer impose upon the people.

Many of the Brethren wished again to resume the work of Masonry in Vermont, and thought it desirable that it should be done under the old organization; as they had made provision for keeping it up to the then present date. Bro. Grand Master Nathan B. Haswell, who had held the Grand Lodge together for so many years (blessed be his memory), called a meeting of the Officers of the Grand Lodge, to be held at Mason's Hall, in Burlington, January 14, 1846, at which time and place the Grand Officers met and the Grand Lodge of Vermont resumed its legitimate functions and prestige, and has continued to do so ever since; and, notwithstanding the great trials and persecutions inflicted upon Masonry as an institution, and upon individuals, the Grand Lodge of Vermont stands to-day upon a higher pinnacle than ever before.

The "Green Mountain Boys" will ever maintain the honor and glory of their great antecedents.

Florida.

Originally, after the discovery by Ponce de Leon in 1513, Florida belonged to the Kingdom of Spain. The country was settled by Huguenots in 1562, and permanently occupied by Spaniards in 1565, at St. Augustine. It was ceded to Great Britain in 1763, again to Spain in 1783, and finally to the United States in 1819, and admitted to the Union in 1845.

The origin of Masonry in Florida is somewhat vague, and the writers on the history of Masonry do not agree as to when it was first introduced into that country. In 1768, the Grand Lodge of Scotland erected a lodge, No. 143, at East Florida and appointed Governor James Grant Prov. G.M. for North America, southern district.[266]

A "memorial from the Brethren of St. Andrew's Lodge, No. 1, late of West Florida; now of Charlestown, South Carolina, with sundry papers relative thereto," was presented to the Grand Lodge of Pennsylvania, July 8, 1783. Of this lodge nothing more is known.

When the Grand Lodge of Pennsylvania responded to the memorial and a Charter was issued, it was forwarded to the W. Master of another lodge with instructions to ascertain if the W. Master and members of the said lodge were of the Ancient and Honorable Fraternity, and consented to be under that jurisdiction. In 1768, the Grand Lodge of Scotland granted a Charter to a lodge in East Florida.

There is no trace whatever of such a lodge.

Brother Mackey indicates that Lodge No. 30, chartered by the Grand Lodge of South Carolina (Ancients), at St. Augustine, East Florida, became "extinct in consequence of a decree of the King of Spain." No. 56, at Pensacola, was chartered by the Grand Lodge of South Carolina (date is unknown). It also became extinct.

The same Grand Lodge, June 30, 1820, chartered Floridian Virtues Lodge, at St. Augustine, in place of No. 30, and which also ceased to work in 1827. June 29, 1821, that Grand Lodge revived No. 56 at Pensacola, by the name of Good Intention Lodge, No. 17, which

---

[266] Gould, voi. vi., p.403.

became extinct in 1825. January 3, 1824, that Grand Lodge issued a Charter to La Esperanza Lodge, No. 47, at St. Augustine, which is supposed to be a revival of No. 30.

From the reprint of the Proceedings of the Grand Lodge of Florida, the committee on the reprint say that the first lodge in East Florida was St. Fernando, at St. Augustine, warranted by the Grand Lodge of Georgia, about 1806. As South Carolina had issued a Charter as early as 1804, consequently this one could not have been the first.

Jackson Lodge, at Tallahassee, was chartered by the Grand Lodge of Alabama, December 19, 1825. On December 15, 1827, it was suspended and the Charter was forfeited, December 8, 1829; it was, however, placed in good standing on the payment of its arrearages of dues.

Washington Lodge, at Quincy, was chartered by the Grand Lodge of Georgia, December 2, 1828; also the same Grand Lodge chartered Harmony Lodge, at Marianna, December 8, 1829. July 5, 1830, these three lodges met and framed and adopted a constitution, July 6th, and the Grand Officers were elected and installed. With the exception of the Territory of Michigan, this was the first Territorial Grand Lodge; and as the first one in Michigan did not continue very long, Florida Grand Lodge, now existing, may claim to be the first formed in a Territory.

Kentucky.

Kentucky being originally a part of Virginia, up to 1792, jurisdiction over it was exercised by that State.

November 17, 1788, Lexington Lodge was chartered by the Grand Lodge of Virginia. The following lodges also derived their authority from the same Grand Lodge, viz.: November 25, 1791, Paris Lodge was chartered; Georgetown Lodge received a dispensation, January 9, 1796, and a Charter, November 29, 1796, a dispensation was issued to Hiram Lodge, September 20, 1799, and a Charter was granted, December 11, 1799; a dispensation was issued to Abraham's Lodge, at Shelbyville, in the latter part of 1799 or commencement of 1800.

Representatives from these five lodges met September 8, 1800, at Lexington, and determined that it was expedient, necessary, and agreeable to Masonic constitution, that a Grand Lodge should be established for that State. The convention then issued a call for a second convention for October 16, 1800.

This convention, composed of the above five lodges by their representatives, met, and after organizational elected their Grand Officers, who were then installed.

District of Columbia.

This district, containing originally one hundred square miles, was set apart by Act of Congress, approved July 16, 1790, for the capital of the United States: being partly in the State of Maryland, on the north and east side of the Potomac River, and on the south and west side of that river, in the State of Virginia.

Prior to that date a lodge had been organized by the Grand Lodge of Maryland, in the town of Georgetown, situated on the west bank of Rock Creek, April 12, 1789, by the name of Potomac Lodge, No. 9.

For some reasons, now unknown, this lodge ceased to work. October 23, 1795, the Grand Lodge of Maryland granted a Warrant to another body of Masons (probably many of them had been members of No. 9), which was named Columbia, No. 19. This lodge also ceased its labors, and another lodge was warranted by the Grand Lodge of Maryland, by the name of Potomac Lodge, No. 43, which last lodge continued with the name and number as stated, until the Grand Lodge of the District of Columbia was constituted, February 11, 1811, when the same name being continued, the number was changed to 5, and is the same at the present time.

Federal Lodge, No. 15, was chartered by the Grand Lodge of Maryland, September 12, 1793. By Act of Congress, the District of Columbia having been laid out and the public buildings for the several departments being under construction, especially the Capitol of the United States, the city of Washington having also been laid out, many private residences were being constructed, and the population was greatly increased.

The corner-stone of the Capitol was laid September 18, 1793, with Masonic ceremonies, conducted by the President, Brother George Washington, who came up from Alexandria, accompanied by Alexandria Lodge, No. 39, and was joined by Potomac Lodge, No. 9. Federal Lodge, No. 15, although its Warrant had been issued a few days previous to this occasion, and in consequence of its not having been duly instituted, could not join in the ceremonies, although the Brethren were present as spectators. The gavel used on that occasion, made by one of the workmen, of a piece of marble similar to that used in the building, was presented to General Washington; after the ceremonies it was given by him to the Worshipful Master of Potomac Lodge, No. 9, and is in the possession of that lodge at the present time.

Brooke Lodge, No. 47, being located in Alexandria, Va., after the formation of the Federal District, was chartered by the Grand Lodge of Virginia.

Alexandria Lodge, No. 29, also located in the city of Alexandria, was originally chartered by the Grand Lodge of Pennsylvania, February 23, 1783, but soon after the institution of the Grand Lodge of Virginia, October 13, 1778, this lodge withdrew from her allegiance to the Mother Grand Lodge of Pennsylvania, by her consent, and received a Warrant from the Grand Lodge of Virginia, under the name of Alexandria Lodge, No. 22, dated April 28, 1788, with George Washington, Esquire, late Commander-in-Chief of the forces of the United States of America, as Worshipful Master.

Columbia Lodge, No. 35, in Washington City, was chartered by the Grand Lodge of Maryland, November 8, 1803; Washington Naval Lodge, No. 40, also in Washington City, was also chartered by the Grand Lodge of Maryland, May 14, 1805.

December 11, 1810, a convention was held by the five lodges above mentioned, viz.: Federal, No. 15; Brooke, No. 47; Columbia, No. 35; Washington Naval, No. 40; and Potomac, No. 43. Alexandria Lodge, No. 22, declined to join in this movement and was sustained by the Grand Lodge of Virginia, and quietly acquiesced in by the Brethren in the District of Columbia. This convention adjourned to January 8th, and again to February 11, 1811, when the organization of the Grand Lodge of the District of Columbia was fully completed, The several lodges surrendered their charters to their Mother Grand Lodges, and charters were issued to them by their own Grand Lodge, their numbers being changed to 1, 2, 3, 4, and 5, according to original dates. Of these five lodges, all are in existence and are in a flourishing condition, except Brooke Lodge, No. 2, of Alexandria, which returned to the Grand Lodge of Virginia when that part of the District of Columbia was retroceded to the State of Virginia, and soon thereafter ceased to labor.

www.ingramcontent.com/pod-product-compliance
Lightning Source LLC
Chambersburg PA
CBHW071146160426
43196CB00011B/2028